(Mis)Understanding Political Participation

The practices of participation and engagement are characterised by complexities and contradictions. All celebratory examples of uses of social media, e.g. in the Arab spring, the Occupy movement or in recent LGBTQ protests, are deeply rooted in human practices. Because of this connection, every case of mediated participation should be perceived as highly contextual and cannot be attributed to one (social) specific media logic, necessitating detailed empirical studies to investigate the different contexts of political and civic engagement. In this volume, the theoretical chapters discuss analytical frameworks that can enrich our understanding of current contexts and practices of mediated participation. The empirical studies explore the implications of the new digital conditions for the ways in which digitally mediated social interactions, practices and environments shape everyday participation, engagement or protest and their subjective as well societal meaning.

Jeffrey Wimmer is Professor in the Institute of Media, Knowledge and Communication at Augsburg University, Germany.

Cornelia Wallner is a postdoctoral researcher in the Department of Communication Science and Media Studies at Ludwig-Maximilians-University Munich, Germany.

Rainer Winter is Professor of Media and Cultural Theory and head of the Institute of Media and Communication Studies at Klagenfurt University, Austria.

Karoline Oelsner is a researcher in the Department of Public Relations and Communication of Technology at Ilmenau University of Technology, Germany.

Routledge Studies in European Communication Research and Education

Edited by Claudia Alvares
Lusofona University, Portugal
Ilija Tomanić Trivundža
University of Ljubljana, Slovenia
Fausto Colombo
Università Cattolica del Sacro Cuore, Milan, Italy

Series Advisory Board: Nico Carpentier, François Heinderyckx, Robert Picard and Jan Servaes

https://www.routledge.com/Routledge-Studies-in-European-Communication-Research-and-Education/book-series/ECREA

Published in association with the European Communication Research and Education Association – ECREA (www.ecrea.eu), books in the series make a major contribution to the theory, research, practice and/or policy literature. They are European in scope and represent a diversity of perspectives. Book proposals are refereed.

For a full list of titles in this series, please visit www.routledge.com.

(Mis)Understanding Political Participation

Digital Practices, New Forms
of Participation and the Renewal
of Democracy

**Edited by Jeffrey Wimmer,
Cornelia Wallner, Rainer Winter
and Karoline Oelsner**

Routledge
Taylor & Francis Group

LONDON AND NEW YORK

First published 2018 by Routledge

2 Park Square, Milton Park, Abingdon, Oxfordshire OX14 4RN
52 Vanderbilt Avenue, New York, NY 10017

Routledge is an imprint of the Taylor & Francis Group, an informa business

First issued in paperback 2019

Library of Congress Cataloging_in_Publication Data
CIP data has been applied for.

ISBN: 978-1-138-65878-3 (hbk)
ISBN: 978-0-367-87664-7 (pbk)

Typeset in Sabon
by codeMantra

Contents

Introduction

Jeffrey Wimmer, Cornelia Wallner, Rainer Winter and Karoline Oelsner

Participation as a Moving Target

It is commonly accepted that political participation and civic engagement are cornerstones of a vital democratic system. Each generation believes in the singularity of their era and the therein expressed characteristics. Even present times do not constitute an exception to the rule because many authors diagnose immense and accelerating social as well as technological processes of change, which they mainly connect to "the Internet". However, due to media and cultural change, new forms and possibilities of participating in the formation of society are appearing constantly for every individual. For approximately 25 years, the epistemological interest of a continually growing research area within communication and media studies as well as pedagogy, political science and sociology is in how these new forms of participation are used and how they could be judged in comparison to the traditional forms of civic engagement and participation. The current practices of engagement and participation are characterised by huge ambiguities. Despite the evidence of growing disenchantment with institutional politics, electoral turnouts in some countries are increasing. Despite increased possibilities for participation through online media, these are often dismissed as 'clicktivism'. Despite celebratory discourses on the uses of social media in the Arab spring, the Occupy movement, the Pussy Riot case, the same-sex marriage debates in France and the UK and in LT+ protests, they were and are often grounded and performed in particular physical spaces. Despite their possibilities for challenging mainstream media, online media technologies are still mostly profit-driven. Going beyond established academic discourses about the decline of citizens' political participation in institutional politics and the rise of alternative forms of political participation, this book aims to explore the issues, platforms, actions, locations and motivations of politically active citizens today. It discusses the opportunities and challenges that new conditions entail for the ways in which digitally mediated social interactions, practices and environments shape everyday participation, engagement or protest, and analyzes their implications for politics, culture and society.

Participation in Everyday (Media) Life

The concept of participation has multiple meanings, of which only a few central dimensions from a social-scientific perspective will be mentioned in this introduction (see Carpentier 2011). In general, participation represents a normative concept whose public relevance and scheme is interpreted differently in various approaches (for more details, see Ferree et al. 2002). Starting with participation-centric theories of democracy, the concept of participation is usually related to individual action, which is characterised by gratuitousness, missing personal material purposes and an orientation towards the common good. Participation can therefore be understood as a practice or everyday activity that is exercised by citizens in specific situations. In this context, the term refers to a continuum of different phenomena which can range from false forms or illusions to latent and manifest, implicit and explicit forms of participation, including types of self-government (for more details, see Arnstein 1969; Adler and Goggin 2005; Ekman and Amna 2012; Carpentier 2016; Villi and Matikainen 2016). While the concept of engagement emphasises voluntary commitment for a commonwealth, participation refers to official inclusion of citizens in political decisions through forms of voice, involvement and codetermination. With this broadly defined understanding of participation, a selective distinction between engagement and participation also is rather difficult, which leads to the fact that both expressions are partially used synonymously. Additionally, participation and engagement must not be confined to the political sphere. In media pedagogy, participation represents a guiding principle (Buckingham 2003) that is more important than ever, e.g. in the field of political (youth) education (see Loader 2007). Finally, the concept of (e-)participation is currently used in public discourse as an e-government tool (Sæbø et al. 2008). This refers to the use of information and communication technologies to simplify processes of public administration and government (top-down participation) or a whole variety of bottom-up online participation not initiated by established political actors, such as the government (for a synoptic overview, see Boulianne 2009; Marichal 2013; Boulianne 2015; Skoric et al. 2016).

All conceptual dimensions of participation are similar in that they cannot be understood without media in today's societies. Participation in and through media (Carpentier 2011) refers to the various available options for access, interaction and participation relating to different kinds of public spheres. From this perspective, publics do not represent only the audience of political institutions, moreover, they are actively constructing the political public sphere(s) as well. Based on this, Habermas (1989) argues that while media organisations are the institutional core of political publicity in modern societies, participation should be the fundamental foundation of democracy. Dahlgren (2006, 274) convincingly argues:

> The public sphere does not begin and end when media content reaches an audience; this is but one step in larger communication and cultural chains that include how the media output is received, made sense of and utilized by citizens.

Following this path, participation can be understood as appropriation of public communication, which can take different forms across different levels of organisational complexity and activity. Examples include: the emotional movement of citizens, the public resonance of media offers (so-called "follow-up communication"), or even the interaction between citizens, ranging from interpersonal face-to-face conversations or discussions via forums, micro-blogging, etc. on the micro-level, through larger organisational publics, movements and events on the meso-level, and to the general communicative construction of political public sphere(s) on the macro-level. The possibilities for citizens to produce their own media content, e.g. citizens' media, or in the form of participatory online communication must also be critically taken into account (e.g. Rodriguez et al. 2014). In the currently unfolding digital media society, the dichotomous distinction between "citizens", "consumers" and "recipients", as has often been the norm in democratic theory and political communications research, is no longer sufficient. This is the case today because publics (who is actively involved in communicative relations in both old and new ways) are the (inter-)active audiences of participatory citizenship and vice versa (Couldry 2004).

Public participation always involves questions of power, conflict as well as (in)equality (see Fraser 1992; Warner 1992; Mouffe 1999). Castells (2007) discusses basic power shifts from a sociological point of view, and, until now, the state and established institutions have had privileged access to media and, hence, a noticeable advantage. This is rapidly changing in the so-called network society. The individual's communicative basis no longer consists of monopolised mass media publics or vertical communication, but of horizontal, social, spatial and interdisciplinary communication networks that are anchored in civil society. This leads to a new form of social communication, which Castells calls "mass self-communication". From an enthusiastic perspective, being on the Internet, producing, disseminating and receiving information are increasingly self-determined. Research in this area is concerned with the possibilities for access and interaction of citizens, with a focus on both subjectively perceived and structural constraints. While research unanimously identifies a greater variety of opportunities for media participation and engagement, these communication processes and their consequences have been evaluated diametrically for a long time. On the one hand, utopian views include the implication and revitalisation of social and political participation in public communication, and the emergence of so-called produsers (e.g. Bruns 2006), or even a fifth estate in the context of transnational Internet communication (Dutton 2009), which slowly, but inevitably, surpasses traditional power institutions (executive, judicial, legislative) in its communicative power. In other studies, the negative effects of new possibilities are put forward, such as increased emergence of idiosyncratic and personal publics (Schmidt 2014) and their highly selective information spheres, also known as "filter bubbles" (e.g. Sunstein 2001; Pariser 2011).

From a more idealistic and optimistic perspective, Jenkins et al. (2009) see the current transformation as the beginning of a period of transmedia and transnational participatory culture. This is due to the fact that technical possibilities of the social web ease political engagement in a simple and playful manner, and hence, political participation becomes part of everyday media habits in the long term: "Welcome to convergence culture, where old and new media collide, where grassroots and corporate media intersect, where the power of the media producer and the power of the media consumer interact in unpredictable ways" (Jenkins 2006, 2). On countless platforms, people with similar private, cultural and political interests get together to share their knowledge, interact with each other and work together. Initially related to the area of popular culture and entertainment communication, Jenkins (2010, s.p.) argues that, under certain circumstances, all digital communication media and media technologies function as "Civic Media" respectively, "any use of any technology for the purposes of increasing civic engagement and public participation, enabling the exchange of meaningful information, fostering social connectivity, constructing critical perspectives, insuring transparency and accountability, or strengthening citizen agency".

Bruns (2006) is also advocating a similar argument in his approach to produsage – the merging of individual usage and production processes. He postulates that networked communication of the social web, and the resulting self-organised and collaborative production of media content, can be regarded as the beginning of political practices because they open up a mass media compatible and hierarchically structured political sphere. The phenomenon of "political consumerism" illustrates that these new forms of participation can no longer be understood without taking media into account. Digital communication media are used in a variety of ways, such as networking, self-presentation or the knowledge management of new, more or less everyday political practices (see Ward and de Vreese 2011).

Although Jenkins is given credit for being one of the first authors to have impressively and sustainably demonstrated the potential and contexts of participatory media cultures, his strongly subject-centered diagnosis can be criticised as not differentiated enough, and therefore too optimistic, for at least three reasons (for more details, see Hay and Couldry 2011). On the one hand, the economic and political influences on the collaborative production of participation communication, for the purpose of exploitation, are dismissed. Authors, such as Fuchs (2013) are arguing that the economic and political motives and contexts of the collaborative production of participatory communication on the social web should be questioned. For example, participation in form of Facebook's fans pages or YouTube channels is largely driven by economic interests that most users are not fully aware of. On the other hand, it is also not concurrent that in the context of increasing privatisation of the media structures, current public structures on the Internet cannot comprehensively guarantee social engagement even in a digital age. Thus, traditional civic media, for example free radio channels, still play a central role in implementing of the fundamental right on free expression in mass media because civic involvement is still not reducible on the Internet and the established mass media still determines public and political agendas. Finally, in contrast to the idealistic perspective, or against the larger communicative power of so-called participator communication, it could be argued that a "power law" applies to the Internet's attention and influence as well (see Barabási 2002; Watts 2003). In theory, it is possible that everyone publishes their opinions online, however, the technical structure of digital platforms and the logic of search engines ensure that only a small amount of online content on the net is actually utilised by a larger number of users (from the perspective of mediatisation theory, see Krotz 2017). The KONY 2012 campaign illustrates a prototypical example that journalistic attention and audience resonance cannot be oversimplified. Many campaigns are waves of viral attention that disappear just as quickly as they appear (see Wimmer 2014, 60ff.). According to critics of the Internet, digital communication leads to a preference for already established actors as well as a fragmentation of public discourse (see Friedland et al. 2006). At the same time, findings in audience research suggest that media change is not necessarily associated with more interactive media reception; there can also be discrepancies in mediatised participation. Coleman and Ross (2010, 154) describe this as a "glaring paradox of contemporary democracies". The audience has more communicative and media opportunities to participate: "question their rulers; challenge official information; contribute to mainstream media; produce their own media and speak for themselves". However, their empirical work also finds that due to the increasing lack of political inclusion, a kind of communication and media disinclination is demonstrated: "feeling distant from elites; ignored by the media; unheard by representatives; constrained in public speech and utterly frustrated by the promises of democracy". On a structural level, Schmidt (2015) identifies a new "participation paradox", which describes the growing gap between participation in, with and on the Internet. Hence, social media would allow new forms of participation in the sense of self-centred codetermination due to the commercial interests and self-management of users.

The current preoccupation in media and communication studies with engagement and participation is characterised by a more analytically differentiated view (e.g. Carpentier and Dahlgren 2011; Curran et al. 2012; Jenkins and Carpentier 2013; Kaun et al. 2016). Therefore, although participation and engagement can be researched as a case sui generis, it sharpens the blurred picture to contextualise political participation in the light of current changes (Dahlgren and Alvares 2013), especially considering the last push of mediatisation through digitalisation (for more details, see Hepp 2013; Hepp and Krotz 2014). In addition to sociopolitical change, the new possibilities and forms of participation that digital media technologies provide are instigators of changing relationships between politics and citizens, between media institutions and their audience, or even between media content and their users. This transformation of participation roles and the possibility of interactive, and hence, mainly horizontal communication processes, does not only affect the media sphere, but it can also be seen in all areas of society (especially in the political system). Digital communication media and technologies in their effective power are no longer, anywhere out there', but right, among us' because audiences are appropriating them into their everyday life quicker and more expansively than ever before. In this way, media and cultural change are accompanied by a complex and ambivalent participation potential, which clearly contradicts notions of technical determinism or symptomism (see groundbreaking Williams 1990). This is because the greatest difference between digital and traditional public spheres cannot be traced back to the technological nature of the Internet, but to its social use (Splichal 2009, 400f., for a current case study, see Lazer 2015). For example, the term "Facebook revolution" is highly inaccurate if it is solely based on the technical potential of certain social web applications. Hepp (2012, s.p.) concurs with this notion:

> It is not the social web that leads to something. Rather, it is the people on the streets, who articulate (...) since Seattle and the globalization-critical movement protest that followed Genoa in Germany. But what has changed is that these protests on the streets are comprehensively mediated – permeated for the media as well as by them. Digital media, which is always accessible through mobile phones, is certainly playing a role: people in the streets are organizing their protests via Facebook, tweeting the most important events and communicating continuously through SMS to avoid the police.

It is apparent that mediated political participation – similar to other mediatised everyday practices – can still be understood as a local activity (even in times of mediatisation and globalisation), always subject to specific local, regional or national requirements. However, the manner in which political participation is organised, carried out and communicated, and, the context in which it takes place, can change dramatically and become segmented according to various related groups. According to Dahlgren (2004, 7), the media revolution did not erase political interest in the majority of individuals, but rather merely shifted their understanding and "[they] developed other modes of political engagement". Thus, especially among young individuals, a different political awareness and understanding of participation can be observed in their media practice (e.g. Bennett 2008; Olsson and Dahlgren 2010). Through self-criticism, evaluations of current youth surveys conclude that the traditional categories of political interest and political orientation among young people cannot capture parts of their political behavior and political understanding. Indeed, a recent synopsis of online media practices only represent a fraction of the many different forms of digital participation and protest. Still, it clearly points out three further processes of the continuation, transformation and replacement of traditional participatory practices (see Wimmer 2014). On the one hand, this includes the mediatisation of participation and protest such as successful civil society agenda building on the social web through YouTube videos (e.g. the 2012 prominent case of the ACTA debate). On the other hand, entirely new forms of counter-publicity and protest emerge, such as virtual sit-ins in online game worlds ("transformation") (see Poor and Skoric 2014). These processes contribute to a significant increase of both the sub-political and the subcultural constitution of the public sphere, which has integrative as well as dividing consequences for the political sphere as a whole. From a normative point of view, nevertheless, it is still feared that taking part in several digital protest activities and other forms of participation are not always serious or indicative of mobilisation (slacktivism). An example of how to deal constructively with this phenomenon is provided by the US administration. In response to a seemingly insane online petition to build a functioning replica of the Death Star from Star Wars, the head of the White House's science and space department published a message laden with Star War references. Perhaps this was done in order to motivate "consumer citizens" of the digital age to more tangible participation:

> If you do pursue a career in a science, technology, engineering or math-related field, the Force will be with us! Remember, the Death Star's power to destroy a planet, or even a whole star system, is insignificant next to the power of the Force.[1]

Structure of the Book

The book consists of three sections, the first entitled *Practices of participation and citizenship*. It deals with the question of how citizens, especially digital natives, engage politically in their everyday life, what possibilities they experience and how they realise them. In their chapter *(New) Forms of digital participation? Toward a resource-model of adolescents' digital engagement,* Annika Schreiter, Sven Jöckel and Klaus Kamps present findings from a paper-pencil survey at two German schools with students from the 5th to 13th grade. They develop a model of political online-communication by using three steps: reception, discussion and participation. Thereby, they explain how adolescents' resources, such as political interest, family and school background, predict these steps of political online participation. Veronika Kalmus, Ragne Kõuts-Klemm, Mai Beilmann, Andu Rämmer and Signe Opermann present a long-term empirical research in *Long-lasting shadows of (post)communism? Generational and ethnic divides in political and civic participation in Estonia.* The results of their survey provide a brief overview of the dynamics in general levels of political and civic participation between 2002 and 2014 in Estonia, focusing on generational and ethnic differences in political and civic activism. According to the assumption that the 'political' expands into all spheres of social life and, thereby, new forms of engagement emerge, this section also takes a closer look at everyday practices of mediated participation and citizenship, critically re-assessing traditional definitions of what is considered 'political'. In *Enhanced .-visibility. The experience of civic engagement in social media,* Maria Francesca Murru discusses the question of what is considered as 'political', but focuses on social networking sites. Her arguments are based on an empirical study conducted in Italy. She identifies four ideal types of public visibility of the self on Facebook, each type being an original combination of personal and political publicness. Her findings suggest that the existing relationship between social media and political participation cannot be uniquely grasped at the level of ends-oriented activism or conscious, well-aware acts of civic engagement. As an another example for an everyday practice that becomes 'political' is illustrated in Sigrid Kannengießer's study *'I am not a consumer person' – Political participation in repair cafés,* where she deals with the repairing of media technologies both as a form of pro-dusage as well as a form of political participation. Her study focuses on the question of why people participate in Repair Cafés, why they want to repair their devices and what they think is the societal significance of these events. The section also deals with new theoretical concepts, such as the concept of 'intimate citizenship', which refers to issues and debates on intimate and sexual politics in society. Sander De Ridder and Sofie Van Bauwel apply this framework in their chapter *Intimate citizenship politics and digital media: Teens' discourses, sexual normativities and popular social media.* They discuss how young people between 14 and 18 years negotiate intimate citizenships and everyday sexually mediated lives on digital platforms. They report on empirical insights from a four-year research project exploring intimate storytelling practices among young people in popular social media websites in Belgium.

Practices of participation are situated within different contextual constraints. Most notably, representations in media contextualise the way we engage ourselves and vice versa. Our engagement decontextualises the structures and meaning of media and communication, and, over the *longue durée* our culture, society and history. The study on different media contexts which frame participation raises the critical question of how the development of participation and citizenship practices can be characterised through a series of continuities and discontinuities. Beyond the mere praising of new possibilities through social media, the second section *Mediated representations of participation and citizenship* tries to show the wide scope of mediated participation and its inherent complexity by looking at entirely different media contexts, ranging from traditional media as the press to the special case of talk shows or the highly contested public sphere of twitter. Maria Kyriakidou, José Javier Olivas Osuna and Maximillian Hänska Ahy discuss in their chapter the role of the Indignados, a social movement in the European press against the economic crisis in Europe. Enabled by social media, these alternative movements are still subject to the media logic of mainstream press for their public representation and reach. Drawing upon an empirical study of the national press in Spain, Greece and Germany, this chapter discusses the role of media in reporting and framing the movement in Europe. Udo Göttlich and Martin R. Herbers take a closer look at forms of mediatised political participation of television talk show audiences in Germany in their chapter *Speak your mind: Mediatized political participation through second screens*. Based on analyses of television show's websites and their Facebook channels, they present a preliminary case study on the new participatory features of mediated public discourse on second screens. In their study *"My body, my decision". The abortion debate and twitter as a counterpublic sphere for women in Turkey* Perrin Öğün Emre and Gülüm Şener, analyse the role of Twitter in a current abortion law debate that protests the bio-political acts of the Turkish government. Elena Pilipets and Rainer Winter in their chapter *Repeat, remediate, resist? Meme activism in the context of the refugee crisis* show the potential of digital memes for contemporary media activism. Focusing on the resonances between two competing political visions on migration regarding the current refugee debate, they look at proliferating refugee memes in the perspective of the concepts of re- and premediation.

The third section, *(Re-)Framing participation and citizenship,* discusses how the emergence of online media changes the concept of political participation. Information search and information flows online are quite different from offline mechanisms. The media repertoire of citizens is widening and low-threshold forms of participation appear, such as sharing videos. Also, researchers can use new methods and technologies to analyse all these new phenomena of political participation.

With traditional approaches and methods often not able to capture this changing environment, there is a need for new approaches. Therefore, this section presents productive analytical frameworks to understand the transgression of political participation and citizenship in the digital age, and tests whether traditional models are still applicable. Julie Uldam and Anne Kaun suggest in their chapter *Towards a framework for studying political participation in social media* the contours of an analytical framework for studying political participation in social media. Their approach considers the context of political participation in social media, paying particular attention to (1) affordances, (2) power relations, (3) practices and (4) discourses by drawing on Couldry's model of a socially oriented media theory. This model considers media in the context of other social institutions that shape our sense of reality, and questions media's overemphasised role in constructing social reality. Thereby, they explore the role of online media technologies in facilitating civic resilience and social innovation. In *Protest or collaboration? How perceived opportunities and constraints shape the activities of anti-infrastructure citizen action groups,* Marco Bräuer and Jens Wolling present a conceptual framework for the analysis of the actions applied by citizen action groups against infrastructure projects using two dimensions: protest and collaboration. The framework is based on case studies dealing with anti-infrastructure protests in Germany on a local level. Based on a classification of activities, differences in the repertoires of the protest groups can be identified not only between the groups, but also between different phases in the policy making cycle, and between different national contexts. They suggest the concept of opportunity structures as an appropriate approach to explaining these differences. Two chapters in this section deal with migration. The chapter *Rethinking otherness and cultural citizenship: Cosmopolitanism and new platforms* by Elke Grittmann and Tanja Thomas concentrates on the concept of 'cosmopolitanism'. They develop a systematic framework for identifying different forms of cosmopolitan openness in online communication. In the empirical part of their chapter, they analyse three different online platforms that are used and organised for migrants and refugees. The chapter demonstrates that the concept of critical cosmopolitanism can serve as a starting point to discuss and broaden the concept of Cultural Citizenship, and enables us to introduce questions of mediatised self-presentation, visibility, voice and participation. In their chapter *Mapping the 'search agenda': A citizen-centric approach to electoral information flows* Filippo Trevisan, Andrew Hoskins, Sarah Oates and Dounia Mahlouly discuss, how search engines help voters escape the information hegemony of election campaigns and traditional media coverage. They explore key Internet search trends for electoral information in the United Kingdom, the United States and Italy by using an innovative methodology that maps the informational trajectories of key events in each campaign. They do so by combining publicly available

Google Trends data (www.google.com/trends) with the analysis of relevant coverage in traditional mass media outlets.

Note

1 Source: https://www.wired.com/2013/01/white-house-death-star/ (accessed March 1, 2017).

References

Adler, R. P., and Goggin, J. (2005). Civic Engagement? *Journal of Transformative Education*, 3(3), 236–253.

Arnstein, S. R. (1969). A ladder of citizen participation. *Journal of the American Institute of Planners*, 35, 216–224.

Barabási, A.-L. (2002). *Linked: The new science of networks*. Cambridge, MA: Perseus Publishing.

Bennett, W. L. (ed.) (2008). *Civic life online: Learning how digital media can engage youth*. Cambridge, MA: MIT Press.

Boulianne, S. (2009). Does internet use affect engagement? A meta-analysis of research. *Political Communication*, 26, 193–211.

Boulianne, S. (2015). Social media use and participation: A meta-analysis of current research. *Information, Communication & Society*, 18(5), 524–538.

Bruns, A. (2006). Towards produsage: Futures for user-led content production. In F. Sudweeks, H. Hrachovec, and C. Ess (eds.), *Proceedings: Cultural attitudes towards communication and technology* (275–284). Perth, WA: Murdoch University.

Buckingham, D. (2003). *Media education – Literacy, learning and contemporary culture*. London, UK: Polity Press.

Carpentier, N. (2011). *Media and participation. A site of ideological-democratic struggle*. Bristol, UK: Intellect.

Carpentier, N. (2016). Beyond the ladder of participation: An analytical toolkit for the critical analysis of participatory media processes. *Javnost – The Public*, 23(1), 70–88.

Carpentier, N., and Dahlgren, P. (2011). *Theoretical horizons of participation. Communication Management Quarterly*, 6(21), 7–12.

Castells, M. (2007). Communication, power and counter-power in the network society. *International Journal of Communication*, 1, 238–266.

Coleman, S., and Ross, K. (2010). *The media and the public: "Them" and "us" in media discourse. Communication in the public interest*. Malden, MA: Wiley-Blackwell.

Couldry, N. (2004). The productive 'consumer' and the dispersed 'citizen'. *International Journal of Cultural Studies*, 7(1), 21–32.

Curran, J., Fenton, N., and Freedman, D. (eds.) (2012). *Misunderstanding the Internet*. London, UK: Routledge.

Dahlgren, P. (2004). Theory, boundaries and political communication. The uses of disparity. *European Journal of Communication*, 19(1), 7–18.

Dahlgren, P. (2006). Doing citizenship: The cultural origins of civic agency in the public sphere. *European Journal of Cultural Studies*, 9(3), 267–286.

Dahlgren, P., and Alvares, C. (2013). Political participation in an age of mediatisation. Towards a new research agenda. *Javnost – The Public*, 20(2), 47–66.

Dutton, W. H. (2009). The fifth estate emerging through the network of networks. *Prometheus*, 27(1), 1–15.

Ekman, J., and Amnå, E. (2012). Political participation and civic engagement: Towards a new typology. *Human Affairs*, 22(3), 283–300.

Ferree, M. M., Gamson, W. A., Gerhards, J., and Rucht, D. (2002). Four models of the public sphere in modern democracies. *Theory and Society*, 31(3), 289–324.

Fraser, N. (1992). Rethinking the public sphere. A contribution to the critique of actually existing democracy. In C. Calhoun (ed.), *Habermas and the public sphere* (109–142). Cambridge, MA: MIT Press.

Friedland, L., Hove, T., and Rojas, H. (2006). The networked public sphere. *Javnost – The Public*, 13(4), 5–26.

Fuchs, C. (2013). *Social media: A critical introduction*. Los Angeles, CA: Sage.

Habermas, J. (1989). *The structural transformation of the public sphere. An inquiry into a category of bourgeois society*. Cambridge, MA: MIT Press.

Hay, J., and Couldry, N. (eds.) (2011). Rethinking convergence/culture. *Special issue of Cultural Studies*, 25(4/5), 473–486.

Hepp, A. (2013). *Cultures of mediatization*. Cambridge, UK: Polity Press.

Hepp, A., and Krotz, F. (eds.) (2014). *Mediatized worlds: Culture and society in a media age*. London, UK: Palgrave.

Jenkins, H. (2006). *Convergence culture: Where old and new media collide*. New York, NY: NYU Press.

Jenkins, H. (2010). *Civic media: A syllabus*. http://civic.mit.edu/blog/henry/civic-media-a-syllabus.

Jenkins, H., and Carpentier, N. (2013). Theorizing participatory intensities: A conversation about participation and politics. *Convergence*, 19(3), 265–286.

Jenkins, H., Purushotma, R., Weigel, M., Clinton, K., and Robison, A. J. (2009). *Confronting the challenges of participatory culture. Media education for the 21st century*. Cambridge, MA: MIT.

Kaun, A., Kyriakidou, M., and Uldam, J. (2016). Political agency at the digital crossroads. *Media and Communication*, 4(4), 1–7.

Krotz, F. (2017). Explaining the mediatisation approach. *Javnost – the Public*, 1–16. doi:10.1080/13183222.2017.1298556.

Lazer, D. (2015). The rise of the social algorithm. *Science*, 5, 1090–1091.

Loader, B. (ed.) (2007). *Young citizens in the digital age: Political engagement, Young people and new media*. London, UK: Routledge.

Marichal, J. (2013). Political facebook groups: Micro-activism and the digital front stage. *First Monday*, 18(12), 1–18.

Mouffe, C. (1999). Deliberative democracy or agonistic pluralism? *Social Research*, 66(3), 746–758.

Olsson, T., and Dahlgren, P. (eds.) (2010). *Young people ICTs and democracy. Theories, policies, identities and websites*. Göteborg, Sweden: Nordicom.

Pariser, E. (2011). *The filter bubble. What the internet is hiding from you*. London, UK: Viking.

Poor, N., and Skoric, M. M. (2014). Death of a guild, birth of a network: Online community ties within and beyond code. *Games and Culture*, 9(3), 182–202.

Rodriguez, C., Ferron, B., and Shamas, K. (2014). Four challenges in the field of alternative, radical and citizens' media research. *Media, Culture & Society*, 36(2), 150–166.

Sæbø, Ø., Rose, J., and Flak, L. S. (2008). The shape of eparticipation. Characterizing an emerging research area. *Government information quarterly*, 25(3), 400–428.

Schmidt, J.-H. (2014). Twitter and the rise of personal publics. In K. Weller, A. Bruns, J. Burgess, M. Mahrt, and C. Puschmann (eds.), *Twitter and society* (3–14). New York, NY: Peter Lang.

Schmidt, J.-H. (2015). Die sozialen Medien und das Partizipationsparadox. In K. Voss, and P. Hurrelbrink (eds.), *Die digitale Öffentlichkeit. Band II*. Hamburg, Germany: Friedrich-Ebert-Stiftung.

Skoric, M. M., Zhu, Q., Goh, D., and Pang, N. (2016). Social media and citizen engagement: A meta-analytic review. *New Media & Society*, 18(9), 1817–1839.

Splichal, S. (2009). 'New' media, 'old' theories: Does the (national) public melt into the air of global governance? *European Journal of Communication*, 24(4), 391–405.

Sunstein, C. (2001). The daily we. Is the Internet really a blessing for democracy? *Boston Review*. http://bostonreview.net/BR26.3/sunstein.php.

Villi, M., and Matikainen, J. (2016). Participation in social media: Studying explicit and implicit forms of participation in communicative social networks. *Media and Communication*, 4(4), 109–117.

Ward, J., and de Vreese, C. (2011). Political consumerism, young citizens and the Internet. *Media, Culture & Society*, 33(3), 399–413.

Warner, M. (1992). The mass public and the mass subject. In C. Calhoun (ed.), *Habermas and the public sphere* (377–401). Cambridge, MA: MIT Press.

Watts, D. J. (2003). *Six degress: The science of a connected age*. New York, NY: Norton.

Williams, R. (1990). *Television: Technology and cultural form*. London/New York, NY: Routledge.

Wimmer, J. (2014). Zwischen Fortführung, Transformation und Ablösung des Althergebrachten. Politische Partizipationskulturen im Medienalltag am Fallbeispiel KONY 2012. In R. Biermann, J. Fromme, and D. Verständig (eds.), *Partizipative Medienkulturen. Positionen und Untersuchungen zu veränderten Formen öffentlicher Teilhabe* (49–68). Wiesbaden, Germany: VS Verlag.

Part I

Practices of Participation and Citizenship

1 (New) Forms of Digital Participation? Toward a Resource Model of Adolescents' Digital Engagement

Annika Schreiter, Sven Jöckel and Klaus Kamps

Resources for Political Engagement

A growing body of literature on the use of online media (boyd 2014; Kupferschmitt 2015; Lenhart et al. 2015; Livingstone et al. 2015; Livingston and Sefton-Green 2016) paints a rather straightforward picture of how young people turn to online media regarding political questions. Online participation or even seeking online for information surrounding politics in general accounts only for a very small part of the online activities of adolescents. We wonder why this should be the case and – to address this book's title – whether this finding is not due to a specific form of misunderstanding new forms of political engagement and participation.

The possible answers to these two questions are ambivalent. One answer might quite simply be that adolescents use social media and acquire meanings from their 'convergent media ecology' unevenly (Mascheroni 2013). They may not see a specific sense in using the internet in the political realm – even though the options of online participation, information, empowerment and organisation are vast and manifold and the hopes for new models of democratisation are accordingly high (Rheingold 2000). Another (potential) answer might be that in terms of political participation we tend to analyse things with regard *only* to classic categories such as following traditional news media or debating politics offline (Bennett 2008). Therefore, we ask, how, why and under which circumstances adolescents become involved with politics online (up to the point where they factually participate and initiate in political debates). These questions will be addressed in this chapter. In other words, instead of complaining about the marginal share of politics in the 'online world' of adolescents, we focus on the resources used (and their specific contexts) when (new) forms of political engagement effectively occur. Therefore, our general research question reads: What resources may explain the political online engagement of (German) adolescents? For the purpose of this chapter we concentrate on the results of the last study out of a series of three conducted in Germany from 2011 to 2013.

An Engaged Youth Perspective

Our normative approach to the phenomenon of digital participation is a participatory perspective on democracy. It views engagement in politics and the community in general as the backbone of a thriving society. Citizens are seen (and compelled) as active members of a political association in which they are not only interested but also obliged to enhance and influence it in many different ways. The more the members of a society participate and the wider the variety of their activities, the better for the community (Barber 1984; Putnam 1993). Following this perspective, a similar view is taken on adolescents. Bennett (2008) describes two different ways in which – roughly speaking – the participation of young people is seen. First, the *disengaged youth paradigm,* the decline of voter turnouts and other traditional forms of participation are seen as a threat to democracy. Adolescents are described as widely detached from politics and society. Nontraditional forms of participation like ethical boycotts or digital participation are seen as less important – or are even left out of the equation. Even when adolescents rally on the streets – mostly organised through social media – this is often not seen as political but as deviant, as danah boyd (2014, 207) outlines for the case of the high-school student protests against immigration laws in 2006. By contrast, the *engaged youth paradigm* focuses on new forms of (digital) participation: "[...] [T]his paradigm emphasizes the empowerment of youth as expressive individuals and symbolically frees young people to make their own creative choices" (Bennett 2008, 3). At the same time, the need for traditional forms of participation such as voting as a core act of representative democracies is diminished (Bennett 2008; Bennett et al. 2009). In this chapter, we follow the engaged youth paradigm but hold a critical view on the balance between creative, as well as new forms of participation and the need for citizens that participate on an institutional level and in traditional ways.

Bennett (2008) further describes a change in citizenship itself. He argues that on the one hand there still exists a traditional citizen type, the so-called *dutiful citizen.* These citizens think of participation as their political obligation and prefer traditional, government-centred forms such as voting or joining civil organisations or political parties. They follow the mass media and have a profound trust in governmental organisations, politicians and most of the media. In contrast, on the other hand, *actualizing citizens* are generally wary of these. They prefer topic-centred, creative forms of participation organised in loose (digital) networks. They do participate; not out of a feeling of duty but because they prefer to in another context or because of a specific subject (Table 1.1).

These two types of citizen are just a rather broad depiction of a subtle shift in citizenship. They are by no means selective, and they are not exclusively separating 'younger' and 'older' citizens. Of course, a lot of

Table 1.1 Typology of Citizens

Dutiful Citizens	Actualizing Citizens
Obligation to participate in government-centred activities	Higher sense of individual purpose
Voting as the core democratic act	Personally-defined acts are more important (e.g., consumerism)
Becomes informed by following mass media	Mistrust of media and politicians is reinforced by negative mass media environment
Joins civil society organizations or parties, employing one-way conventional communication	Favours loose networks of community action maintained by interactive information technologies and social ties

Source: Bennett (2008, 14).

adults participating as actualizing citizens and adolescents can belong to the dutiful type (Bennett et al. 2009, 106–107). But this differentiation helps to outline the difficulties in describing digital participation in terms of a political idea or even a theory based on dutiful citizens alone.

The concept of actualizing citizens explains how young people become engaged in politics and why they might be sceptical of traditional forms of participation. However, it does not explain whether and why they actually participate. This question stands in a long tradition of research (Milbrath 1965; Verba and Nie 1972). In addition, the specific question of how political participation may evolve in adolescence has also been of major interest (Norris 2003; Ogris and Westphal 2006; Albero-Andrés et al. 2009; Quintelier 2015), and more recently also with a focus on digital participation (Bakker and de Vrees 2011; Lim and Golan 2011; Rauschenbach et al. 2011; Spaiser 2012; Wagner 2014). Again, most of these studies simply describe different forms of (digital) participation but not how the antecedents and constraints of political participation may be explained. In this chapter, we employ and propose a *resource-based approach* to fill this gap. This approach is based on the *standard socioeconomic model of participation* (Verba and Nie 1972), which assumes that participation is influenced by socioeconomic factors like demographic attributes, financial resources, education and individual factors (such as a sense of democratic duty or self-efficiency). This model describes a politically active elite which is mainly male, middle-aged, highly educated and with high income (Verba and Nie 1972, 13–14; Brady et al. 1995, 271; Leighly 1995, 183–184). Brady et al. (1995) specified this model to a resource-based approach in which participation is explained by the resources *time*, *money* and *civic skills* like rhetorical or interpersonal skills. These skills are acquired during childhood and adolescence, but may be further developed in adulthood, for example, through civic engagement, which stands in close relation to political participation.

We see political participation as a special form of civic engagement concerning political processes and decisions. Civic engagement has a broader meaning and is comprised of activities like doing work for the local community. Following Ekman and Amnå (2012, 289–292), political participation comprises more manifest forms of activity that directly aim at influencing political decisions. Civic engagement, on the other hand, is a latent individual and collective form of action aimed at influencing circumstances in society outside the direct personal surroundings, for example, voluntary work for the local community (Figure 1.1).

Drawing upon this approach, we related those resources to adolescence and to online engagement. First, we eliminated the resources *time* and *money*. Adolescents' time is highly structured by activities they cannot influence such as school or their parents' wishes. It may also be questioned whether one can obtain *valid* answers to the question, "How much free time do you have?" The availability of money depends partly on the income of parents but also on educational choices (e.g., Feil 2004, 38–39). In addition, the German Shell Youth Study of 2015 shows that money-related activities like donating are hardly carried out by adolescents (Schneekloth 2015). Civic skills, in contrast, are mainly acquired during adolescence via the main agents of political socialisation: education and partaking in school, peers and families (Brady et al. 1995; Jenkins 2009; Quintelier 2015). We therefore consider them as *the* resources of young people for political participation; and because our focus lies on engagement online, we also added experience with online media and social network sites (SNS) as a resource for digital engagement. This is

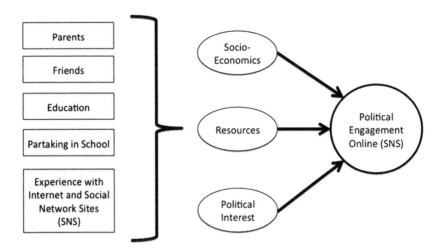

Figure 1.1 A resource model for adolescents' political participation online.

based on the results of several studies indicating that people who frequently use the internet also tend to use it more for political purposes (Bakker and de Vreese 2011; Emmer et al. 2011; Spaiser 2012; Quintelier 2015). Sociodemographic variables and general political interest as a key resource are understood as additional ways of explaining digital participation.

Pre-studies and Developing a Measure of Political Participation on SNS

This study is the third in a series of three. For the purpose of this chapter, we focus on the last analysis but will briefly summarise the previous two in order to introduce our method. The first study was a paper-and-pencil questionnaire (February 2012) on forms of online engagement. We included six forms of online participation, derived from a major youth study in Germany titled 'Aufwachsen in Deutschland' (AID:A) [Growing up in Germany[1]], including taking part in a flash mob, a mail bombing or signing an online petition (Gaiser and Gille 2012). In addition, we asked for seven social network forms of engagement[2] (e.g., writing a statement in an online discussion or following a political party in a social network; Jöckel et al. 2014). Following Ekman and Amnå (2012), these forms lie in between political participation and civic engagement. They do not really aim at influencing political processes or decisions, but are still connected to the political sphere and potentially influence it. This study consisted of 452 German students (10–18 years, M_{age} = 12.65, SD = 1.73, 54% female).

The second study was a qualitative interview study on adolescents' perspectives on politics. Fourteen students from different school types in Germany, all aged 16 or 17 years, were interviewed about their perspectives on politics, (online) participation and their media use (Potz 2014).

In both studies it became evident that – in line with the results of the AID:A study – most forms of online participation are hardly carried out. Between 5% and 10% of the participants had at least once used one of those forms. We further found that about one tenth of the participants had no knowledge of such activities. In contrast, especially low-level forms of social media activities, like taking part in an online discussion, were used more often – up to 35% of the participants had used them at least once and they were far better known as well (Jöckel et al. 2014, 156). As a consequence of these findings, we ask for forms of online participation that are known to adolescents and far more connected to their everyday online and social media behaviour. We subsequently reconstructed our measure of political participation online and used the broader term of political engagement online in the following chapter, which includes participation in a strict sense but also low-level forms on SNS that cannot be accounted for as political participation, but still have a connection to the political sphere like following a political Facebook page. It is of course debatable to what extent we might view these forms as *engagement* and not merely as practices of political *communication*. As online engagement is prone to low-level forms, which can be described as 'micro-activism' or 'sub-activism', we view it as a first step into more action-oriented and more complex forms of engagement and even participation (c.f. Bakardjieva 2009; Marichal 2010; Ekmann and Amnå 2012).

Following recent approaches on the development of political online engagement (Emmer et al. 2011), we distinguished three crucial aspects that may be carried out in and through the use of SNS. On the basic level (1), SNS are a tool to convey political information. Political news is shared online through Facebook and Twitter. For adolescents, SNS might become vital news platforms and complement news from traditional journalistic platforms (Wagner 2014). Yet, it is an inherent feature of SNS that political news (2) is not only consumed but often enough also commented. Again, this resembles the offline world, only that discussions are now no longer taking place in the 'salon', the proverbial political arena of deliberative democracy, but in online forums and SNS. Thus 'information' is considered to be the first and perhaps fundamental function of political participation on SNS, which is then followed by 'discussion'.

As a final consequence (3), *participation*, in a strict sense, is described as the final form of engagement online: This includes becoming active on SNS, for example, founding a political group to inspire others.

Based on our two pre-studies, we came up with a measure of these three forms of political engagement on SNS: *Information*, *Discussion* and *Participation*.

Our Main Study – Method and Procedure

The main study was conducted in late 2012/early 2013. We had access to all students from a German high school in the same area in which our two pre-studies had already been conducted. Again, we carried out a paper-pencil survey in classroom contexts. We interviewed all students that used SNS. Out of a total of 473, we identified 329 students that used SNS, resulting in mostly younger students (grades 5 and 6) being screened out. Our sample ranged from 10 to 20 years of age and 52% of participating students were female. Average age was 15 years (SD = 2.25). We employed a standardised questionnaire with some questions identical with study 1, but our main measures – as mentioned above – were newly constructed for this study.

We specified our main research question and asked: What resources can explain political engagement of adolescents on SNS? For this, we relied (1) on a broad range of measures for adolescents' resources as described above and (2) our three types of political engagement on SNS: *Information*, *Discussion* and *Participation*. The latter became our dependent variables, while the resources acted as independent measures.

Based on the resource model of political participation we included sociodemographic variables (age, gender) as controls but were basically interested in the impact of the civic skills. In this chapter, we first looked at political interest as one underlining factor whose impact has been shown in many different studies (e.g., Spaiser 2012; Wagner 2014; Schneekloth 2015). It was measured with one item 'How much are you interested in politics' (1 = high, 6 = low) ($M = 3.51$, SD = 1.55, $n = 304$). As political discussions are indeed an indicator of political engagement, we argue that for the specific form of online engagement, offline forms may become crucial resources. Thus, as a second factor, we see offline discussion of politics with family and friends. We measured this with four individual one-item measures, each rated on a '1 = often' to '6 = never' scale. We asked how often they discussed politics with their parents ($M = 3.43$), at school ($M = 3.92$) and with friends ($M = 4.17$). Another set of resources related to prior forms of civic engagement offline. Here, the school is one of the most crucial places where adolescents might practice engagement. We measured *Partaking in School* with a combined additive index of four potential activities: classroom spokesperson, member of a student assembly, head of a student assembly and mediator ($M = 0.66$). The last resource we accounted for was to what extent students were accustomed to doing things in their SNS. We could rely on a *Habit Strength for Social Networks Scale* developed from LaRose and Eastin (2004): a combined index of five items rated on a 1–6 scale ($M = 3.43$, $\alpha = 0.854$).

For our dependent measure, we developed three additive index scores; one for *Information*, one for *Discussion* and one for *Participation*. From our pre-studies – particularly our standardised study – we knew that some forms of participation are rarely used: We therefore did not employ a rating scale but came up with a scale that resembles – but should not be mistaken with – a so-called Guttman scale. A typical Guttman scale consists of a list of yes-or-no items, which are ranked regarding their difficulty, so that each item is expected to be more difficult to be accepted. For instance, item 1 states, "Nuclear power is risky"; item 2 states, "Nuclear power cannot be controlled"; and item 3 finally expresses, "The use of nuclear power needs to be forbidden". Participants accepting item 3 are also expected to accept items 1 and 2 and those that only accept item 2 are also expected to accept item 1. We followed the logic of employing yes-or-no type of answers but were not interested in attitudes but in actual behaviour, thus each sub-dimension (*Information, Discussion, Participation*) consisted of behaviours we expected most participants to have carried out but also types of behaviour that only few adolescents would have already done. We then summed up the number of behaviours each adolescent had carried out for each of the three sub-dimensions of political participation on SNS.

For *Information*, we employed four types of behaviours: (1) to click on a link on a political topic, (2) to read a friend's political statement, (3) to like a political website (organisation, politician) and (4) to join a political group on a SNS. Reliability of the scale was mediocre, which can be explained by the yes-no-type answer structure ($\alpha = 0.526$, $n = 329$).

For *Discussion*, we used five items: (1) to share or forward a link on a political topic, (2) to like or comment a link to a political topic, (3) to like or comment a friend's political statement, (4) to post, comment or like something on the wall of a political group, (5) to like, comment or post something on a political SNS ($\alpha = 0.733$, $n = 329$).

For *Participation*, we employed four items: (1) to post a link to a political topic, (2) to post a political statement on an own SNS, (3) to create a SNS for a political topic and (4) to found a political SNS group ($\alpha = 0.597$, $n = 329$).

We then transferred all scores to a 0–4 scale, with 4 the highest level of participation. As expected, rather than to *participate* in a strict sense ($M = 0.32$; $SD = 0.71$), adolescents were more likely to engage through *information* ($M = 1.29$; $SD = 1.11$) than through *discussion* ($M = 1.08$; $SD = 1.18$).

Empirical Results

In order to answer our research question concerning how far adolescents' resources predict their political engagement on SNS, we conducted three hierarchical regression analyses for each of the three different sub-dimensions of political SNS engagement individually. The advantage of hierarchical regressions lies in the fact that we are able to investigate the impact of a broad set of interconnected variables. Therefore, we start with our control measures and in each next step we add a set of variables that we are interested in, moving from the most general to the most specific ones. Thus, variables entered in a later step only become significant predictors if they explain some part of variance that has not yet been explained before.

We carried out our regression models with five blocks each. Block 1 was comprised of sociodemographic control variables (age, gender). Blocks 2 to 5 then included our resources, starting with the political interest measure as the broadest predictor. Political discussion (parents, school, friends online, friends offline) became the third block. Only then did we enter our more specific variables into the equation: Block 4 was comprised of our Habit Strength measure as an indicator for how accustomed adolescents have become to SNS. The final block then accounted for engagement shown in school.

Even though we took a rather broad, exploratory approach, we had some expectations based on the character of each of our resources. We knew, for instance, that sociodemographic variables play a crucial role in predicting political participation. Yet, we expected that if other resources were accounted for, the impact of sociodemographic variables would diminish, as it is often not a matter of gender that boys are deemed to participate more than girls but more likely a matter of political interest (Quientelier 2015; Schneekloth 2015). Second, we expected political interest to be a critical predictor for all types of political participation on SNS. Political discussions will play a more important role for predicting political discussions on SNS, and partaking in school, if at all, will have an impact on participation forms that require more investment on part of the adolescents. Tables 1.2–1.4 give an overview of the key findings of our regression models.

Empirically, our assumptions are strengthened: We see that sociodemographic variables play only a minor role in predicting *Political engagement on SNS*. They are solely a significant predictor for *Information*. In this study, the older our participants are, the more likely they will inform themselves politically on SNS. *Political Interest* is

Table 1.2 Predicting Political Participation on SNS: Information.

	Beta	t-Value	Δr^2 for Block
Block 1			
Age	0.172	2.72***	
Gender	0.068	1.13	
			$r^2 = 0.116$***
Block 2			
Political interest	−0.290	−4.21	
			$\Delta r^2 = 0.098$***
Block 3			
Discussion parents	−0.040	−0.621	
Discussion friends	−0.059	−0.836	
Discussion school	−0.030	−0.452	
			$\Delta r^2 = 0.007$
Block 4			
Habit strength	−0.194	−3.36	
			$\Delta r^2 = 0.036$***
Block 5			
Participation school	0.042	0.74	
			$\Delta r^2 = 0.001$
Model	$F(8,234) = 10.19$***, (adj.) $r^2 = 0.233$		

p-Values: *** $= p < 0.001$; ** $= p < 0.01$, * $= p < 0.05$, (*) $= p < 0.1$.

Table 1.3 Predicting Political Participation on SNS: Discussion.

	Beta	t-Value	Δr^2 for Block
Block 1			
Age	−0.042	−0.632	
Gender	0.088	1.38	
			$r^2 = 0.017$
Block 2			
Political interest	−0.151	−2.06*	
			$\Delta r^2 = 0.051***$
Block 3			
Discussion parents	−0.147	−2.16*	
Discussion friends	−0.043	−0.573	
Discussion school	−0.019	−0.043	
			$\Delta r^2 = 0.024$
Block 4			
Habit strength	−0.247	−4.01***	
			$\Delta r^2 = 0.058***$
Block 5			
Participation school	0.093	1.54	
			$\Delta r^2 = 0.009$
Model	$F (8,234) = 5.50***$, (adj.) $r^2 = 0.130$		

p-Values: *** = $p < 0.001$; ** = $p < 0.01$, * = $p < 0.05$, (*) = $p < 0.1$.

indeed a, if not *the,* most crucial resource. *Political Interest* explains around 5%–10% of the total variance of each of the three forms of *Political engagement on SNS.* For *Participation,* it even becomes the sole significant predictor. *Political Discussions* only play a significant role for explaining *Discussion;* and here, it is only the amount of discussions carried out with one's parents: The more adolescents discuss politics with their parents, the more they engage in political discussions on SNS. Interestingly, *Habit Strength* plays a significant role for both *Information* and *Discussion* but not for *Participation.* The more adolescents are accustomed to using SNS, the more they use it for political information and political discussion. *Partaking at School* did not have an impact on any of the three political engagement forms on SNS. Even so, we have to acknowledge that as expected its effect – albeit not significant – was strongest for *Participation* (p-level as $p = 0.101$).

Looking further into our empirical findings, we see that the overall explanation of variance decreases from *Information* to *Discussion* to *Participation.* Yet, our findings lead the way to a more appropriate

Table 1.4 Predicting Political Participation on SNS: Participation.

	Beta	t-Value	Δr^2 for Block
Block 1			
Age	−0.036	−0.520	
Gender	−0.049	−0.737	
			$r^2 = 0.012$
Block 2			
Political interest	−0.195	−2.55*	
			$\Delta r^2 = 0.046$***
Block 3			
Discussion parents	−0.061	−0.86	
Discussion friends	−0.088	−1.14	
Discussion school	0.087	1.18	
			$\Delta r^2 = 0.013$
Block 4			
Habit strength	−0.077	−1.20	
			$\Delta r^2 = 0.006$
Block 5			
Participation school	−104	1.64	
			$\Delta r^2 = 0.011$
Model	$F(8,234) = 1.52$***, (adj.) $r^2 = 0.056$		

p-Values: *** = $p < 0.001$; ** = $p < 0.01$, * = $p < 0.05$, (*) = $p < .1$.

conceptualisation for predicting all forms of *Political engagement on SNS*.

A Reconceptualisation of Political Engagement on SNS

Our study sets out to find predictors for different forms of political engagement on SNS among adolescents. We are rather successful in explaining the sub-dimension *Information* (overall explanation variance 23%) mainly by two resources: *Political Interest* and *Habit Strength of SNS Use*. For *Discussion*, we may add *Political Discussion with Parents*. And for *Participation* only *Political Interest* remains a significant predictor. Yet, the two lower-key forms of political engagement may also explain *Participation*. *Information* and *Discussion* may indeed be employed to explain the more complex form of *Participation*. We can thus employ our resource model to carve out an empirically grounded path model, where we employ our resource to explain each of the three forms of political engagement on SNS, but also add the explanatory path between the three forms as described in Figure 1.2.

Empirically, we modelled this as a path model that allows multiple interrelated correlations. Figure 1.3 gives an overview of the empirical results. We only included paths that remained significant on the $p < 0.05$ level.

We now see the interrelation between our three participation measures. *Information* is a very strong predictor for *Discussion*, which in itself then becomes a predictor for *Participation*. With respect to the resources, we have to adjust our model: *Political Interest* only remains a significant predictor for *Information* but not for the other two participation forms. The *Political Discussion with Parents* remains a weak, yet significant predictor for *Discussion*. Interestingly, *SNS Habit Strength* is a significant predictor for both *Information* and *Discussion*.

Moving beyond the *statistical* analysis: What does this result tell us in plain words? First, we can describe the political engagement of adolescents on SNS as a three-stage process. Adolescents use SNS to inform themselves about politics. Thereby, two resources play an important role in explaining that adolescents use SNS for information purposes: general political interest and *SNS Habit Strength*. If both are higher, so is the use of SNS for the purpose of gathering political information. This process is then also influenced by age – but not so much by gender as a sociodemographic variable. We understand *Political Interest* as a civic skill and

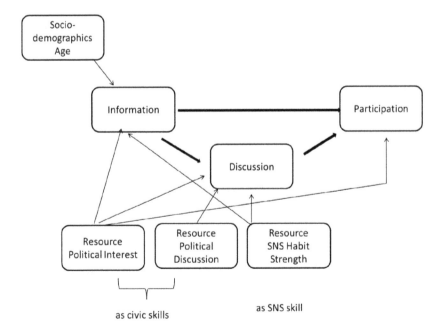

Figure 1.2 A theoretical path model of political engagement.

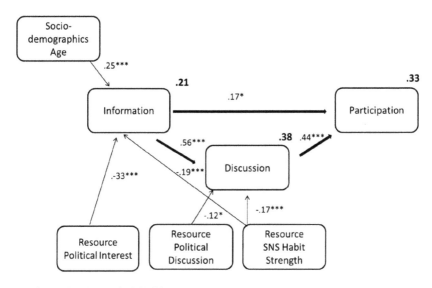

Based on a ML-estimation Path Model
p-Values: *** = p <.001; ** = p <.01, * = p <.05, (*) = p <.1.
Explained Variance in bold
Standardized Regression Weights

Figure 1.3 Empirical path model of political engagement.

SNS Habit Strength as a SNS skill: We thus conclude that both are essential to employ SNS for political information purposes. This *Information* sub-dimension of political engagement is the most common form found among adolescents and it then becomes the precondition for other more complex forms. For instance, it becomes the strongest predictor for political discussions on SNS. Hence, if we use SNS for political information, the chances are increased that we will also engage in political discussions on SNS. Again, the way we are used to employing SNS, that is *SNS Habit Strength*, remains a predictor for this type of political participation on SNS. Furthermore, we see some indications regarding the transfer from the offline to the online world: If adolescents discuss politics with their parents, they are more likely to discuss politics on SNS. Those adolescents who engage in political discussions on SNS are also more likely to engage in the most challenging form of political engagement on SNS: The actual participation through generating own political content.

Crucial Role of Political Interest

In this chapter, we sought to explain the political engagement of adolescents on SNS through a resource-based model of political engagement and participation. Following the framework of the engaged youth paradigm, we argued that even low-level political actions on SNS that are less time- and resource-consuming (such as posting or likening political content) could be seen as some type of political engagement and hence (proto-) political participation.

Following the findings from previous research, we concentrated on three sub-dimensions of political engagement on SNS. Here, we deliberately included low-level actions such as liking, commenting or even only reading political information on a SNS. We found that while the use of SNS for political information was rather prominent, more engaging forms such as using it for political discussions or for the actual creation of political content remain limited.

Second, we carved out crucial resources we considered relevant as predictors of political engagement on SNS among adolescents. On the one hand, these resources were seen as civic skills, such as the general interest in politics or the frequencies of political discussion among friends and parents. On the other, we also included as a SNS skill the habit strength of adolescents' SNS use. In addition, we expected civic engagement in school to play a direct role for political engagement on SNS.

Empirically, we found that political interest plays a crucial role for all types of political engagement on SNS but particularly for *Information*. We also found that the more complex forms of political engagement on SNS become more difficult to predict. Yet, knowing which resources impact which type of participation helped us to come up with a procedural model of political engagement on SNS. This model accounts for the fact that low-level forms of engagement may be seen as a foundation for more challenging participatory forms. What we learn from this procedural model is that political engagement on SNS should be considered as a stage process, with different resources explaining each step individually. However, such a stage-model partially supports the engaged youth paradigm: Small-scale actions such as reading a political article sent from a friend does not in itself lead to much political activism, but it is the foundation for more engaged forms of engagement, first through political discussions and then through actual creative actions. Civic skills learned without digital media, through discussions with parents but also through the development of a general interest in politics. SNS-related skills support this process as well.

From a normative perspective, adolescent's political engagement is still low and leaves plenty of room for development. But the model we present in this chapter argues that when we consider forms of low-level activity (also called micro-activism), for example commenting and liking of political statements on SNS, substantially higher levels of political engagement are found. Thus, these forms of low-level activity are more than just a mere substitute for elaborate political engagement and participation offline: Our findings clearly indicate that they may be fundaments for more complex forms of participation online. Insofar, we understand a necessity for further research in analysing the origins of the underlying resources (political discussions with friends, family and in school).

As a consequence of our research, we urge to have an open mind to new and seemingly low-level forms of political engagement and participation. Decreasing partisan memberships and low voter turn-out among young voters are not so much a sign of lacking political engagement but are perhaps indicative of a gradual shift in the way politics are perceived by young people. There is no longer a distinc-tion between the offline and the online world, and this is particu-larly true for the political realm of adolescents. Some forms of their engagement might not even be seen in themselves as being political but we could demonstrate that even liking and sharing political con-tent is a basis for more complex forms of political engagement. For the adolescents in our sample, the questions remained rather vague and abstract. It may be interesting to see how far our model will be supported if applied to concrete forms of political action. For us, perceiving online engagement not as political can indeed be viewed as a misunderstanding of political participation.

Notes

1 Forms were (1) signing an online petition, (2) taking part in a mailing cam-paign, (3) taking part in a flash mob, (4) participating in an email bomb, (5) taking part in an online demonstration, (6) supporting the election cam-paign of a party online.
2 Forms were (1) befriending a politician on a Social Network Site, (2) adding your political views to your personal profile, (3) using a political logo as pro-file picture, (4) writing a political statement into your status, (5) following the page of a political party, (6) following the page of a political organisa-tion, (7) taking part in a political discussion on a Social Network Site (e.g., in a group).

References

Albero-Andrés, M., Olsson, T., Bastardas-Boada, A., and Miegel, F. (2009). *Young people, the Internet and civic participation. A qualitative analysis of European web-based civic participation among young people.* CivicWeb Deliverable 17, London. Accessed August 1, 2017. www.civicweb.eu/images/stories/reports/civicweb%20wp11%20final.pdf.

Bakardjieva, M. (2009). Subactivism: Lifeworld and politics in the age of the internet. *The Information Society,* 25(2), 91–104.

Bakker, T. P., and de Vreese, C. H. (2011). Good news for the future? Young people, internet use, and political participation. *Communication Research,* 38(4), 451–470.

Barber, B. R. (1984). *Strong democracy: Participatory politics for a new age.* Berkeley, CA: University of California Press.

Bennett, W. L. (2008). Changing citizenship in the digital age. In W. L. Bennett (ed.), *Civic life online: Learning how digital media can engage youth* (1–24). Cambridge, MA: MIT Press.

Bennett, W. L., Wells, C., and Rank, A. (2009). Young citizens and civic learning: Two paradigms of citizenship in the digital age. *Citizenship Studies*, 13(2), 105–120.

boyd, d. (2014). *It's complicated. The social lives of networked teens.* New Haven, CT and London: Yale University Press.

Brady, H. E., Verba, S., and Schlozman, K. L. (1995). Beyond SES: A resource model of political participation. *American Political Science Review*, 89(2), 271–294.

Ekman, J., and Amnå, E. (2012). Political participation and civic engagement: Towards a new typology. *Human Affairs*, 22(3), 283–300.

Emmer, M., Vowe, G., and Wolling, J. (2011). *Bürger online. Die Entwicklung der politischen Online-Kommunikation in Deutschland* [Citizens online. The evolution of political online-communication in Germany]. Konstanz: UVK.

Feil, C. (2004). Mythen und Fakten zur Kommerzialisierung der Kindheit [Myths and facts about the commercialization of childhood]. *ZSE: Zeitschrift für Soziologie der Erziehung und Sozialisation*, 24(1), 33–48.

Gaiser, W., and Gille, M. (2012). Soziale und politische Partizipation. Trends, Differenzierungen, Herausforderungen [Civic and political participation. Trends, differentiations, challenges]. In T. Rauschenbach and W. Bien (eds.), *Aufwachsen in Deutschland*. AID:A – Der neue DJI-Survey (136–159). Weinheim and Basel: Beltz Juventa.

Jenkins, H. (2009). *Confronting the challenges of participatory culture.* Cambridge, MA: MIT Press.

Jöckel, S., Kamps, K., and Potz, A. (2014). Digitale Partizipation Jugendlicher [Digital participation of adolescents]. In J. Einspänner-Pflock, M. Dang-Anh, and C. Thimm (eds.), *Digitale Gesellschaft – Partizipationskulturen im Netz* (148–168). Berlin: LIT.

Kupferschmitt, T. (2015). Bewegtbildnutzung nimmt weiter zu – Habitualisierung bei 14- bis 29-Jährigen. Ergebnisse der ARD/ZDF-Onlinestudie 2015 [Rising use of moving pictures – Habitualization in the use of 14- to 19-year olds. Results of the ARD/ZDF-Online-Study 2015]. *Media Perspektiven, 9*, 383–391.

LaRose, R., and M. S. Eastin. (2004). A social cognitive theory of Internet uses and gratifications: Toward a new model of media attendance. *Journal of Broadcasting and Electronic Media*, 48(3), 358–377.

Leighly, J. E. (1995). Attitudes, opportunities and incentives: A field essay on political participation. *Political Research Quarterly*, 48(1), 181–209.

Lenhart, A., Smith, A., Anderson, M., Duggan, M., and Perrin, A. (2015). Teens, technology & friendships. Video games, social media and mobile phones play an integral role in how teens meet and interact with friends. Pew Research Center, August, 2015. Accessed August 1, 2017. http://www.pewinternet.org/2015/08/06/teens-technology-and-friendships/

Lim, J. S., and Golan, G. J. (2011). Social media activism in response to the influence of political parody videos on YouTube. *Communication Research*, 38(5), 710–727.

Livingstone, S., Mascheroni, G., and Staksrud, E. (2015). *Developing a framework for researching children's online risks and opportunities in Europe*. London: EU Kids Online.

Livingston, S., and Sefton-Green, J. (2016). *The class: Living and learning in the digital age*. New York, NY: New York University Press.

Marichal, J. (2010). *Political Facebook groups: Micro-activism and the digital front stage. Presented at the Internet, politics, policy 2010: An impact assessment*. Oxford. Accessed August 1, 2017. http://ipp.oii.ox.ac.uk/sites/ipp.oii.ox.ac.uk/files/documents/IPP2010_Marichal_Paper.pdf.

Mascheroni, G. (2013). Performing citizenship online: Identity, subactivism and participation. *Observatorio, 7*(3), 93–119.

Milbrath, L. W. (1965). *Political participation: How and why do people get involved in politics?* Chicago, MI: Rand McNally.

[Mpfs] Medienpädagogischer Forschungsverbund Südwest. (2015). *JIM 2015. Jugend, Information, (Multi-) Media. Basisuntersuchung zum Medienumgang 12- bis 19-Jähriger*. [Adolescents, information, (multi-)media. Basic research on the media use of young people from 12 to 19 years]. Accessed August 1, 2017. www.mpfs.de/fileadmin/JIM-pdf15/JIM_2015.pdf.

Norris, P. (2003). *Young people & political activism: From the politics of loyalties to the politics of choice?* Cambridge, MA: Harvard University. Accessed August 1, 2017. www.hks.harvard.edu/fs/pnorris/Acrobat/COE.pdf.

Ogris, G., and Westphal, S. (2006). Politisches Verhalten Jugendlicher in Europa [Political Behavior of Adolescents in Europe]. *Aus Politik und Zeitgeschichte, 53*(47), 7–17.

Potz, A. (2014). Let's talk about politics! Eine qualitative Studie zum Politikbegriff Jugendlicher. [A qualitative study on the understanding of politics of adolescents]. In D. Frieß, J. Jax, and M. Michalski (eds.), *Sprechen Sie EU? Das kommunikative Versagen einer großen Idee* (239–258). Berlin: Frank & Timme.

Putnam, R. D. (1993). The prosperous community. Social capital and public life. *The American Prospect, 13*(4), 35–42.

Quintelier, E. (2015). Engaging adolescents in politics: The longitudinal effect of political socialization Agents. *Youth & Society, 47*(1), 51–69.

Rauschenbach, T., Begemann, M.-C., Bröring, M., Düx, W., and Sass, E. (2011). *Jugendliche Aktivitäten im Wandel. Gesellschaftliche Beteiligung und Engagement in Zeiten des Web 2.0* [Changing activities of adolescents. Civic participation and engagement in times of Web 2.0]. Dortmund: Forschungsverbund Deutsches Jugendinstitut und Technische Universität Dortmund. Accessed August 1, 2017. www.forschungsverbund.tu-dortmund.de/fileadmin/Files/Engement/Abschlusberic ht_Engagement_2_0.pdf.

Rheingold, H. (2000). *The virtual community. Homesteading on the electronic frontier*. Cambridge and London: MIT.

Schneekloth, U. (2015). Jugend und Politik: Zwischen positivem Gesellschaftsbild und anhaltender Politikverdrossenheit [Adolescence and politics: Between a positive view on society and continuous political cynism]. In Shell Deutschland Holding (ed.), *Jugend 2010: Eine pragmatische Generation behauptet sich* (157–199). Frankfurt a.M.: Fischer.

Spaiser, V. (2012). Empowerment or democratic divide? Internet-based political participation of young immigrants and young natives. *Information Polity, 17*(2), 115–127.

Verba, S., and Nie, N. H. (1972). *Participation in America. Political democracy and social equality.* Chicago and London: The University of Chicago Press.

Wagner, U. (2014). Jugend, Information und Partizipation online. Zur Differenzierung von Beteiligungsformen im Internet [Adolescence, information and participation online. Differentiating forms of participations on the internet]. In J. Einspänner-Pflock, M. Dang-Anh, and C. Thimm (eds.), *Digitale Gesellschaft – Partizipationskulturen im Netz* (169–189). Berlin: LIT.

2 Long-Lasting Shadows of (Post)Communism? Generational and Ethnic Divides in Political and Civic Participation in Estonia

Veronika Kalmus, Ragne Kõuts-Klemm, Mai Beilmann, Andu Rämmer and Signe Opermann

Political and Civic Participation in Estonia

The first years after the collapse of communism witnessed diminishing participation in politics everywhere in Central and Eastern Europe (Howard 2002; Fuchs and Klingemann 2006). Since then, the relative weakness of post-communist civil society has become almost an axiomatic knowledge in social scientific literature, supported by cross-regional empirical studies (World Values Survey; see Inglehart 2006). Several hypothetical scenarios and remedies to the situation have been proposed, among them generational change, improvement of economic conditions and living standards, encouraging state initiatives and policies, and, more recently, placing hopes on unprecedented opportunities provided by online participation and social media activism. Long-term empirical research to map actual trends and developments is, however, scarce.

This chapter explores patterns of political and civic participation in Estonia in a dynamic perspective, covering the period between 2002 and 2014. Our research interest stems from two different points of departure. On the one hand, it can be assumed that post-communist civil societies are suffering from similar kinds of post-totalitarian trauma (Sztompka 2004). On the other hand, it is likely that dissimilar political and socioeconomic development paths after the collapse of the Soviet bloc have contributed to the formation of different civic participation patterns in Eastern European countries.

We focus on Estonia, a former republic of the Soviet Union. We assume that the background of being the most liberal part of the Soviet Union and the peaceful restoration of independence in 1991 has been a facilitator of the development of civil society in its post-communist era. Moreover, Estonia was the first among the former Soviet Republics to begin post-communist reforms (Norkus 2007) and experienced one of the fastest political and economic transformations in Eastern Europe (Vihalemm and Kalmus 2008). Specifically, the highly liberal economic reforms carried out in the 1990s have been highlighted as the key component of the accelerated movement of Estonia on the transitional path. Closely related to the economy-dominated transformation paradigm, technological development has been a crucial component of Estonian transition. Internetisation has become one of the central symbols of the rapidly changing society, leading to a widely held perception of Estonia as a leading e-state (Runnel et al. 2009).

Political analysts have expressed different opinions about Estonia. On the positive side, Grzymala-Busse (2007) considers the political development of Estonia to be rather successful, compared with many other Eastern European countries. Rose and Munro (2003), however, evaluated the political processes in post-socialist countries from a different angle and reached a more critical conclusion. According to their comparative surveys, the political culture in Estonia can be characterised by the domination of voters who do not trust political parties, and by weak party institutionalisation, which means that voters cannot hold their government accountable. This argument concerning the deficit of accountability is supported by Lagerspetz' (2001) assessment regarding the weakness of civil society institutions in Estonia where a low number of active voluntary associations are unable to form a significant counterbalance to party politics.

These, partly contradictory, developments make Estonia a promising case for a closer inspection of the presumed healing process from post-totalitarian trauma and restoration of civil society. We will examine participation in institutional politics (exercised mainly through identification with and interest in political parties and voting), civic participation and engagement (for instance, participation in civic organisations, and various political and civic actions organised by them), as well as usage of the internet and social media networks for the purpose of engaging in political and civic life. As social trust is often regarded as a prerequisite and cornerstone of a viable civil society (Newton 2007), we will also present trends in generalised social trust, and trust in state institutions. In taking a comprehensive survey-based approach to civic and political engagement, this chapter contributes to understanding participation in its various forms as a set of practices and dispositions that may presumably form different patterns and assemblages. Furthermore, our analysis of the developmental trends of political and civic engagement in a particular context of social transformation provides an additional perspective for mapping and interpreting the ambiguities of participation.

In terms of sociodemographic analysis, we focus on two, presumably most-salient factors. First, in the context of profound societal changes, disparate socialisation experiences of different age cohorts have been theorised as playing a prominent role in the formation of historical or social generations characterised by distinctive generational consciousness (Mannheim 1927, 1952) and, we may say, habitus (Edmunds and Turner 2002). Substantial intergenerational differences in post-socialist societies have been emphasised, in particular, by Sztompka (2004) and Marada (2004), and demonstrated in previous studies of Estonian transition culture, namely the analyses of identity and value patterns (Kalmus and Vihalemm 2008; Vihalemm and Kalmus 2008). Furthermore, previous studies of civic engagement and participatory performance (Rikmann et al. 2012) clearly suggest that civic activities of Estonian inhabitants can be distinguished across age groups.

Second, the transition of Estonia has an ethnic aspect. Estonia is a multi-ethnic society where the titular group, ethnic Estonians, forms 69% of the population, and Russians as the biggest group among ethnic minorities form 25% of the people (Põder 2015). Most of the Russians who settled in Estonia in Soviet times came 'as a result of coerced immigration by the Soviet authorities' (Vihalemm and Kalmus 2008, 906). When the former Soviet Union disintegrated and the Estonian Republic was restored as an independent state, the sociopolitical status of the Russians changed. Thus, in the transformation period, Estonian Russians have faced a double challenge of coping and self-determination, both in terms of transition and the Estonian nation-state (Vihalemm and Kalmus 2008), which presumably has an effect on their political and civic engagement.

This chapter seeks to answer the following research questions:

1   What are the general trends of political and civic participation in Estonia in the observed period of social transformation? What are the main differences and similarities between generations, and between the ethnic majority and minority groups?
2   How can Estonian people be divided into types of political and civic participation? How can these types be characterised in terms of generational and ethnic divisions, and media use, including social media activities?

Theoretical and Empirical Context

The weakness of post-communist civil society, evidenced, for instance, in relatively low levels of organisational membership, has been emphasised since the early 1990s (Howard 2002; Halpern 2005). This criticism stems, on the one hand, from the fact that the hopes for a quick blossoming of post-communist civil society were idealistically high. Historical experience, however, has shown that after the collapse of totalitarian regimes (e.g., the Nazi regime in Germany after the World War II) people are rather reluctant to participate in any organisation because of the negative experiences of mass organisations they were forced to join (Howard 2002; Offe and Fuchs 2002). Furthermore, the fear about the declining civic engagement, especially among the young people, is present also in contemporary Western societies where people are less inclined than before to vote, to join political parties, to campaign for social causes, or to trust political process (Banaji and Buckingham 2013; Banaji and Cammaerts 2014; Sloam 2014). Therefore, the low levels of civic participation in the former Soviet bloc may be part of bigger and more global trends of declining civic engagement.

The diminishing trend of civic participation in the Western world, though, is not unanimously taken as an axiomatic knowledge. The forms of political and civic participation are shifting as classical forms of participation (e.g., organisational membership) are losing their importance and new forms are gaining more popularity. Information seeking, information providing, information retrieving and information interpretation are considered more and more as forms of political participation (Micheletti 2006). Especially young people are seen as being prone to these changes, and sometimes high hopes are put on new media and the internet as a means of revitalising civic life (Banaji and Buckingham 2013; Sloam 2014; Sveningsson 2014). Bennet et al. (2011), for example, acknowledge that young people's political participation today is rather defined by peer content sharing and social media use, and not so much by the models of political and civic participation of earlier generations.

However, there is also a more critical perspective towards new avenues opened by online participation. Sveningsson (2014) studied young Swedes' understandings of social media and found that even the youth who were rather interested in civic and political issues were quite sceptical about using social media in relation to politics and considered online political activities less authentic than their offline equivalents.

Nevertheless, as the different modes of handling information are increasingly important forms of political participation (Micheletti 2006), the choices people make in their everyday media consumption become more important than ever before. Wolfsfeld et al. (2016, 2096) claim that 'in today's high-choice media environment, individuals and groups with the highest level of political interest are more likely to develop richer political information repertoires that involve exploiting both digital and traditional ways of searching for political information. Individuals and groups with richer political information repertoires can be expected to have higher levels of political knowledge, efficacy, and participation'. We may, thus, conclude that besides traditional ways of information seeking and participation, digital skills and new forms of engagement are becoming increasingly important for varied political and civic participation.

Before online participation became an issue, institutional and generalised social trust, volunteerism, and participation in civic organisations were often regarded as the cornerstones of a strong civil society (Putnam 2000; Howard 2002; Putnam 2002; Halpern 2005). Information seeking, news consumption, and trust may be considered the foundations of civic life today as well (Banaji and Cammaerts 2014). As trust is equally important for classical civic ideals and new online participation, we focus on this concept in more detail.

Newton (2007) distinguished between social and political trust: the former referring to trust in other people and the latter to trust in institutions on the basis of people's sense of the performance of institutions. Newton suggests maintaining a clear conceptual distinction between the social and the political to explore the social foundations of politics. Generalised trust in other people, in institutions, and in media are all positively related to political participation. Furthermore, active and diverse media use is related to more active participation in social life and higher trust in institutions (Kõuts et al. 2013).

Different forms of trust are unevenly distributed between groups of people and between different countries (Delhey and Newton 2005; Beilmann and Lilleoja 2015). In post-communist countries, the levels of generalised trust in other people, in institutions and in media are relatively low (Lovell 2001; Delhey and Newton 2002; Howard 2002; Kõuts et al. 2013; Beilmann and Lilleoja 2015). Estonia, however, forms an exception to this pattern. Generalised social trust levels are rather high in Estonia, resembling the patterns in German- and English-speaking countries in Europe more than the other former Eastern bloc countries (Beilmann and Lilleoja 2015). Kõuts et al. (2013, 86) emphasise that

> when compared to other European countries, the level of institutional trust in parliament, government and all media types in Estonia is significantly higher than the EU average; it is not only almost the highest among EEC countries, but it is also comparable with 'old' EU countries, although it does not reach the level of Scandinavian nations.

For the purposes of this chapter, it is also important to outline the trajectory of Estonia in the cross-national context. About two decades ago, several comparative studies characterised post-communist societies in Europe as a rather coherent group (see, e.g., Howard 2002; Inglehart 2006; Pettai et al. 2011). These studies concluded that despite different religious and cultural heritage these societies shared a common powerful experience of life under the communist rule, and nearly the same length of such domination imprinted all societies in a similar way. Inglehart (2006, 67) revealed that 'most central and east European publics rank substantially lower on survival/self-expression values – a syndrome of tolerance, trust, well-being, and emphasis on self-expression that is closely linked with democracy'. He, nevertheless, also reported that 'large differences exist between value systems of the historically Catholic or Protestant ex-communist societies of central and Eastern Europe, and the historically Orthodox ex-communist societies' (Inglehart 2006, 67). The position of Estonia in the Inglehart's value system is, thus, determined by two opposite factors: as a former Soviet Republic, it was exposed to the impact of Communist rule, while the Protestant cultural heritage probably makes it more responsive to the development of civil society.

Representative Survey "Me. The World. The Media"

The analysis is based on data from a representative survey "Me. The World. The Media", carried out every third year since 2002 by the Institute of Social Studies, University of Tartu, in cooperation with market research companies. The survey (a self-administered questionnaire, combined with an interview) covers the Estonian population aged between 15 and 79. We apply a proportional model of the general population (by areas and urban/rural division) and multistep probability random sampling (realised through primary random sampling of settlements with a proportional likelihood related to the size of the settlement, followed by random sampling of households and individuals). In addition, a quota is applied to include a proportional number of representatives of the ethnic majority and the minority, differentiated according to the preferred language of the survey interview (Estonian or Russian, respectively). In order to alleviate the differences between the representativeness of the sample model (based on demographic statistics data) and the survey outcome, the collected data were weighted by the main sociodemographic attributes (gender, age, ethnicity, education, and place of residence).

This chapter draws mostly upon two waves of the survey: the first, which took place from December 2002 to January 2003 (n = 1,470; age range 15–74), and the fifth, conducted in August–September 2014 (n = 1,503; age range 15–79).

To analyse generational differences in political and civic participation, we cut the sample into five age groups, each covering 12 years. The five groups represent age cohorts rather than delineating social generations in Mannheim's (1927, 1952) sense: the groups are large and internally heterogeneous, and the cut-off points in the continuum of birth years were chosen for statistical reasons. The age groups are of comparable size and, as the distance between two measurements is almost 12 years, it is possible to observe how nearly the same birth cohorts' positioning vis-à-vis each other has changed in this period (see Table 2.1). Furthermore, in following Spitzer's (1973) advice, we assume that, if age-specific differences are historically significant, they will reveal themselves wherever the cut-offs are made in the continuum.

Table 2.1 Dynamics in Political and Civic Participation by Generations and Ethnic Groups in 2002 and 2014 (%)

	Year of survey	All	15–27	28–40	41–53	54–66	67–74 (79)	Sig.	Estonians	Estonian Russians	Sig.
Years of birth	2002	1928–1987	1975–1987	1962–1974	1949–1961	1936–1948	1928–1935				
	2014	1935–1999	1987–1999	1974–1986	1961–1973	1948–1960	1935–1947				
N	2002	1470	352	367	326	291	134		940	509	
	2014	1503	309	239	304	348	304		1028	475	
Social trust (agree that most people can be trusted)	2002	24	20	22	29	26	16	*	25	20	NS
	2014	36	32	36	40	36	34	NS	36	35	NS
Identify themselves with an existing political party in Estonia	2002	59	57	56	58	65	67	NS	64	49	**
	2014	65	49	64	66	69	76	**	66	65	NS
Are not interested in politics, are not familiar with the political parties	2002	26	29	30	26	18	22	NS	23	32	**
	2014	21	33	22	17	17	14	**	20	22	NS
Do not remember whether they voted in last local elections	2002	30	35	36	34	19	19	**	31	30	NS
	2014	6	9	5	6	3	6	**	5	6	NS
Do not remember whether they voted in last parliament elections	2002	24	27	31	25	15	10	**	22	27	NS
	2014	9	15	11	8	5	6	**	9	7	NS
Do not participate in any civic organisation	2002	69	74	71	66	68	63	**	69	70	NS
	2014	42	41	40	39	44	43	NS	38	50	**

Note: * p < 0.01; ** p < 0.001 (based on Cramer's V).

Political and civic participation as well as media use characteristics were measured by a number of original single indicators on the basis of which several cumulative indexes were calculated to aggregate the data and highlight more general trends. All indicators were collectively developed by the research group of the Institute of Social Studies; theoretical concepts and inductive reasoning in mapping the emerging real-life phenomena (e.g., forms of online engagement) were employed in operationalisation. We use descriptive statistics and the analysis of variance (ANOVA) to determine statistically significant differences between the generation groups and between Estonians and Estonian Russians. To create a typology of political and civic participation, we used K-means cluster analysis based on index variables.

The Dynamics of Political and Civic Participation

Rising Levels of Social Trust

The beginning of our period of observation, the early 2000s, coincides with the time of active preparations for accession to the EU and NATO. Lauristin and Vihalemm (2009, 14) characterise the sociopolitical milieu of that period in Estonia by deepening contradictions

> between the interests of the new social agencies (national business circles, the academic community, unions of medical professionals and teachers, new farmers, local municipalities) and the political agenda pursued by the government, referring to the external demands shaped by the EU pre-accession *acquis communautaire.*

In the atmosphere of rising tensions and dissatisfaction, the media expressed growing distrust in public institutions, the parliament and the government.

Our data reveal that the low tide in social atmosphere was followed by steady recovery: trust in state institutions grew in the period of 2002–2014 (Figure 2.1). The only exception to this pattern is a small decline in trust in the institution of president that can be explained by differences in the political personas of two presidents. Nevertheless, we may conclude that Estonian citizens at large have become more satisfied with the functioning of the state and democracy. No significant intergenerational differences in institutional trust exist. Ethnic Estonians and Estonian Russians, however, are rather different in this matter: the ethnic majority trusts state institutions more than the Russian-speaking minority does. This is not surprising; in the early 1990s, after the dissolution of the Soviet Union, the minority rather lost than won when compared to ethnic Estonians (Hansson 2001). Persisting shadows of this experience are reflected in our data regarding political trust.

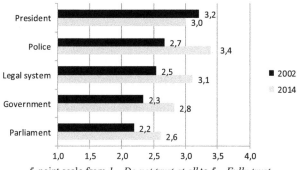

Figure 2.1 Average trust in state institutions in 2002 and 2014.

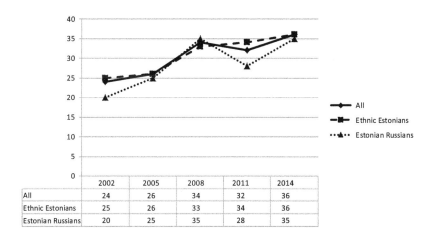

Question: "Generally speaking, would you say that most people can be trusted?"
(Can be fully trusted + Can usually be trusted; %)

Figure 2.2 Dynamics in generalised social trust by ethnic groups in 2002–2014.

Levels of generalised social trust have also grown slowly but steadily in the observed period (Figure 2.2). Differences between ethnic groups existed, with Estonian Russians being somewhat less trusting in 2002 and 2011, but the contrasts have levelled by the end of the period. Furthermore, no statistically significant differences between generations manifest in 2014 (Table 2.1). The cohort dynamics reveals that two younger generations, in particular, have gained in their belief that most people can be trusted. We may interpret such a comprehensive increase in the level of generalised social trust as sign of a growing sense of perceived security and a favourable seedbed for the development of civic culture in society.

Changes in Political Participation

In the middle of the 1990s, after exhaustive reforms, interest in politics was low in all Baltic States: only approximately a quarter of the Estonian population indicated that politics occupied a high rank in their life, and the figure was even lower among Estonian Russians (Titma and Rämmer 2006). Our analysis reveals that the proportion of people who share the views of one political party or another has slightly grown, whereby increased identification with political parties can largely be attributed to steeply growing interest in party politics among Estonian Russians (Table 2.1). Furthermore, in 2014 somewhat less people said that they were not interested in party politics, and differences between Estonians and Estonian Russians had levelled in this aspect, too. Such a remarkable expansion of identification with political parties among the Russian minority refers, to some extent, to the equalisation and democratisation of Estonian political culture. While Estonian Russians found themselves in a plight after the collapse of the Soviet Union (Kymlicka 2000), their changed attitudes refer to adjustment with the political system. Ethnic Estonians and the Russian minority, however, feel affinity with different political parties: in particular, the central-left populist Central Party gathered an increasing number of Russian votes during the observed period.

The expansion in political identification is evident among all age groups, except the youngest respondents, 15- to 27-year-olds, who demonstrated a lower level of interest in party politics in 2014 than their counterparts in 2002 did (Table 2.1). This trend is in line with the declining conventional political engagement among young people in Western societies (Banaji and Buckingham 2013; Banaji and Cammaerts 2014; Sloam 2014). The intra-cohort dynamics, however, show that all four comparable generation groups have become more prone to identification with political parties in 12 years of maturation. That period marks stabilisation (or even stagnation) of the political system in Estonia. The ruling Reform Party has been the most successful political player for years, and the main opposition force, the Central Party, has also steadily enjoyed high support. Previous research, too, has revealed a clear connection between political identification and support for the political system (Delhey and Tobsch 2000; Kõuts 2004).

Participation in voting as the most basic form of conventional political engagement shows a trend similar to that of social trust and interest in party politics. Pettai et al. (2011) noted on the basis of the European Value Study that electoral participation in Estonia dropped noticeably after the founding elections of the early 1990s, being lowest in 1999 when only 41% of respondents reported having voted in national parliament elections. Lower levels of participation at the end of the 1990s can be explained by political alienation and voter fatigue (Pettai et al. 2011), and by post-communist disappointment (Howard 2002). The 2000s saw a slight but steady increase in electoral participation, which reached 55% of turnout in 2011. Besides rising levels of social trust and political identification, the introduction of e-voting in Estonia has contributed to electoral participation: about one third of the electorate, irrespective of ethnicity, age or income, uses this option as a convenient means of political participation (Vassil et al. 2015).

As attitudes towards voting can be even more telling than voting behaviour, we focus our trend analysis on the issue of remembering participation in the last parliamentary and local elections (Table 2.1). A sharp decline in the share of people who did not remember whether they voted or not in the last elections is noteworthy, being similar in the case of both election types and ethnic groups as well as across all four comparable age cohorts. Except for 15- to 27-year-olds who display a more apathetic attitude than older age groups in 2014, the overall trend suggests that political participation has occupied an increasingly crucial role in Estonian citizens' lives by the end of the observed period.

Changes in Civic Engagement

In the middle of the 1990s, participation in voluntary organisations was low in all post-communist societies. Howard (2002) explains this by three factors: mistrust towards all kinds of organisational membership due to bad experiences of forced membership in communist-era organisations; general post-communist disenchantment; and the persistence of friendship networks that had formed in the Soviet period to cope with a shortage economy. Hansson (2001), however, has noted that in Estonia the majority of such exchange networks were disconnected in the 1990s.

Our data reveal that participation in civic organisations has grown substantially in 12 years (Table 2.1). In 2002, more than two thirds of Estonian citizens did not report membership in any union or organisation. Twelve years later, less than half of Estonian people had remained outsiders in this respect. It should be noted, however, that the most common civic associations in Estonia are apartment and consumer co-operatives: the latter have a long historical tradition, and formation of apartment cooperatives is prescribed by law. In 2014, nearly one third of Estonian citizens participated in apartment and/or consumer cooperatives, whereby in older age groups the participation level in this type of associations reached 40%.

It is also noteworthy that membership in civic organisations has increased substantially – more than 30% – among the two youngest age groups. The youngest respondents (aged 15–27) participate, first and foremost, in sports clubs or other sport-related organisations, and in choirs, dance clubs, or other art and culture organisations. It is important to note that the participation rates among the youngest generation are boosted by very high participation among 15- to 19-year-olds, while young people aged 20–27 are somewhat less active in civic society. Boulianne and Brailey (2014, 376) report a similar trend among Canadian youth: 'While secondary schools have successfully promoted volunteerism among teenagers, the effects are short-lived' as levels of civic engagement drop steeply when young people graduate from secondary schools and enter universities.

Over the observed period, a significant gap between ethnic Estonians and the Russian minority emerged: half of Estonian Russians (compared to 38% of the ethnic majority) do not participate in any civic organisation. Estonians prevail in almost all types of organisations, except in apartment and consumer cooperatives, and religious organisations, which are more popular among the Russian minority.

Participation in Civic and Political Activities: Real-Life Versus Digitally Mediated Forms

Our data from 2014 allow juxtaposing traditional ways of participation in civic and political actions and activities with online forms of political engagement (Table 2.2). The analysis reveals that over past years more than one third of Estonian people have participated in different activities and actions organised by civic organisations and associations. All in all, participation in civic events and activities is a bit more common than engagement in political actions. Most popular forms of participation are massive clean-up actions, charity, and taking part at memorial events, but also signing protests or petitions.

So far, digitally mediated forms of political engagement have not reached the popularity level of real-life activities. For instance, signing petitions on the internet is less common than its offline counterpart even among the youngest age groups. This tendency may be indicative of the perception of real-life political activities as being more authentic than identical online practices. Furthermore, the relatively modest level of digitally mediated political engagement can be explained by the fact that the youngest generations, while being the most active internet users, are more prone to personal and entertainment-related online activities than the institutional aspects of digital communication (Kalmus et al. 2013).

Differences between age groups are of a more qualitative nature, depending on the type of personal resources needed for participation in particular activities. The oldest generations are more active in participating at memorial events and the ones organised by church, which tend not to demand too much personal initiative and input. Middle-aged citizens prefer collection bees, while younger people are more active in participating in sports events and voluntary work. All observed forms of digitally mediated political engagement decrease linearly with growing age, reflecting the overall pattern of age-based digital stratification

Table 2.2 Participation in Civic and Political Actions and Activities in 2014 (%)

	All	15–27	28–40	41–53	54–66	67–79	Sig.	Estonians	Estonian Russians	Sig.
Civic actions and activities										
Garbage collection bees, home decoration bees	38	37	33	42	43	31	*	40	32	*
Helping the needy with money, things, clothes	37	31	45	42	37	29	NS	41**	26**	**
Memorial events	36	35	28	30	40	44	**	40	27	**
Public sports events (rallies, races, ski marathons, etc.)	22	41	30	26	13	5	**	26	14	**
Concerts, family events, etc. organised by church	18	14	14	17	20	22	*	20	12	**
Voluntary work	17	26	17	19	13	11	**	21	8	**
Political actions and activities										
Signing a protest or a petition	37	38	41	39	35	33	NS	45	20	**
Participation at a public meeting where political or social problems were discussed	30	27	20	29	35	32	NS	37	14	**
Wearing a sign or a ribbon with political message or using a sticker	16	17	15	19	15	14	NS	13	23	**
Approaching personally a politician or a high official with ideas or proposals	13	11	15	13	14	14	NS	17	5	**
Participation in demonstration	13	10	8	14	14	15	NS	14	10	NS
Online political engagement										
Signing petitions on the internet	19	28	27	23	14	6	**	25	7	**
Joining a support or protest campaign with political content on Facebook or other social networks	18	36	24	16	8	5	**	21	10	**
Participation in political discussion on the internet (writing articles, sending e-mails, posting comments)	16	25	19	18	10	8	**	19	9	**

Note: * p < 0.01; ** p < 0.001 (based on Cramer's V).

in Estonia, and the fact that older age groups are more deprived of the opportunity of interacting with political actors and institutions via new media (Kalmus et al. 2013).

Compared to intergenerational variety, ethnic differences are more systematic and striking. Estonian Russians have engaged significantly less in almost all civic and political activities, except participating in demonstrations and wearing signs or ribbons with a political message. The latter's popularity among the Russian minority can be associated with the Ribbon of Saint George that symbolises the emerging search for Russian identity in historical and iconic symbols. Some other cultural factors play a role in ethnic differences in civic and political participation. For instance, the higher power of loyalty among Russians helps to explain their lower levels of protest behaviour, for instance, signing protests or petitions, which manifested already in the early 1990s (Titma and Rämmer 2006). Most of the ethnic differences in participation levels, however, seem to reflect the minority's lesser social resources, such as looser ties with state institutions (Ehin 2009) and less extensive social capital (Hansson 2001).

Typology of Citizens

This section employs cluster analysis to identify distinct types of political and civic participation based on the 2014 data. As input indicators for the cluster analysis, we used eight aggregated indices formed on the basis of a number of single indicators. Those index variables measure, at a higher level of generalisation, frequency of engagement in various types of civic and political activity (general interest in politics and the level of political activity, participation in civic organisations, and participation in civic actions), and relevant attitudes and predispositions (political apathy and ignorance; trust in state institutions; general social trust; opinion that a citizen's voice counts; and self-evaluated level of being informed about national and local matters; see Table 2.3).

After testing different algorithms (hierarchical and K-means clustering) and combinations of variables, the best model was calculated by using the K-means method. A four-cluster solution turned out to be the clearest and the best for interpretation. Furthermore, the results of ANOVA were explored to check whether the solution served the principle of maximising differences between the clusters, and whether the differences in all input variables were statistically significant.

The following section describes the four types of citizens in terms of political and civic participation (Figure 2.3), ethnic and age composition, media use, and engagement in civic and political activities on social media (Table 2.3). The types differentiate, first and foremost, on the dimension of conventional institutional versus non-institutional participation that is reflected in the names of the types. Furthermore, the

Table 2.3 Characterisation of Citizen Types (Percentages and Mean Values)

	Active Citizen	Orderly Citizen	Sceptical Citizen	Alienated Citizen	All
Ethnicity**					
Estonians	27	26	28	20	100
Estonian Russians	11	24	20	45	100
Age					
15–27	23	26	26	25	100
28–40	25	31	23	21	100
41–53	26	22	26	26	100
54–66	20	22	26	32	100
67–79	17	26	25	31	100
Indices of media use (mean values)					
Frequency and versatility of reading newspapers**	3.56	2.87	3.10	2.47	2.97
Reading news on the internet**	3.09	2.50	2.61	2.06	2.54
Frequency and versatility of using computers**	3.30	2.75	2.84	2.29	2.77
Functional versatility of social media usage**	2.79	2.19	2.27	1.87	2.25
Engagement in civic and political activities on social media					
Have shared news media stories, posted links to news, or comments or questions about the news on social media*	45	30	30	22	31
Have posted information about political issues, commented on a political issue or figure, contacted with some politician on social media	12	8	8	4	8
Follow some association, civic initiative, NGO or network on social media**	42	21	25	13	24
Have given feedback to a state institution or municipality, or answered their questions on social media**	20	8	9	4	10

Note: * $p < 0.01$; ** $p < 0.001$.

typology manifests a clear distinction between ethnic Estonians and Estonian Russians, while intergenerational differences are not significant.

Active Citizen (type 1): The first cluster embraces the smallest share of citizens (22%) and demonstrates the highest level of civic and political engagement. While the most distinguishing features of this citizen

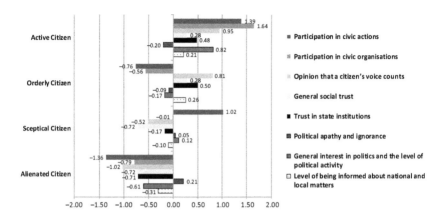

Figure 2.3 Typology of citizens (mean differences from the average).

type are participation in civic organisations and non-institutionalised actions, they also demonstrate the highest level of interest in politics and conventional political activity, which harmonises with their strong belief that the voice of every individual matters in society and a high degree of social trust. This actively engaged and well-adapted citizen type is more common among the ethnic majority. When it comes to the age composition, middle-aged people are slightly over-represented, while belonging to this type is somewhat less common among the elderly. Active Citizens are the most intensive users of both traditional and new media, and are, by far, most active on social networking sites regarding all observed forms of digitally mediated civic and political engagement.

Orderly Citizen (type 2): The second type comprises one fourth of the Estonian population. This type is, first and foremost, characterised by a high degree of social trust and optimism regarding the functioning of democracy and the political system. Orderly Citizens are moderately inclined towards institutional means of political participation, while being more prudent regarding civic engagement and non-institutional participation. The type is rather well balanced in terms of ethnic and age composition, with a slight predominance of 28- to 40-year-olds. Individuals of this type are eager to keep themselves informed about local and national events in the country, and they are moderately active in using traditional and new media age, as well as in political participation via social networking sites.

Sceptical Citizen (type 3): The third cluster involves, equal to the second type, one fourth of Estonian citizens. Their most characteristic feature is active political participation in non-conventional ways (protest actions, campaigns, demonstrations, etc.), based on onetime individual judgement. Their scepticism regarding the political system and functioning of democracy manifests in below-average levels of trust indicators and belief in the power of a citizen's voice. The ethnic majority is slightly over-represented in the Sceptical type. Although Sceptical Citizens are, compared to the second type, more active users of traditional and new media, their self-evaluated level of being informed about local and national affairs is more modest, remaining slightly below the average. The pattern of political engagement via social media, however, is almost identical to that of Orderly Citizens.

Alienated Citizen (type 4): The fourth and the largest citizen type embraces 28% of the Estonian population, and can be described as rather estranged or alienated from political and civic participation. They are characterised by the highest level of political apathy and the lowest levels of political and civic engagement, social trust, belief in the functioning of democracy, and knowledge of current affairs. Belonging to this type is much more common among the ethnic minority; also, the two oldest age groups are slightly over-represented in the Alienated Type. The modest civic and political engagement is echoed in the lowest levels of media usage and, compared to the other types, less frequent political activities on social media.

To conclude this section, we point out that active-minded individuals are more likely to be engaged in both political and civic participation, use various media channels to keep themselves informed of current issues at national and local levels, and contribute to political discourses and interactions on social media. The emergent availability of alternative forms of participation, including digitally mediated social interactions, does not function independently of the individuals' mind, lifestyle and habitus to create a higher level of engagement. It can only support an existing potential.

Towards Democratic Political and Civic Participation Patterns

Our trend analysis showed that the observed 12-year period and, in a wider perspective, the whole epoch of post-socialist rehabilitation has witnessed development towards democratic political and civic participation patterns. 'Return to the Western world' (Lauristin and Vihalemm 1997) manifests in several aspects. Trust is no longer a missing resource in Estonia: albeit slowly, trust in state institutions as well as in other people has increased. In line with the stabilised political system, citizens' political identification and electoral participation have strengthened and crystallised in coherent patterns – among ethnic Estonians as well as the Russian minority. Similarly, attitudes towards the importance of conventional political engagement, manifested in remembering one's participation in the last elections, have proliferated in 12 years under scrutiny. Furthermore, participation in civic organisations has grown substantially.

Alongside these positive developments, some shadows of the (post) communist past are still detectable. Although membership in civic organisations has been boosted, more than two fifths of Estonian people have remained outsiders in this respect. The total share of the two more passive citizen types (Sceptical and Alienated Citizens) slightly outstrips that of more active types (Active and Orderly Citizens). Even more significantly, a clear inter-ethnic divide in civic participation has emerged with Estonian Russians being, in general, more prudent and rather 'silent protesters' than actively transforming and agentive. As more than 80,000 of the Russian-speaking inhabitants do not have Estonian citizenship yet (Enterprise Estonia 2016), the 'challenge of the Russian minority' (Lauristin and Heidmets 2002) remains acute in the establishment of a more balanced and sustainable civic society.

Several previous accounts of intergenerational differences in post-socialist societies have blamed older generations that were socialised in a particular socialist milieu as being the bearers of cultural legacies of (post)communism with all its sins, and placed hopes for improvement on younger generations who have been 'basically insulated from the cultural impact of the Communist system' (Sztompka 2004, 193). Other social scientists like Howard (2002) are more sceptical and tend to believe that it is being over naïve to hope that participation in civic activities will increase automatically, if new demographic cohorts replace the older generations at the central positions in a society. According to Howard, prior experiences under communist rule do not work only upon elder generations, but impinge also younger generations that were socialised in post-soviet society, 'as socialization comes both from the current institutional setting and from one's parents, teachers, and peers, all of whom can contribute to reproducing the same patterns of attitudes and behaviour' (Howard 2002, 166).

Our data, including the results of the cluster analysis, demonstrated that generation groups do not differentiate in the extent of civic participation; intergenerational division lines, however, do exist in the kind of organisations, actions and activities, that is, qualitative features of *civicness*. On the one hand, intergenerational differences are shaped by the unequal shares of personal resources needed for participation in particular activities. On the other hand, and more in line with the arguments of Sztompka (2004) and Marada (2004), our analysis revealed some tendencies of younger generations to be more oriented towards civic participation through individual contribution and with the aim of actively reshaping the future living environment. The trend of declining identification with political parties among the youngest age group is in line with the decrease in conventional political engagement among young people in Western societies (Banaji and Buckingham 2013; Banaji and Cammaerts 2014; Sloam 2014).

Our analysis contributed to uncovering one of the most common misunderstandings of participation by showing that new opportunities of digitally mediated participation have not created completely new forms or patterns of political or civic engagement. Rather, active citizens employ these opportunities as complementary means to support and upgrade their existing forms of participation. We may say that instruments of e-participation (such as e-voting, online platforms for signing petitions, social media affordances for joining political movements and initiatives, etc.) supplement more traditional modes of engagement in a natural way. While all forms of digitally mediated participation are much more common among younger generations, echoing the overall pattern of age-based digital stratification in Estonia (Kalmus et al. 2013), older age groups are also coming around to the new opportunities. Time will show whether the forms of digitally mediated engagement facilitate tearing away from the remaining shadows of (post)communism and building a more harmonious and viable civic society.

Acknowledgement

The preparation of this chapter was supported by the Estonian Science Foundation Grant No. 8527 and personal research funding (PUTJD570) from the Estonian Research Council and the institutional research funding (IUT20–38) from the Estonian Ministry of Education and Research. The research subject is part of and will be further developed within the H2020 project on Constructing AcTiveCitizensHip with European Youth: Policies, Practices, Challenges and Solutions [CATCH-EyoU]. The CATCH-EyoU project has received funding from the European Union's Horizon 2020 Research and Innovation Programme under Grant Agreement No. 649538. The chapter reflects only the authors' view. The Research Executive Agency of the European Commission is not responsible for any use that may be made of the information it contains.

References

Banaji, S., and Buckingham, D. (2013). *The civic web: Young people, the internet, and civic participation.* Cambridge, MA: MIT Press.

Banaji, S., and Cammaerts, B. (2014). Citizens of nowhere land: Youth and news consumption in Europe. *Journalism Studies, 16*(1), 115–132.

Beilmann, M., and Lilleoja, L. (2015). Social trust and value similarity: The relationship between social trust and human values in Europe. *Studies of Transition States and Societies, 7,* 19–30.

Bennet, W. L., Wells, C., and Freelon, D. (2011). Communicating civic engagement: Contrasting models of citizenship in the youth web sphere. *Journal of Communication, 61,* 835–856.

Boulianne, S., and Brailey, M. (2014). Attachment to community and civic and political engagement: A case study of students. *Canadian Review of Sociology, 51*(4), 375–388.

Delhey, J., and Newton, K. (2002). *Who trusts? The origins of social trust in seven nations.* WZB discussion papers, FS III 02–402. Accessed August 1, 2017. http://econstor.eu/bitstream/10419/50209/1/350527032.pdf.

Delhey, J., and Newton, K. (2005). Predicting cross-national levels of social trust: Global pattern or Nordic exceptionalism? *European Sociological Review, 21*(4), 311–327.

Delhey, J., and Tobsch, V. (2000). *Understanding regime support in new democracies.* WZB discussion papers FS III 00–403. Accessed August 1, 2017. http://econstor.eu/bitstream/10419/50203/1/324448260.pdf.

Edmunds, J., and Turner, B. S. (2002). *Generations, culture and society.* Buckingham, PA: Open University Press.

Ehin, P. (2009). Political support and political participation: Comparison of Estonians and non-Estonians. In M. Lauristin (ed.), *Estonian human development report 2008* (91–95). Tallinn: Estonian Cooperation Assembly.

Enterprise Estonia (2016). *Citizenship.* Accessed August 1, 2017. http://estonia.eu/about-estonia/society/citizenship.html.

Fuchs, D., and Klingemann, H.-D. (2006). Democratic communities in Europe: A comparison between East and West. In H.-D. Klingemann, D. Fuchs, and J. Zielonka (eds.), *Democracy and political culture in Eastern Europe* (25–66). London: Routledge.

Grzymala-Busse, A. (2007). Rebuilding Leviathan: Party competition and state exploitation in post-communist democracies. New York: Cambridge University Press.

Halpern, D. (2005). *Social capital.* Cambridge, UK: Polity Press.

Hansson, L. (2001). *Networks matter: The role of informal social networks in the period of socio-economic reforms of the 1990s in Estonia.* Jyväskylä: University of Jyväskylä.

Hooghe, M., and Marien, S. (2013). A comparative analysis of the relation between political trust and forms of political participation in Europe. *European Societies, 15*(1), 131–152.

Howard, M. M. (2002). The weakness of postcommunist civil society. *Journal of Democracy, 13*(1), 157–169.

Inglehart, R. (2006). East European value systems in global perspective. In H.-D. Klingemann, D. Fuchs, and J. Zielonka (eds.), *Democracy and political culture in Eastern Europe* (67–84). London: Routledge.

Kalmus, V., Talves, K., and Pruulmann-Vengerfeldt, P. (2013). Behind the slogan of "e-state": Digital stratification in Estonia. In M. Ragnedda, and G. Muschert (eds.), *The digital divide: The internet and social inequality in international perspective* (193–206). London: Routledge.

Kalmus, V., and Vihalemm, T. (2008). Patterns of continuity and disruption: The specificity of young people's mental structures in three transitional societies. *Young, 16*(3), 251–278.

Kõuts, R. (2004). Social integration in the post-socialist society: The case of Estonia. Gdansk-Berlin: Humboldt Universität Berlin.

Kõuts, R., Vihalemm, P., and Lauristin, M. (2013). Trust in the context of audience fragmentation. *CM: Communication Management Quarterly, 26,* 77–102.

Kymlicka, W. (2000). Estonia's integration policies in a comparative perspective. In A. Laius, I., Pettai, and I. Proos (eds.), *Estonia's integration landscape: From apathy to harmony* (29–57). Tallinn: Jaan Tõnissoni Instituut.

Lagerspetz, M. (2001). Consolidation as hegemonization: The case of Estonia. *Journal of Baltic Studies*, 32(4), 402–420.

Lauristin, M., and Heidmets, M. (eds.). (2002). The challenge of the Russian minority: Emerging multicultural democracy in Estonia. Tartu: Tartu University Press.

Lauristin, M., and Vihalemm, P. (2009). Internal and external factors influencing Estonian public agenda during two decades of post-communist transformation. *Journal of Baltic Studies*, 40(1), 1–29.

Lauristin, M., Vihalemm, P., Rosengren, K. E., and Weibull, L. (eds.). (1997). *Return to the Western world: Cultural and political perspectives on the Estonian post-communist transition*. Tartu: Tartu University Press.

Lovell, D. W. (2001). Trust and politics of post-communism. *Communist and Post-Communist Studies*, 34(1), 27–38.

Mannheim, K. (1927, 1952). The problem of generations. In P. Kecskemeti (ed.), *K. Mannheim essays on the sociology of knowledge* (276–320). London: Routledge & Kegan Paul.

Marada, R. (2004). Social construction of youth and formation of generational awareness after socialism. In P. Mareš (ed.), *Society, reproduction and contemporary challenges* (149–68). Brno: Barrister and Principal.

Micheletti, M. (2006). Communication and political understanding as political participation. In M. Eduards, C. Linde, and A. Segerberg (eds.), *State of welfare: Politics, policies and parties in the post-national welfare society* (1–15). Stockholm: Stockholm University. Accessed August 1, 2017. www.statsvet.su.se/polopoly_fs/1.133039.1366808279!/menu/standard/file/micheletti_communication_and_political_understanding_as_political_participation.pdf.

Newton, K. (2007). Social and political trust. In R. J. Dalton, and H.-D. Klingemann (eds.), *The Oxford handbook of political behavior* (342–361). Oxford: Oxford University Press.

Norkus, Z. (2007). Why did Estonia perform best? The North–South gap in the post-socialist economic transition of the Baltic States. *Journal of Baltic Studies*, 38(1), 21–42.

Offe, C., and Fuchs, S. (2002). A decline of social capital? The German case. In R. D. Putnam (ed.), *Democracies in flux: The evolution of social capital in contemporary society* (189–243). New York: Oxford University Press.

Pettai, V., Auers, D., and Ramonaite, A. (2011). Political development. In M. Lauristin (ed.), *Estonian human development report 2010/2011, Baltic way(s) of human development: Twenty years on* (144–164). Tallinn: Estonian Cooperation Assembly.

Põder, K. (ed.). (2015). *Statistical yearbook of Estonia 2015*. Tallinn: Statistics Estonia. Accessed August 1, 2017. www.stat.ee/90733.

Putnam, R. D. (2000). Bowling alone: The collapse and revival of American community. New York: Simon and Schuster.

Putnam, R. D. (2002). Democracies in flux: The evolution of social capital in contemporary society. New York: Oxford University Press.

Rikmann, E., Hinno, K., Vallimäe, T., and Lagerspetz, M. (2012). *Kodanikualgatust toetavad väärtused ja käitumismustrid Eesti elanikkonnas 2011–2012: Uuringu raport*. [Civil Society in Estonia: Values and Behavioral Patterns in 2011–2012: Study Report]. Tallinn: Tallinn University.

Rose, R., and Munro, N. (2003). *Elections and parties in new European democracies.* Washington, DC: CQ Press.

Runnel, P., Pruulmann-Vengerfeldt, P., and Reinsalu, K. (2009). The Estonian tiger leap from post-communism to the information society: From policy to practice. *Journal of Baltic Studies, 40,* 29–51.

Sloam, J. (2014). 'The outraged young': Young Europeans, civic engagement and the new media in a time of crisis. *Information, Communication & Society, 17,* 217–231.

Spitzer, A. B. (1973). The historical problem of generations. *American Historical Review, 78*(5), 1353–1385.

Standard Eurobarometer 83 (2015). Accessed August 1, 2017. http://ec.europa. eu/COMMFrontOffice/PublicOpinion/index.cfm/Survey/getSurveyDetail/ instruments/STANDARD/surveyKy/2099.

Sveningsson, M. (2014). "I don't like it and I think it's useless, people discussing politics on Facebook": Young Swedes' understandings of social media use for political discussion. *Cyberpsychology: Journal of Psychological Research on Cyberspace, 8*(3), article 8.

Sztompka, P. (2004). The trauma of social change: A case of postcommunist societies. In J. C. Alexander, R. Eyerman, B. Giesen, N. J. Smelser, and P. Sztompka (eds.), *Cultural trauma and collective identity* (155–195). Berkeley, CA: University of California Press.

Titma, M., and Rämmer, A. (2006). Estonia: Changing value patterns in a divided society. In H.-D. Klingemann, D. Fuchs, and J. Zielonka (eds.), *Democracy and political culture in Eastern Europe* (277–307). London: Routledge.

Vassil, K., Solvak, M., and Ehin, P. (2015). More choice, higher turnout? The impact of consideration set size and homogeneity on political participation. *Journal of Elections, Public Opinion & Parties,* 26(1), 78–95.

Vihalemm, T., and Kalmus, V. (2008). Mental structures in transition culture: Differentiating patterns of identities and values in Estonia. *East European Politics and Societies, 22*(4), 901–927.

Wolfsfeld, G., Yarchi, M., and Samuel-Azran, T. (2016). Political information repertoires and political participation. *New Media & Society, 18*(9), 2096–2115.

3 Enhanced Inter-visibility. The Experience of Civic Engagement in Social Media

Maria Francesca Murru

An Open Question

The way in which political participation is affected and eventually promoted by the use of social networking sites (SNSs) is a widely investigated topic. However, a general consensus on the capability of these platforms to encourage citizens' engagement is still missing. As always, the case with new communication media (Simonson 1996; Peters 1999), the emergent strands of thoughts have been articulated into the opposition between optimistic and pessimistic positions. On the one hand, several comprehensive inquiries demonstrate that the active use of social media can offer cheap and motivating pathways to participation by generating more flexible forms of political involvement and more effective instruments for spreading information. A recent study by Gil de Zúñiga et al. (2014) demonstrated that the exposure to political information and social interactions on social media steers citizens on a path of political expression which may lead to political participation. One of the strongest arguments posited by the more optimistic side is that SNSs act as a leveller of political participation (Holt et al. 2013; Xenos et al. 2014) in that they are effective in engaging audiences traditionally characterised by lower levels of political engagement such as youngsters and people with lower socio-economic status or isolated citizens. On the other hand, other studies have pointed out the negative consequences that social media can have on participation like the exacerbation of individualism, a fierce polarisation of debate and a growing slacktivism. Fenton and Barassi (2011), for instance, argue that the kind of self-centred participation that is enhanced by SNSs, far from being empowering, can represent a threat for collective endeavour of political change. According to Morozov's popular thesis (2011), social media enforce slacktivism because the kind of small-scale type of activism they support distracts from the hard, on-the-ground work of movement activism. Between the two extreme positions, the great majority of research supports the third hypothesis of a normalisation trend according to which internet and SNSs are supposed to simply confirm existing participatory patterns. Among them, Gustafsson (2012) has demonstrated that the use of social media does not in itself bring previously disengaged people to become actively involved in political discussions. Those people that are not members of interest organisations prefer to remain passive, even when they are exposed to political content and to explicit requests for participation. In the same line, the analysis of polarisation in social media discussions realised by Heatherly et al. (2017) has shown that party identification moderates the relationship between SNSs use and involvement in cross-cutting discussions, indicating that US Republicans participate more frequently than Democrats in cross-cutting exchanges on social media.

However, structuring the debate by means of confronting pessimistic and optimistic views has the misleading result of ignoring the unexpected emergence of new forms of political participation that are not already codified by traditional interpretative frames. An alternative path of exploration could come from an inductive turn where the adoption of a 'cultural-diagnostic approach' (Nieminen 2006) allows a temporary suspension of normative judgments while sharpening the comprehension of the cultural and sociological preconditions of the phenomenon. The present chapter aims at working exactly in this direction through the discussion of a set of theoretical and empirical resources that can help to understand some of the fundamental dynamics that are involved in the relationship between political participation and online media. First, it will draw on a circumscribed overview of most recent literature to clarify what exactly is the kind of political participation that is taking place through and within social media. While it is undeniable that social networking platforms can be decisive tools for ends-oriented activism and traditional political participation aimed at influencing institutions and public opinion, there are several indications showing how they mainly act as breeding ground for a kind of civic participation that is more expressive than instrumental. This implies that an exhaustive comprehension of the phenomenon can only start from moving the focus from rational deliberation to meaning-making processes where self-expression and self-reflexivity are considered as values in themselves. One way of avoiding misunderstandings in researching mediated political participation thus consists of mobilising concepts that are in tune with the observed phenomenon and the stakes to which people directly involved give their heed. The second argument that will be developed in the chapter posits that we risk misunderstanding the relationship between social media and discursive participation if we presume that social media directly shape the forms of political talk and discussions they are currently hosting. What they are rather doing consists of affecting the modes of social inter-visibility, which in turn constitute the conditions of possibility for political interactions to happen and develop. By discussing the findings of a qualitative research on styles of discursive engagement on social media, the chapter will show how the relevance of social media can be better appreciated in the opening of several modes of *publicness* which result from the contingent combination between the technical affordances of the platforms and the social conventions that structure their frames of usage.

Political Participation and Social Media

The path towards a 'cultural-diagnostic' approach can start from the recognition that the relationship between SNSs and citizen engagement is differentiated according to the types of activities people engage in through and within social media. Through a meta-analytic review of empirical research published from 2007 to 2013, Skoric et al. (2016) have shown that expressive, informational and relational use of social media has a positive relationship with civic engagement and its three subcategories (social capital, civic engagement and political participation). On the other hand, they found little empirical evidence concerning the identity and entertainment-oriented uses of social media and their relationship with citizen engagement. According to the authors, this pattern of findings can be explained by the non-anonymous or pseudonymous quality of the social media settings where the acts of political expression are always personalised and identity-focused:

> given the number of potential social settings and overlapping audiences on egocentric networks, citizens engaging in political expression need to develop a broader repertoire of political selves which triggers a process of inadvertent civic learning and may lead to spillover effects on real-world political action.
>
> (Ivi 23)

It is precisely by virtue of the 'nonymous space' (as opposed to anonymous) that Facebook offers to its users and which allows the performances of 'would be selves' (Marichal 2013) that many scholars have started to argue that the heart of the relationship between internet and political participation is constituted by the 'new' forms of participation that are emerging from activities made possible by the internet. In line with the plea by Papacharissi (2011) for a reconsideration of the praxis of citizenship, Marichal (2013) suggests that political participation on and through social media takes the prevailing form of 'middle-level acts of political participation online that do not carry with them goals of full-scale activism but requires political engagement in a deeper and reflective way'. In providing a safer space to perform political identities, convey political views and eventually park negative feelings of alienation, social media appear to be the privileged incubator of 'expressive rationality' (Svensson 2011), intended as a form of discourse that is centred on processes of identification, self-realisation and self-expression rather than aimed at achieving instrumental ends. More than towards instrumental politics, the analytical focus should be oriented to politics as a meaning-making process where the will to self-express, self-reflect and identify is a value in itself and prevails on the product of action or deliberation that could eventually arise from interactions. This stronger emphasis on expressivity over deliberation constitutes an increasingly relevant aspect of the most widespread interpretative frameworks that are currently applied to contemporary politics. In 2002, Norris spoke of a 'democratic phoenix', arguing that the disengagement from traditional forms of political participation paved the way to the emergence of unconventional participatory practices. Already in 1998, Bennett described the phenomenon of lifestyle politics as a way to articulate political meanings around lifestyle values and personal narratives. The increasing centrality of the personal and the emotional has been interpreted by Van Zoonen (2005) as a process of intimization of politics where private feelings and emotion become the stuff of public politics. Analysing 'citizens as everyday-makers', Bang (2005) showed that the simple act through which people speak out about themselves should be considered as an enactment of citizenship in that it allows paths of personal and collective recognition. In the same line, Kim and Kim (2008) draw on Habermas' theory of communicative action and Buber's concept of dialogue to argue that formal and non-purposive everyday political talk is the cornerstone of democratic participation because it allows people to construct the concept of the self and other, the sense of community and public reason. Considering the rise of these self-centred and expressive forms of participation, Casteltrione (2015) has proposed to update the traditional definition of political participation (Verba et al. 1995) so as to include such activities as informal interactions or political consumerism that are not explicitly aimed at influencing government action but that reflect individuals' interest and personal involvement in politics.

What is then clear from this literature review is that the expressive forms of political participation that prevail on social media exist prior and beyond them, but nevertheless find in their relational and performative spaces a perfect breeding ground. The theoretical and empirical path that will be deployed in the rest of the chapter is aimed at understanding the ways in which the new online social settings are 'mediating' the sociological possibilities for political interactions. The notion of 'mediation' is understood here in the sense attributed to the term by Silverstone (1999), as the introduction of new material and symbolic thresholds within the open-ended process of meaning-making. More than on dialogic qualities, on styles and content spectrum of public discussions on SNSs, the attention will be placed on the modes of *publicness* as one of the conditions of possibility through which political discourses and interactions on political issues emerge on social media. As will be explained in next paragraph, *publicness* is intended here as a form of mediated intersubjectivity by virtue of which the visibility that is inherent to both the process of the self and the access of generalised others is shaped by new and contingent combinations of technical affordances and cultural conventions.

The Intersubjective Bases of Political Talk

As we have seen in the previous paragraph, cultural approaches to the role of informal talk in civic life have demonstrated that the nature of social settings can hinder or facilitate political talk. The rich ethnographic study on several civic and political groups realised by Eliasoph (1998) revealed that political talk is repressed in more public settings. While in private settings, people don't disdain to be actively involved in political discussion; however, when addressing a public or a media they deliberately avoid speaking about politics because they are afraid to put sociability at risk. She observed a process of 'political evaporation' which relegates issues of justice and common good as well as historical and institutional analyses to the background context of conversations among a few relatives or friends. Hayes et al. (2006) showed how the disposition towards self-censorship in political conversation can be explained in the light of both personality characteristics and of the perceived 'publicness' of a given setting of political interaction. According to Thorson (2014), social settings matter for political talk because they provide people with cues about appropriate social behaviour and appropriate speech styles within the group, and as such, they offer a shared ground, a shared schema that serves as a basis for action (Goffman 1959). Even more deeply, it can be argued that the conditions of possibilities for political interactions to take place and freely deploy are rooted in the intersubjective bases of sociality. Citizenship as 'communal belonging is not, in the first instance, a matter of choice but rather of mutual interference' (Crossley 2001, 42), of the ineluctable mutual interference that ties together social actors who share the same space and the same scarce resources. Following the theoretical path that has been developed and detailed by Crossley (1996, 2001), we can further specify the way in which this mutual interference is deployed in the intersubjective fabric of social processes by drawing upon Mead's theory of self-hood and Schütz's notion of social regions. In Mead's theory (1934), the self is the emergent product of social interaction where subjects, through the symbolic interpretations of actions, gestures and languages of the others, negotiate the *Me*, that is the self, viewed from the point of view of the generalised other and vehicle of social reproduction, with the *I*, that is the self's most creative dimension, irreducibly specific and innovative. Two elements are fundamental in that process: The involvement in the symbolic world of a particular speech community, which allow subjects to think and simultaneously have access to their own objectified thoughts, thus gaining a critical distance from them and consequently from themselves; the capacity of seeing themselves from the point of view of the others, taking their role and assuming their external perspective. Mead's account is complemented by the notion of social typifications introduced by Schütz (Schütz and Luckmann 1973), which allows to grasp how the attitude of the generalised other is generated and grasped by the subject. The peculiar structure of this lifeworld, and the available tools for shaping and flexibly navigating it, determines conditions and forms through which the self gains access and involvement in the different entities populating his or her universe. Schütz describes the lifeworld as structured in an interlocking range of zones of anonymity: 'the breadth of variations in my experience of the social world extends from the encounter with another man to vague attitudes, institutions, cultural structures and humanity in general' (Schütz and Luckmann 1973, 61). The experience of the otherness is thus organised through a continuum of social typifications that are differentiated by a specific degree of immediacy and generalisation and that range from people personally met and immediately reachable to those abstract social entities that can only be imagined indirectly through myths or media narrations.

> Communication media with different affordances and the use genres they engender help individuals traverse this continuum and establish social engagements infinitely variable in closeness, content and intensity. The Internet has proven to be a particularly versatile vehicle for navigating the structures of the social world.
>
> (Bakardjieva 2009, 97)

Brighenti (2010) underlines how the dynamics of socialisation and symbolic reproduction that sustain the lifeworld hold an intrinsic dimension of visibility which pertains to the process of subjectivisation and objectivisation (Brighenti 2010, 46). We can find it both in the different degrees of visibility through which the various generalised others become perceived and experienced by the subject, and in the objectification of the Me through which the self become conscious of oneself by way of symbols and internalisation of other's gaze. In the next section, it will be shown that social media are working exactly at the level of this inter-visibility and that they translate it into several modes of *publicness* as a result of the contingent combination between the technical affordances of the platforms and the expectations, languages and social conventions that structure their frames of usage.

Social Media and Intervisibility

According to one of the most recent and renowned definitions, social media are constituted by

> a networked communication platform in which participants (1) have uniquely identifiable profiles that consist of user-supplied content,

content provided by other users, and/or system-provided data; (2) can publicly articulate connections that can be viewed and traversed by others; and (3) can consume, produce, and/or interact with streams of user generated content provided by their connections on the site.

(Ellison and boyd 2013, 158)

They represent a tool of perpetual connection with friendship networks and, at the same time, they offer bridges of connection with weak ties, allowing to explore them in relation to their public profiles and the place they occupy within different social networks. Larsson (2015) has identified four main modes of communication that are fairly similar across different platforms: broadcasting, redistributing, interacting and acknowledging. The modes of broadcasting and interaction entail the actions of sending a message respectively to a network of followers or to one single person. The modes of distributing and acknowledging constitute more complex acts that can mix together one-to-many and one-to-one communication and that have become distinctive features of the kind of social connections that can be established through social media. The act of redistributing posts or tweets made by others indicates that the value attributed to them is so high that they are considered as worth sharing more widely. From the point of view of those actors that aim at spreading their messages beyond their networks, this kind of feedback can be very attractive because it can trigger a *viral* diffusion within which each addressee acts in turn as a loudspeaker of the original message. The act of acknowledging entails the favourite marking of a tweet or the liking of a Facebook post and can be considered as a minimal feedback whose meaning subtly varies depending on specific relational contexts.

These four modes of communication are the building blocks of two main practices that are carried out within social media. *Presencing* is one of them and can be considered as one of the larger family of practices that are oriented to social media. *Presencing* involves a 'a whole set of media-enhanced ways in which individuals, groups and institutions put into circulation information about, and representation of, themselves for the wider purpose of *sustaining a public presence*' (Couldry 2012, 50). As a complex practice, it can serve different needs; it can be a tool of self-promotion, a site for exerting a kind of public agency when other opportunities are precluded or just a basic way for keeping in touch when circles of friends or relatives are spatially dispersed. Public *presencing* is something more than publishing content on a bulletin board or calling for the attention of friends and acquaintances; it has rather to do with the display of an 'objectification of oneself' (ibid.) that is supported by digital resources and that makes up for one's immediate bodily invisibility. Social media provide subjects with an expressive frame that can articulate relationally and temporally the process of objectification of the self. Feedback from the others, more or less anonymous, is included and standardised by platforms designs in the form of *likes, comments, retweet* or *reply*. However, *presencing* cannot be seen as a mere opportunity that can be enjoyed or eluded according to individual preferences. It is rather an obligatory passage for those users that want to take advantage of the connection opportunities offered by the platforms: 'individuals have no choice but to represent themselves' (Enli and Thumim 2012). This obligatory passage should not be intended as a mere imposition; it is rather a symbolic layer that reframes the process of the self and that is open to several interpretative possibilities. For this reason, it is important to keep the differences between the notion of self-presentation – the presentation of the self we ineludibly carry out in face-to-face socialising (Goffman 1959) – and the concept of self-representation which designates a self-presentation made within a mediated context and drawing on the symbolic resources that are created and circulated there. Transversally to cultural contexts and different platforms, a common trait of social conventions about the 'identity work' (Silfverberg et al. 2011) that users carry out on social media has to do with social conventions on authenticity (Marwick 2013; Uski and Lampinen 2016). Authenticity in social media is encouraged by a platform's policy and by the design of the interface which invites users to express their thoughts in their main personal page. Bakardjieva and Gaden (2011) suggest employing the evocative concept of 'technologies of the self' as a heuristic device that situates Web 2.0 use in a long history of culturally evolved forms of self-constitution. 'Technologies of the self' is a category that has been introduced by Foucault in order to describe all those historically specific practices through which individuals are invited to consider themselves as an object of knowledge or as a field of action. In his words, they

> permit individuals to effect by their own means or with the help of others a certain number of operations on their own bodies and souls, thoughts, conduct, and way of being, so as to transform themselves in order to attain a certain state of happiness, purity, wisdom, perfection, or immortality.
>
> (Foucault 1988, 18)

Foucault underlines that technologies of the self put into play not only the care of the self aimed at attaining some kind of interior welfare, but also and most importantly, a deep and constitutive relationship with the truth towards which the contemporary subject still seems devoted. Starting from a long genealogy of the practices that has created the modern subject from stoicism to first Christianity, Foucault shows that technologies of the self consist mainly of hermeneutical practices aimed at unveiling the truth of the subject, a truth that paradoxically exists as far as it is concealed: 'it is the fact that these features of the self (feelings, memories, instincts) are (represented and also experienced as) concealed that makes them able of attesting a personal truth' (Sparti 1996, 172). Many recent media phenomena seem to slot into that peculiar connection between the subject and the truth, in order to shape it and take advantage of it on the basis of their particular organisational and economical logics. Reality television is one of the most meaningful cases in point; its participants claim for popularity in exchange for the promise of revealing themselves as they really are (Couldry 2010). Conventions on establishing authenticity in social media appear to be meaningful as well. The specific form of appearance that is explicitly encouraged and implied by social media's design seems to correspond to a way of telling about oneself within which the perpetual connection, the phatic or emotional connection become entrenched with the process of the self.

The second big family of social media-related practices is *connecting*. The ability to articulate a list of other users, with whom to share a connection, represents a key differentiating feature of these sites. More than to find new friends, the practices of connecting are about showcasing users' already established networks and viewing others' networks (boyd and Ellison 2007). It is useful to think about the special kind of connectivity that is allowed by social media as a *doing* rather than a *fact*, as something that is constantly performed and enacted both by users and by platforms through click, share, likes and posts (Bucher 2015). One way of practicing connections is that of traversing others' contact lists, looking for shared contacts, making acquaintances closer and more achievable or just monitoring relationships that exist among other users' ties. However, according to Ellison and Boyd (2013), as social media have become mainstream traversing the connections between people to view profiles is no longer the primary way of connecting. What is rather acquiring prominence is the possibility of consuming, producing and/ or interacting with streams of user-generated content provided by one's contacts on the site. Since 2011, Facebook's newsfeed or the landing page on Twitter and Tumblr have been organised as a something like 'social awareness streams' (Naaman et al. 2010) that show both the collection of links, media and texts posted by one's contacts as well as the automated messages about people's actions on the site. Within these new conditions, the act of traversing visible networks starts to follow new exploratory paths whose points of departure prioritise content shared and commented by other users more than their personal profiles. Insofar as they allow users to traverse and explore both their own as well as friends' layers of connection, social media contribute in a more significant manner to the accessibility of the interlocking range of zones of anonymity that each individual has at their disposition. They can increase a peculiar kind of accessibility to the generalised others, making them less anonymous and more achievable. This accessibility is dependent, on the one hand, on visibility and, on the other hand, on listening. Visibility has to do not only with how other users regulate privacy options in order to make their personal profiles and content available to external gazes, but also with how underlying software and algorithmic logics steer users' attention by shaping the order of appearance in their personal News Feed of content generated by their contacts. As a pioneering study by Bucher (2012) on how the Facebook's algorithm, EdgeRank, signifies and makes sense in networked environments has shown, the participatory subject created by the algorithm hinges on an underlying idea of popularity that is not so far from the well-known mass media logics by virtue of which popularity fosters further popularity.

> How many friends are commenting on a certain piece of content, who posted the content, and what type of content it is (e.g. photo, video, or status update) are just some of the factors at work in determining the rank of an Edge (...) The algorithm is based on the assumption that users are not equally connected to their friends. Some friends thus "count more" than others.
>
> (Bucher 2012, 1168)

To be popular enhances the likeness of becoming visible and consequently of generating even more interactions, thus revealing a circular logic that runs counter to the widespread rhetoric about Web 2.0 democratisation effects and the presumed empowerment of marginalised voices. On the other hand, access to previously distant others depends on attitudes of receptivity that mark the practices of online engagement. How long and how much depth we pay attention to the myriad of inputs that are circulated on social media is often an overlooked dimension of contemporary media research, too much of which focused on speaking, voice and opportunities of expression. Crawford (2009) underlines that social media are constantly invoking an efficient listening subject insofar as they collapse the divergent spaces of modernity – working life, family, social life and political life – into the same one location. These new disciplines of listening are creating disparities between what users are technically able to do and the limits of their schedules, desires and bodies. Consequently, new norms, habits and conventions are emerging to manage the gap between disciplinary imperatives and human limits, like for instance the three modes of listening that Crawford (ibid.) identifies as prevailing on social media, namely background listening, reciprocal listening and delegated listening, which give an account of the manifold senses of connection that participants can feel in online space beyond the active attitude of posting, commenting and speaking up that is often overemphasised.

Therefore, what SNSs are doing can be better appreciated as a form of mediation of the intersubjectivity, and more precisely, of that overarching dimension of visibility on which both the process of the self and the access to generalised others rely. The constitutive inter-visibility is thus transposed into a 'socially mediated publicness' (Baym and boyd 2012) where the engagement with differentiated audiences and the exposure to others' gaze are codified by a variable mix of technical affordances and social conventions, as has been clearly shown by the examples on authenticity and forms of listening. The fact that the technical affordances are not univocal prescriptions in their undisputable materiality but are rather filtered by the symbolic frames that make them meaningful (Silverstone and Hirsch 1992) requires one to think about *publicness* in its unavoidably plural character. Plural modes of *publicness* are always possible and their variety needs to be constantly explored and mapped. What should now be clarified is the kind of relationship that ties these new modes of *publicness* to the political interactions that are carried out within social media. The empirical research that will be discussed in the next section will address this relationship in an attempt to grasp and comprehend its constitutive dynamics.

Modes of Publicness and Styles of Dialogue

We have seen that social media enhance social visibility. They allow to arrive at an idea of distant others and to promote the public expressions of personal identities, content and contacts. Their discursive dimension is mainly conversational in that they continuously invite users to like and comment on content posted by other friends and contacts. What are the consequences that this enhanced visibility has on social interactions on political issues? Can we suppose that also the inclination towards public dialogue is enhanced and people are therefore better disposed to publicly disclose their political positions? Or, on the contrary, is talking about politics becoming ever more difficult because the uncontrolled *publicness* allowed by social media increases the risk of encountering disagreement, of experiencing discomfort and offending otherwise peaceful social relationships? Are these 'anonymous' spaces promoting a dialogic culture where fair and inclusive confrontations prevail on elitist and like-minded exchanges? The empirical research presented here will not give an exhaustive and definitive overview of the great variety of political interactions that are taking ground in social media. It will rather explore in depth whether and how the inclination to publicly express political opinions and the attitudes towards dialogue on political issues change according to the different modes of *publicness* that are experienced by the subjects. As already said, various modes of *publicness* can be found as a contingent result of the ongoing negotiation between the technical affordances of the platforms and the different styles of *presencing* and *connecting* actualised by users. More than to the final output, the analytical consideration will thus be placed on the way in which the modes of *publicness* act as conditions of possibility for people to be actively engaged in political interactions on Facebook. A set of in-depth interviews was conducted with a sample of 25 young-adults, aged 20–35 years old and living in urban areas of different regions of Italy. The field has been structured in two rounds. During the first one, 15 people were recruited following one minimal eligibility criteria: that they had published at least one comment on Facebook on political issues in the two weeks before the interviews. They were found through snowball techniques starting from personal acquaintances of the researcher and people that publicly commented on the Facebook walls of prominent Italian newspapers. In the second round, the recruitment was more focused and ten people were selected among those directly engaged in civic and political activism. Again, the snowball sampling technique was applied, asking previously interviewed people to suggest other persons among their circles of friends and acquaintances. Twelve men and thirteen women were interviewed in 2014 and 2015. Interviews lasted approximately one hour. They started with a short life history focused on experiences and opportunities for political socialisation and were then extended to a detailed discussion of SNSs practices and perceptions. Three areas of interest and their mutual relationship were explored during the interviews:

1　The paths of political socialisation, previous and current experiences of political and civic activism,
2　The modes of *publicness*, described as personalised actualisations of the opportunities for self-representation and access to generalised others that are allowed by social media, and
3　The general attitudes towards public discussions on Facebook: How often people pay heed and actively intervene into dialogues on political issues and how much value they attribute to discursive engagements within their overall civic experience.

The findings led to the identification of three types of conversational attitudes, each one characterised by different ways of actualising the opportunities of *presencing* and *connecting* in Facebook. The analysis of data followed the method of theoretical coding, where theoretical concepts constitute the analytical coordinates to interpret the qualitative data that emerge from interviews (Creswell 2007). The first phase of analysis consisted of developing a description of each interviewed person where his/her modes of publicness and general conversational attitudes were contextualised within his/her path of political socialisation and previous civic experiences. Then, the comparisons between single descriptions allowed to grasp patterns of similarities and differences which in turn formed the basis of the typifications. Each of the available descriptions allowed to assess whether the person was similar to any of others previously sorted or whether she/he constituted a new type. The three types have emerged from the theoretical coding as original combinations between specific declinations of the three explored elements. The description of the three types that will be now presented will allow to understand these combinations as patterns of correspondence and mutual conditioning between the attitudes towards public discussions on Facebook, the modes of publicness and the paths of political socialisation.

Impulsive Conversations

People in this group are used to expressing their personal opinions almost on a daily basis in Facebook fan pages of newspapers and political groups without engaging in a real debate or discussion. For them, the self-expression is an end in itself and they pay no attention to the feedback they receive from other people. The discursive engagement in these public conversational spaces is not intended as an occasion for self-clarification, for changing their mindsets or simply confronting themselves with divergent opinions. Insofar as self-expression is the motivating driver of their participation, authenticity of expressed opinions is commonly considered as a value in itself, in no way affected by the kind of interest that their opinions are able to trigger or by the quality of the feedbacks they receive. It seems that for these individuals the merely abstract presence of a generic audience is enough to produce in them a personal perception of being recognised in their subjective distinctiveness. When they enter a public discussion, the divergence between expressed opinions most often takes the form of a fierce opposition with no interest in achieving a possible mediation; on the contrary, disagreement concurs to strengthen self-awareness and the personal gratification that comes from self-disclosure. One respondent said:

> I like commenting news to express my opinion, I have my say and I am not too much interested in what people say after or concerning my comment (...) it's important for me to express my point of view and I really cannot shut up.

When asked about entering a dialogue with another anonymous commenter he said, 'yes, it happened to be confronted with divergent opinions, sometimes I had also conflicts but I never changed my mind, I kept my position and the same was done by my interlocutors'. The kind of *publicness* that these individuals carry out is emotional, impulsive and haphazard. The scaling up of social networks is mainly interactional and not relational; it is constructed on the basis of extemporaneous and isolated interactions within the public spaces of Facebook fan pages and it doesn't draw on a project of relationship. The generalised other is thus made more accessible by social media but does not lose its anonymity. People in this group have not in their background had any rich experiences of civic engagement and in some cases, they also declare to perceive themselves as being insufficiently skilled for a proper discussion on political issues. Moreover, they are not used to speaking about political news with relatives, friends or colleagues; for them, Facebook represents a stage for conveying personal judgments on political issues that would otherwise have been repressed. It is then plausible to suppose that for these people Facebook, as a space of enhanced visibility, constitutes a driver for the display of an emergent political *publicness* that hadn't previously found any concrete opportunity for expression. It seems that the social networking platform has not only offered technical possibilities for *presencing* and *connecting* but also a social grammar of self-presentation that hadn't been previously acquired through traditional paths of political socialisation.

Strategic Discussions

What is deemed as relevant in these cases is not the expression of personal opinions in itself, rather their capacity of stimulating a rich debate on political issues among their contacts. People included in this group have a personal rank of their most successful posts where the success is measured on the basis of the number of involved people and of the liveliness of the discussion. They are not really interested in sharing their personal views; their discursive engagement is more motivated by the will of thematising and problematising the debated issues with convincing and well-articulated arguments. One respondent said:

> I publish posts on political news mainly to fuel an argument, and the controversy often passes from the wall to private messages with people asking me "do you really mean this...?" Two days ago, I published one post like this and it triggered at least 25 comments by people that are not real friends, they are acquaintances that share my political engagement.

People in this group are young members of political parties and movements and they keep a watchful eye on the impressions that other parties' members can get from their Facebook profiles. They are used to discussing about political issues both in their families and group of friends; many of them have career ambitions in the field of politics or political sciences. For these individuals, *publicness* is never impulsive: It is always thought-out because their digital presence is calibrated and shaped according to their imagined publics. Their publics are in no way anonymous; in the majority of cases, they are weak ties that can be potentially strengthened. They use Facebook for scaling up social circles crossing through their networks of acquaintances in a way that is always strategic and well aware. They know how to promote their public image but they do this in a constant relation with the other collectivities in which they aim at being included and for which they aim at becoming credible points of reference. They consider their profile on Facebook as something that should be not coincident but coherent with their whole identity. For this reason, they try to balance the thematic areas of their published content in order to avoid any exclusive focus on any single political issues. Insofar as their lives cannot be reduced to their political engagement, it is important that their Facebook profile faithfully reflects the variety of personal interests and hobbies they enjoy. Political opinions are thus alternated with tastes in music, pictures of recent trips or quotations from the novel they love the most. A respondent said:

> I don't want to speak only about politics, because the risk is that friends start to consider my Facebook profile as a "political profile" and stop to watch at it and to follow it. I try to restrict content related to political issues because I don't want to be boring and I don't want to push away friends that I love to get in touch to but who are not interested in politics.

They prove to be well aware and lucid curators of the plurality of belongings that converge on their social networking profile.

Fair Dialogues

In this category, we have people that pay great attention to the quality of dialogue and arguments. They recognise the democratic value of an inclusive debate where each participant can have their say and eventually change their mind when convinced by reasoned and well-founded arguments. While they are familiar with making use of different digital tools to organise groups discussions – as forums and mailing lists – they are convinced that Facebook offers good opportunities to convey articulated political views with the support of long texts and direct links to informational sources. When asked about the advantages of using Facebook to discuss political issues, one respondent replied:

> written dialogues offers the great advantage of reflecting before writing. When discussions are well thought out, Facebook gives the opportunity of amending your assertions and helps you to articulate your thoughts and to get back to them, maybe change their expressive forms so that they become less ambiguous for those who are reading. Even in face-to-face encounters, in live groups, when it is possible, I write things that are said because when you read them, you catch a more complete meaning.

The people included in this group are used to lending their personal profiles on Facebook to the political causes they support. Several times, they have used their personal image as a sign of endorsement and their status updates as a blackboard to explain and clarify the main points of the political agenda claimed by the movements or political parties they supported. They have high level educational curricula and previous experiences of civic and political activism that have been very relevant for their political biographies. Facebook is an essential tool for the management of their current political engagement, which is distributed among several memberships and cannot rely on a continuous presence because of private and professional commitments. It is used both in the ordinary life as a way to maintain contact with acquaintances and weak ties, but also during extraordinary occasions when there is the need to spread the message and to mobilise people in favour of specific causes. The style of *publicness* they deliberately choose is personal but not private. It is personal in the sense that their Facebook profiles bear witness to a first-person investment of a personal belief and assumption of responsibility. But it's not private because they intentionally avoid publishing any details about their private life, their lifestyles or cultural tastes. Speaking about the boundaries between private and public in social media, one respondent affirmed:

> I don't share personal or professional issues with my Facebook contacts, I use Facebook to achieve my aims (...) I don't use my profile to tell about my private life, I rather express my opinions. I am not interested in becoming popular among my friends, in being followed and appreciated, I explicitly declare what are my thoughts: this is me and who knows me accepts also my decisions and my positions.

The empirical findings presented here have shown how the usage of Facebook has offered to all the interviewed people the opportunity to pluralise their lifeworlds (Lievrouw 2001), by enriching their repertoires of generalised others and by scaling up and navigating in a versatile way the interlocking range of zones of anonymity of their social worlds. However, this same process of pluralisation of lifeworld developed differently and resulted in different outcomes for the three identified types. These differences can be explained in the light of previous experiences of political socialisation but they can also in turn be used as explanatory keys to understanding people's attitudes towards political interactions on Facebook. For people with a weak political background, the opportunity of exploring and flexibly navigating among distant social circles has been concretised into a leap towards an anonymous social space populated by extemporaneous interactions but not by continuous relationships or projects of relationship. However impersonal and sometimes hostile, this social space has allowed these people who were not used to discussing politics with friends, colleagues and relatives, to publicly express their personal opinions on political news in front generalised but reactive publics. The enhanced visibility of Facebook has therefore offered them an opportunity of access to the public space that was not included in their previous paths of political socialisation. Conversely, their lack of interest in dialogue demonstrates how this acquisition of a public self has not coincided with dynamics of mutual recognition or with involvement within a collective frame of action and meaning. On the contrary, in the second and third group the great sensitivity towards the quality of arguments and the mutual enrichment that can result from dialogue is combined with a strategic *publicness* where social networks are scaled up with determined purposes and the practices of *presencing* are always thought out and reflexive.

Social Media, Publicness and Political Interaction

The connection that has been here established between political interactions and the mediation of inter-visibility brings to the foreground a specific dimension of the political that is often disregarded when models of deliberative democracy are applied to online public spheres. This dimension coincides with the ontological dimension of social life and cannot be reduced to the ends-oriented activism that is aimed at influencing institutions and public opinion. It has been described by Hannah Arendt as a *space of appearance* that is constituted as 'a non-territorial and contingently established space that emerges out of people doing things together in the manner of speech and action' (Arendt 1958, 198f.). We can therefore draw on Arendt's political theory to understand this dimension as the communicative context where bystanders make use of performances and discourses to show each other their uniqueness and their ability to undertake original and new actions. What matters is not *what* is said, neither as a specific semantic content nor as a structures of reasoning and argument; it is rather *the act of saying* which is in itself a relational and contextualised act within which each actor communicates their specific uniqueness (Cavarero 2010). It results that the privileged perspective from where to observe the political in its constitution is not focused on conversations' rules, on equity and transparency between interlocutors or granitic orientation towards the best argument, as it happens within deliberative models of public sphere (Habermas 1995, 2006). On the contrary, the focus is on the relational fabric, on the dynamics of connection and disconnection that it makes possible and that are in turn affected by the contingent and material acts of saying. The empirical research presented in this chapter has clearly shown that the attitudes people have towards dialogic opportunities on Facebook are closely connected to the ways in which people make experience of the *space of appearance* as it is mediated by Facebook. The styles of discussion, the dispositions towards diversity and the care towards arguments have appeared to be in consonance with how people concretise the opportunities of *presencing* and *connecting* that are offered by social media. The more the access to generalised other and the self-representation are determined by personal targets and reasoned purposes, the higher is the attention paid to expressive forms and their relational echo. These main findings suggest that the existing relationship between social media and political participation cannot be uniquely grasped at the level of ends-oriented activism or of conscious acts of civic engagement. The difference SNSs are making should also be appreciated in relation to that dimension of the political that is mainly relational and performative and that we have empirically explored as a mode of *publicness* and as a condition of possibility for political interactions to take place. Additional research is strongly needed to achieve a deeper comprehension of the kind of relationship that exists between modes of *publicness* and political interactions and to understand whether and how its constitutive dynamics follow different paths in different cultural contexts. Moreover, when under the lens is the political as a dimension of visibility and appearance, new understandings should be developed to capture the dynamics of power that are thus observed. As the locus where the social territorialises itself tracing thresholds, boundaries, bridges and walls, visibility oscillates between the disempowering pole of control and the empowering pole of recognition (Brighenti 2010). In the same vein, the enhanced visibility of social media can be steered towards control every time that the modes of *publicness* are *re-territorialised* through mechanisms of quantification and classification and the criteria of commercial popularity and self-branding are likely to prevail on the logic of free sharing and personal gratification (Bakardjieva and Gaden 2011; van Dijck 2013). But also, the opposite extreme can be concretised and the enhanced visibility can be territorialised in ways that promote recognition and freedom, as happened for instance during the Iranian uprising in 2009 (Rahimi 2011) when Facebook constituted an alternative spatiality – a third space (Oldenburg 2011) – where oppressive reality had been temporarily suspended and new ways of thinking about the self and the other had been experimented and performed.

References

Arendt, H. (1958). *The human condition.* Chicago, IL: Chicago University Press.
Bakardjieva, M. (2009). Subactivism: Lifeworld and politics in the age of the internet. *The Information Society, 25*(2), 91–104.
Bakardjieva, M., and Gaden, G. (2011). Web 2.0 Technologies of the Self. *Philosophy & Technology, 25*(3), 399–413.
Bang, H. (2005). Among everyday makers and expert citizens. In J. Newman (ed.), *Remaking governance: Peoples, politics and the public sphere.* Bristol, UK: Policy.
Baym, N. K., and boyd, D. (2012). Socially mediated publicness: An introduction. *Journal of Broadcasting & Electronic Media, 56*(3), 320–329.

Bennett, L. W. (1998). The uncivic culture: Communication, identity, and the rise of lifestyle politics. *Political Science & Politics, 31*(4), 741–761.

boyd, D., and Ellison, N. (2007). Social network sites: Definition, history, and scholarship. *Journal of Computer-Mediated Communication, 13*(1): 210–230.

Brighenti, A. M. (2010). *Visibility in social theory and social research.* London, UK: Palgrave MacMillan.

Bucher, T. (2012). Want to be on the top? Algorithmic power and the threat of invisibility on Facebook. *New Media & Society, 14*(7), 1164–1180.

Casteltrione, I. (2015). The Internet, social networking web sites and political participation research: Assumptions and contradictory evidence. *First Monday, 20*(3). Accessed August 1, 2017. http://firstmonday.org/ojs/index.php/fm/article/view/5462/4403.

Cavarero, A. (2010). *A più voci. Filosofia dell'espressione vocale.* Milano, Italy: Feltrinelli.

Couldry, N. (2010). *Why voice matters.* London, UK: Sage.

Couldry, N. (2012). *Media, society, world.* Cambridge, UK: Polity Press.

Crawford, K. (2009). Following you: Disciplines of listening in social media. *Continuum: Journal of Media & Cultural Studies, 23*(4): 525–535.

Creswell, J. W. (2007). *Qualitative inquiry and research design: Choosing among five approaches.* Thousand Oaks, CA: Sage.

Crossley, N. (1996). *Intersubjectivity. The fabric of social becoming.* London, UK: Sage.

Crossley, N. (2001). Citizenship, intersubjectivity and the lifeworld. In N. Stevenson (ed.), *Culture & citizenship* (33–46). London, UK: Sage.

Eliasoph, N. (1998). *Avoiding politics: How Americans produce apathy in everyday life.* Cambridge, UK: Cambridge University Press.

Ellison, N., and boyd, D. (2013). Sociality through social network sites. In W. H. Dutton (ed.), *The Oxford handbook of internet studies* (151–172). Oxford, UK: Oxford University Press.

Enli, G. S., and Thumim, N. (2012). Socialising and self representation online: Exploring Facebook. *Observatorio, 6*(1), 87–105.

Fenton, N., and Barassi, V. (2011). Alternative media and social networking sites: The politics of individuation and political participation. *Communication Review, 14*(3), 179–196.

Foucault, M. (1988). Technologies of the self. In L. H. Martin, H. Gutman, and P. Hutton (eds.), *Technologies of the self: A seminar with Michel Foucault* (16–49). Amherst: Univ. Massachusetts Press.

Gil de Zúñiga, H., Molyneux, L., and Zheng, P. (2014). Social media, political expression and political participation: Panel analysis of lagged and concurrent relationships. *Journal of Communication, 64*(4), 612–634.

Gustafsson, N. (2012). The subtle nature of Facebook politics: Swedish social network site users and political participation. *New Media & Society, 14*(1), 1111–1127.

Goffman, E. (1959). *The presentation of self in everyday life.* Garden City, NY: Anchor Books.

Habermas, J. (1995). Discourse ethics: Notes on a program of philosophical justification. In S. Benhabib and F. Dallmayr (eds.), *The communicative ethics controversy* (60–110). Cambridge, MA: MIT Press.

Habermas, J. (2006). Political communication in media society: Does democracy still enjoy an epistemic dimension? The impact of normative theory on empirical research. *Communication Theory, 16*(4), 411–426.

Hayes, A. F., Scheufele, D. A., and Huge, M. E. (2006). Nonparticipation as self-censorship: Publicly observable political activity in a polarised opinion climate. *Political Behavior, 28*(3), 259–283.

Heatherly, K., Lu, Y., and Lee, J. K. (2017). Filtering out the other side? Cross-cutting and like-minded discussions on social networking sites. *New Media & Society, 19*(8), 1271–1289.

Holt, K., Shehata, A., Strömbäck, J., and Ljungberg, E. (2013). Age and the effects of news media attention and social media use on political interest and participation: Do social media function as leveller? *European Journal of Communication, 28*(1), 19–34.

Kim, J., and Kim, E. J. (2008). Theorizing dialogic deliberation: Everyday political talk as communicative action and dialogue. *Communication Theory, 18*(1), 51–70.

Larsson, A. O. (2015). Comparing to prepare: Suggesting ways to study social media today and tomorrow. *Social Media + Society, 1*(1): 1–2.

Lievrouw, L. (2001). New media and 'pluralisation of lifeworlds': A role for information in social differentiation. *New Media & Society, 6*(1): 9–15.

Marichal, J. (2013). Political Facebook groups: Micro-activism and the digital front stage. *First Monday, 18*(12). Accessed August 1, 2017. http://firstmonday. org/article/view/4653/3800.

Marwick, A. (2013). *They're really profound women; they're entrepreneurs: Conceptions of authenticity in fashion blogging.* Presented at the International Conference on Web and Social Media, Cambridge, MA, July 8.

Mead, H. G. (1934). *Mind, self, and society.* Chicago, IL: The University of Chicago Press.

Morozov, E. (2011). *The net delusion: How not to liberate the world.* London: Allen Lane.

Naaman, M., Boase, J., and Lai, C. H. (2010). Is it really about me? Messages content in social awareness streams. Proceedings of the 2010 ACM Conference on Computer Supported Cooperative Work, Savannah, Georgia, USA.

Nieminen, H. (2006). What do we mean by a European public sphere? In N. Carpentier, P. Pruulmann-Vengerfeldt, K. Nordenstreng, M. Hartmann, P. Vihalemm, and B. Cammaerts (eds.), *Researching media, democracy and participation. The researching and teaching communications series* (105–120). Tartu, Estonia: Tartu University Press.

Norris, P. (2002). *Democratic phoenix: Reinventing political activism.* New York, NY: Cambridge University Press.

Oldenburg, R. (1991). *The great good place.* New York, NY: Paragon House.

Papacharissi, Z. (2011). *A networked self: Identity, community and culture on social network sites.* New York, NY: Routledge.

Peters, J. D. (1999). *Speaking into the air: A history of the idea of communication.* Chicago, IL: University of Chicago Press.

Rahimi, B. (2011). Facebook Iran. *Sociologica, 3*, 1–17.

Schütz, A., and Luckmann, T. (1973). *The structures of the lifeworld.* Evanston, IL: Northwestern University Press.

Silfverberg, S., Liikkanen, A. L., and Lampinen, A. (2011). *I'll press play, but I won't listen: Profile work in a music-focused social network service.* Proceedings of the ACM conference on computer supported cooperative work, Hangzhou, China, March 19–23.

Silverstone, R., and Hirsch, E. (eds.) (1992). *Consuming technologies: Media and information in domestic spaces.* London, UK/New York, NY: Routledge.

Silverstone, R. (1999). *Why study the media.* London, UK: Sage.

Simonson, P. (1996). Dreams of democratic togetherness: Communication hope from Cooley to Katz. *Critical Studies in Mass Communication, 13*(4), 324–342.

Skoric, M., Zhu, Q., Goh, D., and Pang, N. (2016). Social media and citizen engagement: A meta-analytic review. *New Media & Society, 18*(9), 1817–1839.

Sparti, D. (1996). *Soggetti al tempo.* Milano, Italy: Feltrinelli.

Svensson, J. (2011). The expressive turn of political participation and citizenship in convergence culture. *JeDem, 3*(1), 42–56.

Thorson, K. (2014). Facing an uncertain reception: Young citizens and political interaction on Facebook. *Information, Communication & Society, 17*(2), 203–216.

Uski, S., and Lampinen, A. (2016). Social norms and self-presentation on social network sites: Profile work in action. *New Media and Society, 18*(3), 447–464.

Van Dijck, J. (2013). *The culture of connectivity: A critical history of social media.* Oxford, UK: Oxford University Press.

van Zoonen, L. (2005). *Entertaining the citizen: When politics and popular culture converge.* Lanham, MD: Rowman & Littlefield.

Verba, S., Schlozman, K. L., and Brady, H. E. (1995). *Voice and equality: Civic voluntarism in American politics.* Cambridge, MA: Harvard University Press.

We are Social (2016). Digital in 2016. Accessed August 1, 2017. http://wearesocial.com/sg/special-reports/digital-2016.

Xenos, M., Vromen, A., and Loader B. D. (2014). The great equalizer? Patterns of social media use and youth political engagement in three advanced democracies. *Information, Communication & Society, 17*(2), 151–167.

4 'I Am Not a Consumer Person' – Political Participation in Repair Cafés

Sigrid Kannengießer

Repair Cafés from the Perspective of Media and Communication Studies

In Europe, climate change and impacts of the financial and economic crisis over the past few years have provoked a growing awareness regarding the social and environmental effects of the consumer society. This has led to changes in the consumer behaviour of more and more people. Transition Towns, Urban Gardening, Exchange Circles or Repair Cafés are projects in which people criticise the capitalistic consumer society and develop practices aimed at sustainability. One of these projects, Repair Cafés, is the focus of this chapter.

Repair Cafés are new event formats which have spread all over Western European and North American countries within recent years (see a map for many such locations at www.repaircafe.org[1]). At these events, people meet to work together on repairing their objects of everyday life such as electrical appliances, clothing or bicycles – media technologies being among those goods which are brought most often to these events.

While some of the people attending come to offer their services free of charge in the repairing process, others are seeking help to have their things repaired. The idea is to help people to help themselves. The repair events take place for a restricted period of time (usually three to five hours). They take place at different types of location – very often in cafés or community centres. Irrespective of the location, usually coffee and cake or other beverages and snacks are provided to create a sort of café atmosphere even when not actually taking place in cafés. The seating and table arrangements are similar, with the people offering help sitting at tables (except those offering help to repair bicycles), and signs above or on the tables indicating the type of goods in need of repair.

This chapter presents the results of a qualitative study in which I analysed Repair Cafés from the perspective of media and communication studies, focusing especially on the media practices at such events. The organisers of Repair Cafés use the usual media like emails, blogs or social networks to connect and mobilise people. They use "old" media such as flyers or leaflets for the purpose of public relations (see Kannengießer 2018). But in Repair Cafés, media also become the focus of action themselves with people coming to *repair* media technologies and others to have them repaired. They bring with them new devices such as laptops and smartphones as well as old ones like slide projectors and radios. Together with the helpers, the participants open the devices, clean them up, tighten screws and glue them together.

As the practice of repairing media technologies is an action in relation to media, I define the repairing of media technologies as media practice (see ibid.). The central question of a paradigm perceiving media as practice is, 'What, quite simply, are people doing in relation to media across a whole range of situations and contexts?' (Couldry 2004, 119) In the case of Repair Cafés, this question can be answered quite easily: People come to repair their media technologies or have them repaired (whether successfully or not).

The study focused on the media practice of repairing devices, and therefore people bringing broken media technologies and those offering help in maintaining them. Why do people participate in Repair Cafés and repair media technologies? What do Repair Cafés and the practice of repairing mean to the participants? And which relevance do the participants see in the Repair Cafés for a (mediatised) society? Analysing the aims of the participants in Repair Cafés and the meanings they construct, practices of political participation became apparent as people involved want to change the consumer society and strive for sustainability. In this chapter, the results of the study analysing Repair Cafés are discussed, which gave reason to frame the repairing of media technologies as a form of political participation.

Therefore, in a first section of this chapter, the research fields on political participation in media and communication studies as well as the field on repairing and public sites of repair are sketched out as both provide relevant insights for the empirical discussion. Then the methodology is described. In a third part, the results of the empirical study in which Repair Cafés have been analysed from the perspective of media and communication studies are discussed. The focus here is on the results that are relevant for the discourse on political participation in media and communication studies, especially the research field on media practice.

Research on Political Participation in Media and Communication Studies and Public Repair Sites

This chapter discusses an aspect of interrelation between media and political participation which is rarely acknowledged in media and communication studies: What do people actually do with media technologies and in what way are these practices acts of political participation?

The discourse on media and participation has a long tradition in media and communication studies (see, for an overview, Carpentier 2011, 64–131) but the term participation is used in different ways (see ibid., 15–38; Barrett and Brunton-Smith 2014). In this chapter, political participation is defined as voluntary practices by citizens which are aimed at influencing and shaping society (de Nève and Olteanu 2013, 14). The term political participation has to be distinguished from the term engagement: While participation refers to processes in which citizens *actively* take part, the term engagement rather addresses moments of interest and attention (Dahlgren 2009, 80–83; Barrett abd Brunton-Smith 2014, 6). Following this definition, the repairing of media technologies will be discussed as a form of political participation as people *actively* try to transform society while repairing their devices – an aspect which will be discussed below.

The research field on media and participation has gained in relevance and complexity since the establishment of the internet – and especially the development of social media like Twitter and Facebook. Studies discuss and analyse the possibilities of internet media (especially Web 2.0 media and mediated networks) for political participation (e.g. Anduiza 2009; Anduiza et al. 2012; Kavada 2013; Serra et al. 2014; Loader et al. 2014; Cammaerts 2015).

Internet media make it easier for people to participate in the public and political debate than traditional mass media do – especially by creating media content. The neologism 'produser' (Bruns 2008, 2009) grasps the mixture of the role of the user becoming also the producer of media content in internet media. The produser can participate in the public sphere by creating media content, which is what Nico Carpentier identifies as participation *in* media. He (as well as Altheide 1997) distinguishes between participation *in* and *through* media: While participation *in* media deals with participation in the production of media content and the decision-making processes in media organisations, participation *through* media deals with mediated participation in public debate and for self-representation (Carpentier 2011, 67f.).

In discussing what people actually *do with media technologies* and in what way these practices are acts of political participation, it already becomes obvious that limiting the focus of the role of the produser to media *content* is too narrow. The concept of the 'produser' or 'prosumer', combining the roles of producers and consumers (Toffler 1980), can be discussed and analysed more broadly with regard to media and participation, not only taking media content and organisational forms into account but also the material dimension of media technologies.

Produsers or prosumers are relevant concepts in respect of the idea of do-it-yourself citizenship, 'a term intended to highlight the diversity of ways citizenship is enacted and performed' (Ratto and Boler 2014b, 3). In the publication edited by Ratto and Boler (2014a), many case studies analysing do-it-yourself projects are presented. Ratto and Boler (2014b, 5) suggest using the term 'critical makers', thus also encompassing the people involved in Repair Cafés (which I will discuss below) as 'DIY citizens'. Media in this context are relevant as do-it-yourself media, a term used for social media or Web 2.0 media that offer people the possibility to create media content (Lankshear and Knobel 2010, 10f.; Ratto and Boler 2014b, 3).[2] Similar to the concept of the produser is also that of the do-it-yourself citizen. Do-it-yourself media have to be discussed in a broader sense in relation to media so as not only to acknowledge what people do with media content but also what they do with media technologies.

When analysing Repair Cafés, it becomes obvious that political engagement by citizens is not declining, as Peter Dahlgren suggests (2009, 1), but that other or alternative forms of political engagement and participation are established which can be described as unconventional. Unconventional forms of political participation are those which are not traditional like e.g. voting, but rather practices that are not institutionalised (de Nève and Olteanu 2013, 283; Barrett and Brunton-Smith 2014, 7). They are forms of sub-political practices (Beck 1997, 103) 'life politics' (Giddens 1991, 215ff.) or 'subactivism' (Bakardjieva 2009), not organised by political institutions but practiced in everyday life.[3] The concept of unconventional political participation will become relevant in discussing the empirical results of the analysis of Repair Cafés.

Repair and Repair Cafés are mainly analysed in technology and design studies. Here, repair is defined as 'the process of sustaining, managing, and repurposing technology in order to cope with attrition and regressive change' (Rosner and Turner 2015, 59). Steve Jackson 'rethinks repair' and suggests the approach of 'broken world thinking' in media and technology studies, shifting the perspective from the new, growth and progress to erosion, breakdown and decay (2014: 221). He sees a necessity for this shift in current crisis and instabilities and perceives repairing as a way to sustain and restore infrastructures and lives (ibid., 222). I will argue in this chapter on the basis of the results of the empirical study analysing Repair Cafés that repairing is not only a way of dealing with current financial or economic crisis or climate change but that it can also be an act of political participation aimed at the transformation of society.

Daniela K. Rosner and Morgan G. Ames stress the active role of people shaping technologies by repairing. They introduce the notion of *negotiated endurance*, which 'refers to the process by which different actors – including consumers, community organisers and others – drive the ongoing use, maintenance, and repair of a given technology through the sociocultural and socioeconomic infrastructures they inhabit and produce' (Rosner and Ames 2014, 319). By so doing, they stress that the lifecycle of things is rather negotiated by the users in the appropriation process than planned ahead by the people who designed these things (ibid., 329).

Rosner and Ames show that the repair initiatives they analysed in California and Paraguay follow the idea of technical empowerment, which they define as 'knowing more about technology and making more informed choices around technology as a result' (ibid., 326). But the authors also concede that such empowerment rarely emerges in the repair initiatives as often the things are repaired *for* the people seeking help (ibid, 327), which is similar in the findings presented below.

However, this technical empowerment has a political character and repairing can become 'a mode of political action', as Rosner and Turner state (2015, 64f.). They call Repair Cafés 'theaters of alternative industry' (2015) which are 'meant to demonstrate the power of creative re-manufacturing to change the world' (ibid., 65), and whose participants strive for social change, whereupon the change here is seen in questions of egalitarianism and collectivity (ibid., 67).

Charter and Keiller analyse motivations of volunteers in Repair Cafés in a quantitative study: the top three reasons why participants engage in Repair Cafés were encouraging others to live more sustainable lives, providing a valuable service to the community and being part of the movement to improve product reparability and longevity (2014, 5). The authors draw the conclusion that the volunteers act altruistically and that their personal gain is not important to them (ibid., 13). The latter finding is not shared in the results presented in this chapter. Moreover, the results of the qualitative study discussed in this chapter show that the aims of people involved in Repair Cafés are more complex. Furthermore, the results also show that repairing media technologies can be characterised as unconventional participation, which will be the argument of this chapter.

Methodology Used for Analysing Repair Cafés

It is useful to adopt a qualitative approach when analysing the aims pursued by people by repairing their media technologies and the meanings people construct regarding the societal relevance of repairing their devices as well as the relevance of Repair Cafés. The approach of Grounded Theory (Corbin and Strauss 2008[4]) allows for an open procedure and the reconstruction of the perspective of the people involved in Repair Cafés.

As case studies for the qualitative study, I chose three Repair Cafés in Germany which differ regarding the location in which they are organised as well as the background of the organisers: one Repair Café is arranged in a university context in Oldenburg (a mid-sized city in North West Germany); the second one is organised by an artist in the Kreuzberg quarter of Berlin in cooperation with a non-governmental organisation Kunststoffe e.V.[5] (this Repair Café was the first in Berlin and awarded a prize for sustainability by the City of Berlin); and the third one is organised in Garbsen (a small city near Hanover in the North of Germany) by a retired teacher in collaboration with the agency for volunteers of the City of Garbsen. I chose these different case studies to find out whether there might be differences regarding the aims of people involved when they have different backgrounds and the events take place in different settings.

I conducted observations in these Repair Cafés (Flick 2009, 282) in 2014 and 2015 as well as 40 in-depth interviews (Kruse 2008, 53) with the organisers, with people offering help in repairing media technologies and people seeking help in repairing their devices. In addition, interviews were also carried out with two employees of the non-governmental organisation Anstiftung & Ertomis who are working on creating a network among the different repair initiatives in Germany.[6] The observations allowed to follow the (media) practices during these events, and the interviews to reconstruct the perspectives of the people involved.

For the observations and the interviews, guidelines were developed for structuring the observations/interviews to ensure relevant aspects for each of the research questions were considered (ibid.), e.g. why people become involved in organizing or participating in Repair Cafés. Aspects of political participation had not been included in the questions: it was not until analysis of the data that political participation became obvious.

In respect of the theoretical sampling of the interview partners (Corbin and Strauss 2008, 143–158), I chose people among the groups of the organisers, the helpers and people seeking help with differing age, gender, class and educational background.

In respect of the organisers of the Repair Cafés, the social categories of age, gender and educational background varied. People offering help in fixing media technologies also differed in age and educational background: some have a professional background as IT system administrators, e.g. TV technicians or students/teachers of physics or technical education; only a few are autodidacts. Some helpers are unemployed; many are retired, finding a worthwhile task in Repair Cafés. All of the people offering help in fixing media technologies in the Repair Cafés who were chosen as case studies were men.[7]

In respect of the participants seeking help in repairing their media technologies, the social categories varied: People from all age groups and men as well as women coming from different social backgrounds bring their broken devices for repair. But what is significant in respect of all three groups is that rarely people with a migration background participate.[8] I considered these differences in the theoretical sampling.

I coded the interview transcriptions as well as the protocols of the observations along the coding process (open coding, axial coding selective coding) of Grounded Theory (Corbin and Strauss 2008). I developed inductive categories which allowed to sort and compare the data. In the coding process, six main categories became obvious regarding the aims of the people involved and why they organise the Repair Cafés or repair media technologies: conservation of resources, waste prevention, appreciation of the apparatus, technical empowerment, having fun repairing things and economic pressure. In the following, I will focus on the categories and results which led to framing the repairing of media technologies as unconventional (political) participation.

Prolonging the Lifespan of Media Technologies: Conservation of Resources and Waste Prevention

People repair objects of everyday life because they want to prolong the lifespan of these goods. Organisers of Repair Cafés, those offering help in the repairing process and people bringing their broken media technologies for repair share the aims of conserving natural resources as well as waste prevention by not throwing things away and buying new ones.

One participant expresses his motivation for repairing his radio apparatus as follows: 'I think it's a pity and waste of resources to throw these devices away, because they then only become scrap. The material will not even be recycled'. And a 42-year-old electrician offering help in repairing media technologies explains, 'Throwing away does not make sense because electronics often contain valuable resources like coltan, copper, gold'. Also, the organisers share the aim of conservation of resources, as one of the organisers of a Repair Café in Oldenburg said, 'I think especially the repairing of computers is important as they contain resources, because of which people in other countries die. And we should not throw these [technologies] away and buy a new iPhone'. Many organisers and participants point to the harmful and pollutive circumstances and situations of war under which the resources needed for digital media technologies (such as coltan) are extracted.[9] One participant even calls the people producing media technologies 'slaves'.

A second dominant aim of people being involved in Repair Cafés is waste prevention. A woman trying to repair her smartphone explains the relevance of repairing: 'I do not want to pollute our planet with things that are still working, but only have a loose screw'. Another participant explains, 'We would have a better world if more people repair their things [...] because our planet would be less polluted'. And a third participant gazes into the future: 'If our waste pile continue to grow that fast and poisons our groundwater – our children will have to pay for that'.

Organisers, as well as people offering help and bringing broken devices, point to the circumstances on waste dumps in Africa, where people (often children) burn the broken media technologies to retrieve reusable resources while they damage their health and the environment is polluted as poisonous substances end up in soil and groundwater.[10] One of the helpers explains, 'These goods are shipped to Africa where they are burned, which is not very nice for the environment, people and resources'.

The production of waste piles and the situation on waste dumps in Africa provokes emotional reactions: 'That's the bad thing, that old media technologies are brought to disposal sites in Africa and that people there search for noble metal and this shit. That makes me sick', expresses emotionally a 50-year-old man offering help, and a female participant says she is angry that people lived as though there was a second earth. One of the organisers is even aware of the law prohibiting shipping electronic waste to non-European countries; but she also stresses that customs is not able to control the illegal transport – e.g. to waste disposal sites in Ghana.

The responsibility of people is highlighted by many participants, as this citation from a woman, trying to repair her old television set, shows exemplarily: 'climate change [...] we need to practice what we preach, that's why I am doing that [repairing the TV set, S.K. ...] This is my contribution, as far as it is possible'. Many interviewees point to the restricted possibilities and impact they have regarding climate change and the protection of the environment.

Notwithstanding, all the people interviewed do not *not* use media technologies. One organiser stresses that the aim of repairing media technologies is not to disconnect with technological progress, but to decelerate this process in favour of ecology. But especially people offering help in repairing media technologies point to the limits they experience when repairing mainly digital media technologies – sometimes not being able to open the apparatus. Although being aware of the socioecological negative effects the production and disposal of media technologies cause, some participants still try to push this knowledge aside: "One mustn't think about these production processes because if one does, one would not buy electronic devices anymore."

Nevertheless, people involved in Repair Cafés try to avoid the production of new media technologies and disposal of existing ones by prolonging the lifespan of the ones they own by offering help in repairing media apparatuses. The artist organising this event describes the Repair Café as a 'place for escape for things' which would otherwise be thrown away. And one man offering help in repairing media technologies perceives his action as a 'life prolonging practice for electronic devices'. By making the technologies work again, people try to avoid the consumption of new media technologies because many seek the conservation of resources and waste prevention. They are aware of the harmful production processes of media technologies as well as the problematic disposal of old devices. For many, repairing existing media apparatus is a way of contributing towards a sustainable society.

The Repair Café functions not only as a setting in which people share the aims of conserving resources and preventing waste but also as an event through which these ideas are spread. One 21-year old woman helping to organise the Repair Café in Berlin explains that the Repair Café 'awakened' her to not throwing things away but trying to repair them.

Treasured Media Devices and Technical Empowerment

Besides waste prevention and conservation of resources, people also try to prolong the lifespan of their technologies because they value their things and try to empower themselves. Many people involved in Repair Cafés – either as organisers of events or the people offering or seeking help – value existing media technologies and criticise the regular consumption of new devices. A volunteer helping to repair media technologies underlines the amount of work which is put into each device, people inventing, developing and designing the products and others constructing them, which is a reason for him to value his goods and try to maintain them:

> There is an immense amount of work in every device, which we have to acknowledge: People worked on this object, developed it, designed it, people in a factory built it. [...] And I think we value this work of human beings when we try to repair the products that do not function anymore.

One woman bringing her laptop to the repair event stresses the relevance of repairing media technologies by comparing the fixing of these device with the repairing of textiles: 'If your blouse is missing a button, you also do not throw it away immediately'.

Participants bringing their broken media devices stress the value of their existing devices and their personal relation to the technologies they possess: 'I befriend with my smartphone', tells one participant trying to repair his phone and a 76-year-old participant explains that he is attached to his old radio as he grew up with this device. He, as well as many other people seeking help in repairing old media devices, stresses the quality of older media technologies compared to new products. A retired man values his old radio as the quality of the sound was in his view much better than that of a new radio. The same applies to a 30-year old musician repairing his amplifier. While repairing an old cassette recorder, a 74-year-old participant underlines the relevance of older devices when facing technological innovation: he relies on his broken cassette recorder to play his old cassettes.

The repairing of media technologies is not only a media practice as people act in relation to media (see above). It is also a communicative one: People repair their things *together*. As the observation shows, people seeking help often ask about the defects of their devices or problems in the repairing process. Several are keen to learn how to do repairs themselves so they can do it on their own in future. Many volunteers offering help in repairing try to explain this process and teach others how to repair things. Providing a space in which knowledge can be shared is also the intention of the organisers:

> This is our idea; that customers take part in the repairing process [...] to learn how to repair and to understand the process. On the one

hand to appreciate the effort of the people offering help and on the other hand to say to oneself in the future: Have the heart to repair!

The organisers of these events want to build a network among people knowing how to repair and those wanting to learn about their objects and the repairing process. For them, the repairing of media technologies is an act of empowerment which they want to support by organising these events. Still, especially regarding (digital) media technologies, the spread of knowledge also has its limits as several people offering help in repairing media apparatus explain: many people seeking help are either not interested in learning how to do repairs or do not have any talent at all in repairing electronic devices. Moreover, observations in the different Repair Cafés show that people offering help in repairing media technologies often repair things alone without the help of the people who brought the broken items in.[11] Furthermore, repairs are not always successful as either time or spare parts are missing or the devices are no longer repairable.

But it is not only people seeking help who gain knowledge; also, participants offering help underline the increase of knowledge. They stress their interest in media technologies and their aim of gaining knowledge about the technologies while repairing, as a retired man relates during an interview: 'You get to learn many things. [...] "A rolling stone gathers no moss"'. Especially retired people are helping in Repair Cafés. But also, unemployed people or those whose hobby is repairing and engagement with technologies find a space in Repair Cafés where they can pursue their passion. Another retired participant relates that repairing for him is a positive challenge that keeps him young. Retired and unemployed people find a task through the Repair Cafés and the possibility to socialise. Sometimes, people organising Repair Cafés and those offering help also come together for other social meetings in between the repair events like having a barbeque or bowling.

Sharing and spreading the knowledge of repairing, empowering oneself and others, as well as the social dimension of Repair Cafés – chatting about repairs, consumption and ecology or other things – are besides the conservation of resources and waste prevention also aspects of political participation as also these motives aim at transforming society – into a repair culture (Heckl 2013).

The Repair Movement Striving for Cultural Transformation

Many people involved in Repair Cafés try to transform society and try to do that by the practice of repairing. Some of the participants take part in the repair events as they have fun repairing things or for financial reasons as they do not have the resources to buy new media technologies. But the organisers of these events as well as many participants share consumer-critical attitudes and strive for a sustainable society, to which they want to contribute by the practice of repairing. For one particular woman organiser, repairing is a way of 'cheating consumption'. One man offering help in repairing media technologies perceives Repair Cafés as an act against the consumer society. The organisers of Repair Cafés strive for a cultural transformation: 'We cannot talk about sustainability without a culture of repairing, and a fundamental extension of the life-span of technologies', says the 50-year-old initiator of the repair event in Oldenburg. He stresses that a culture of repairing is needed to establish a sustainable society and perceives a need for change regarding identification with technologies:

> We need to have a cultural change, through which it becomes cool again and socially acceptable to walk around with technologies which have signs of use and patina, where the display has scratches or fractures and one says: "This is my good old device, I stand by this, this is my trademark."

And another organiser stresses the cultural relevance of Repair Cafés: 'The Repair Café is very important for our culture, so that we do not continue consuming but repair our things to be able to conserve resources'.

Cultural change is perceived as necessary because of the finiteness of resources: 'It is the idea that we do not throw everything away. [...] It is clear that our way of living does not work forever. So I think it is an important process that people understand to not throw everything away', explains one helper. One participant claims:

> We need to get rid of the 'consumption mentality'. Some people involved in Repair Cafés already share this mentality, as one 27-year old bicycle courier having brought his computer to the Repair Café, describes himself: 'I am not a consumer person'.

Not obeying the logics of the consumer society, repairing is even described as 'disobedience' by one of the organisers who stresses that repairing is a political act as the role of the consumer is negotiated again: 'It is not planned that the consumer is opening and repairing technologies, and this then is already an act of disobedience'.

But are these questions of individual identities or is there a repair *movement*? One of the organisers perceives such a movement, which he defines as sharing a common identity:

> This repair movement [...] constructs its identity on the basis of a certain product aesthetics: [...] Young people having an old Nokia, which is taped and has scratches on the display. That's what they like and that's a political statement for them.

Some of the organisers of Repair Cafés describe themselves and people involved in these events as 'pioneers', breaking with established practices (regarding consumption) and starting a cultural transformation. One of the helpers offering support in repairing smartphones in the Repair Café in Berlin says he wants to 'swim against the tide' by not buying a new smartphone every year. One of the organisers constructs a collective of people involved in Repair Cafés: 'We are starting to rethink and repair things over and over again. Thereby we help to improve the world, conserve resources [...] and live more consciously'. And the owner of the Café in Oldenburg where the Repair Café takes place is proud that this event takes place on his premises:

> I am proud that it [the Repair Café, S.K.] is taken place at my place. Because I think that this is a culture, which will be established all over Germany. And I will be able to say then: I was part of it from the beginning.

But not the act of repairing itself is a pioneer practice as people have always repaired their possessions. But what is new about the repairing done in Repair Cafés is that it happens publicly and that it is politicised: It is framed as a possibility to transform society into a sustainable one.

While some of the people involved in Repair Cafés talk about a 'repair movement', others are more sceptical: 'This [the repair movement, S.K.] will only be a mass movement when we are shaken again through another financial crisis for example'. The organiser stresses that repairing will only become a widespread practice in society if there was the need for it – people not being able to consume anymore.

The German non-governmental organisation Anstiftung & Ertomis (see footnote 3) tries to build a repair movement: they support people organising Repair Cafés in Germany, try to build a network among them (e.g. through annual meetings of people organising repair events), and try to make the repair initiatives visible through a website (www.reparatur-initiativen.de) but also by lobbying. The networking takes place via an online platform on which repair initiatives in Germany can register and through annual face-to-face meetings organised by Anstiftung & Ertomis. Lobbying for the idea of repairing and repair initiatives happens by giving presentations (about repairing and Repair Cafés), when invited by other non-governmental organisations, and taking part in political round tables. The Repair Cafés themselves are also used for lobbying: one organiser explains that he uses these events as a communication strategy to put pressure on the economy and politicians. Repair Cafés are staged as political events.

Four theoretical characteristics of social movements also match a repair movement: shared aims, a shared identity, protest and network character (Ullrich 2015, 9–15ff.). As the results of the study conducted show, actors of Repair Cafés share the aim of sustainability and consumer criticism. Their forms of protests are the repair events and they network not only locally in these events but also translocally on a national level (organised in Germany by Anstiftung & Ertomis). The aim of the repair movement is to transform society into a culture of repair, thereby striving for a sustainable society.

Repairing Media Technologies As Unconventional Political Participation

People participate in Repair Cafés because they want to prolong the lifespan of everyday objects – media technologies being among those goods which are brought most often to these events. Organisers, helpers and participants bringing broken media apparatuses in the case studies chosen share the aims of conservation of resources, waste prevention, appreciation of media devices and technical empowerment.

Still, especially regarding (digital) media technologies, the technical empowerment has its limits: the observations in the different Repair Cafés show that people offering help in repairing media technologies often do the repairs without the help of the people bringing in items for repair. Therefore, the idea of Repair Cafés helping people to help themselves is not always realised. Moreover, the repairs are not always successful as either time or spare parts are missing or the items are no longer repairable (which is discussed as effects of the planned obsolescence).

Nevertheless, by trying to prolong the lifespan of existing media technologies and avoiding the consumption of new devices, as well as striving for technical empowerment, people try to *transform* society. They disobey the logics of the consumer society by not throwing their broken things away and buying new ones, but by holding on to items and maintaining them, thereby trying to contribute to a 'repair culture' (Heckl 2013) and a sustainable society. Therefore, the repairing of media technologies in Repair Cafés can be identified as political participation as people voluntarily try to change society through the practice of repairing their possessions.

Engaging actively with media technologies in Repair Cafés, the consumer becomes a produser (Toffler 1980): people shape media apparatuses by repairing. In this active role, people repairing take the status of citizens – they are 'DIY citizens' (Ratto and Boler 2014b, 5), empowering themselves by engaging with the material dimension of technologies and reflecting on media production, disposal and appropriation.

Media here are not 'do-it-yourself media' in the sense of social media or Web 2.0 media that offer people the possibility to create media content (ibid., 3; Lankshear and Knobel 2010, 10f.). But all media technologies become do-it-yourself media in the context of Repair Cafés as all devices can be shaped.

The political participation during the repair process is neither participation *in* nor *through* media (Carpentier 2011, 67f.). Rather, it is a political participation by acting *with and on* media technologies. What people actually do with media technologies must be acknowledged in media and communication studies when analysing and debating practices and possibilities of political participation and media (see Kannengießer and Kubitschko 2017).

The repairing of media devices is a form of *unconventional* political participation as repairing is not a traditional form of participation organised by political institutions. Rather, it is a form of sub-political practices (Beck 1997, 103) and 'life politics' (Giddens 1991, 215ff.) or 'subactivism' (Bakardjieva 2009) as it is integrated in everyday life. It is a way of doing 'politics with a shopping trolley' (Baringhorst 2012) as people try to avoid (over)consumption. Yet, people participating in Repair Cafés do not refuse to use media devises. Rather, they are practicing an alternative way of media appropriation by having their possessions repaired – an alternative to overconsumption.

Repairing is not a new process nor does it always have political implications (people also repair e.g. due to financial reasons) but the repairing practices analysed in this chapter happen publicly in Repair Cafés, which are staged as public events to debate and advertise for consumer-criticism and alternatives to consumption by the organisers of these events. Many people involved in Repair Cafés admit that these events are only a small step towards a societal change; but they stress that it is *their* contribution.

The results presented here are also transferrable to the repairing of other goods – not only media devices. But repairing media technologies has a special relevance in current mediatised societies, in which the media environment of the people becomes more and more complex and where media gain in importance in all societal areas (Krotz 2009). In mediatised societies, the number of media technologies increases – and thereby also the production and disposal of media technologies. This is what many people involved in Repair Cafés criticise and try to change.

Notes

1 This list is supported by the Dutch foundation Stichting Repair Café, which claims to have invented the concept of Repair Cafés in 2009 (Stichting Repair Café n.d.). Being the origin or not, the format of Repair Cafés has spread and the number of repair events increases. E.g. there are more than 500 repair initiatives in Germany (www.reparatur-initiativen.de).

2 The concept of *citizenship* grasps political participation in relation to different fields. While *civil citizenship* refers to participation of producers or consumers in the economic field, *political citizenship* focuses on participation in political decision making processes, *social citizenship* refers to participation in the welfare state (Marshall and Bottomore 1992), and *cultural citizenship* points to the creative and successful participation in cultures (Hermes and Dahlgren 2006). The latter concept is discussed in media and

communication studies when analysing how citizens use media for participating in society and politics (see e.g. Klaus and Lünenborg 2012).

3 Ekman and Amnå (2012, 290) prefer the term extra-parliamentary forms
  of political participation to unconventional political participation but I stick
  to the term 'unconventional', stressing the sub-political and also creative
  character of these forms of activism.
4 I adopted Strauss' and Corbin's approach of Grounded Theory and not Glaser's.
  For a comparison of both see e.g. Walker and Myrick (2006).
5 Kunststoffe e.V. is a German non-governmental organisation based in Berlin
  that organises projects dealing with the recycling and re-utilisation of any
  material. For further information visit www.kunst-stoffe-berlin.de/en/.
6 Anstiftung Ertomis is a German-registered non-governmental organisation,
  based in Munich, which carries out research on commons and do-it-yourself
  projects and supports initiatives like Urban Gardening or Repair Cafés. For
  more information visit www.anstiftung.de/english.
7 This finding regarding gender was also the case in public sites of repair in
  California, which Daniela Rosner analysed (2013).
8 This finding differs in other Repair Cafés, e.g. which are especially organised for refugees, as e.g. a second repair initiative in Oldenburg, Germany is.
9 See e.g. Bleischwitz et al. (2012); Chan and Ho (2008) for research on the
  harmful and pollutive production processes of technologies.
10 See for an analysis of the effects of e-waste, e.g. Gabrys (2011); Kaitatzi-
   Whitlock (2015).
11 I share this result with Daniela Rosner, who analyses public repair sites in
   California (see above).

References

Altheide, D. L. (1997). Media participation in everyday life, leisure sciences. *An Interdisciplinary Journal, 19*(1), 17–30.
Anduiza, E., Cantijoch, M., and Gallego, A. (2009). Political participation and the internet. *Information, Communication & Society, 12*(6), 860–878.
Anduiza, A., Jensen, M. J., and Jorba, L. (eds.) (2012). *Digital media and political engagement worldwide.* Cambridge, UK: Cambridge University Press.
Bakardjieva, M. (2009). Subactivism: Lifeworld and politics in the age of the internet. *The Information Society, 25*(2), 91–104.
Baringhorst, S. (2012). Politik mit dem Einkaufswagen – Erfolgschancen und Probleme der Politisierung von Konsum. *Argumente*, 2012(2), 44–50.
Barrett, M., and Brunton-Smith, I. (2014). Political and civic engagement and participation: Towards an integrative perspective. *Journal of Civil Society, 10*(1), 5–28.
Beck, U. (1997). *The reinvention of politics: Rethinking modernity in the global social order.* Cambridge, UK: Polity Press.
Bleischwitz, R., Dittrich, M., and Pierdicca, C. (2012). Coltan from Central Africa, international trade and implications for any certification. *Resources Policy, 37*, 19–29.
Bruns, A. (2008). The future is user-led: The path towards widespread produsage. *The Fibreculture Journal, 11/2008.* Accessed August 1, 2017. http://eleven.fibrecul turejournal.org/fcj-066-the-future-is-user-led-the-path-towards-widespread-produsage.

Bruns, A. (2009). „Anyone can edit": vom Nutzer zum Produtzer. In *Kommu nikation@Gesellschaft, 10*(3). Accessed August 1, 2017. http://nbn-resolving.de/ urn:nbn:de:0228-200910033.

Cammaerts, B. (2015). Social media and activism. In R. Mansell and P. H. Ang (eds.), *The international encyclopedia of digital communication and society* (1027–1034). Oxford, UK: Wiley-Blackwell.

Carpentier, N. (2011). *Media and participation. A site of ideological-democratic struggle.* Bristol, UK: Intellect.

Chan, J., and Ho, C. (2008). *The dark side of cyberspace: Inside the sweatshops of China's computer hardware production.* Berlin, Germany. Accessed August 1, 2017. http://goodelectronics.org/publications-en/Publication_2851.

Charter, M., and Keiller, S. (2014). *Grassroots innovation and the circular economy. A global survey of repair cafés and hackerspaces.* Farnham, Surrey, UK: University for the creative arts. Accessed August 1, 2017. http://cfsd.org. uk/site-pdfs/circular-economy-and-grassroots-innovation/Survey-of-Repair-Cafes-and-Hackerspaces.pdf.

Corbin, J., and Strauss, A. (2008). *Basics of qualitative research. Techniques and procedures for developing grounded theory.* 3rd ed. Los Angeles, CA: Sage.

Couldry, N. (2004). Theorising media as practice. *Social Semiotics, 14*(2), 115–132.

Dahlgren, P. (2009): *Media and political engagement. Citizens, communication and democracy.* New York, NY: Cambridge University Press.

Ekman, J., and Amnå, E. (2012). Political participation and civic engagement: Towards a new typology. *Human Affairs, 22*(3), 283–300.

Flick, U. (2009). *Qualitative Sozialforschung. Eine Einführung.* Reinbek bei Hamburg, Germany: Rowohlt-Taschenbuch-Verlag.

Gabrys, J. (2011). *Digital rubbish: A natural history of electronics.* Ann Arbor: University of Michigan Press.

Giddens, A. (1991). *Modernity and self-identity: Self and society in the late modern age.* Stanford, CA: Stanford University Press.

Heckl, W. M. (2013). *Die Kultur der Reparatur.* München, Germany: Carl Hanser Verlag.

Hermes, J., and Dahlgren, P. (2006). Cultural studies and citizenship. *European Journal of Cultural Studies, 9*(3), 259–265.

Jackson, S. J. (2014). Rethinking repair. In T. Gillespie, P. Boczkowski, and K. Foot (eds.), *Media technologies: Essays on communication, materiality, and society* (221–239). Cambridge, MA: MIT Press.

Kaitatzi-Whitlock, S. (2015). E-waste, human-waste, inflation. In R. Maxwell, J. Raundalen, and N. L. Vestberg (eds.), *Media and the ecological crisis* (69–84). Milton Park, UK/New York, NY: Routledge.

Kannengießer, S. (2018). Repair cafés – Consumer critical media practices for cultural transformation. In A. Hepp, U. Hasebrink, and A. Breiter (eds.), *Communicative figurations. Rethinking mediatized transformations.* London, UK: Palgrave.

Kannengießer, S., and Kubitschko, S. (2017). Editorial. Acting on media: Influencing, shaping and (re)configuring the fabric of everyday life. *Media and Communication.* 5 (3), 1–4.

Kavada, A. (2013). Internet cultures and protest movements: The cultural links between strategy, organizing and online communication. In B. Cammaerts,

A. Mattoni, and P. McCurdy (eds.), *Mediation and protest movements* (75–94). London, UK: Intellect.

Klaus, E., and Lünenborg, M. (2012). Cultural citizenship. Partizipation by and through media. In E. Zobl, and R. Drüeke (eds.), *Feminist media. Participatory spaces, networks and cultural citizenship* (197–212). Bielefeld, Germany: transcript.

Krotz, F. (2009). Mediatization: A concept with which to grasp media and societal change. In K. Lundby (ed.), *Mediatization: Concept, changes, consequences* (21–40). New York, NY: Peter Lang.

Kruse, J. (2008). *Reader. Einführung in die qualitative Interviewforschung.* Freiburg, Germany: University of Freiburg.

Lankshear, C., and Knobel, M. (2010). *DIY media. Creating, sharing and learning with new technologies.* Frankfurt a.M., Germany: Peter Lang.

Loader, B. D., Vromen, A., and Xenos, M. A. (2014). The networked young citizen: social media, political participation and civic engagement. *Information, Communication & Society, 17*(2), 143–150.

Marshall, T.H. and Bottomore, T. (1992) *Citizenship and social class.* London: Pluto Press.

Nève, D. de, and Olteanu, T. (2013). Potenziale unkonventioneller Partizipation. In D. de Nève and T. Olteanu (eds.), *Politische Partizipation jenseits der Konventionen* (283–302). Leverkusen, Germany: Verlag Barbara Budrich.

Ratto, M., and Boler, M. (eds.) (2014a). *DIY citizenship. Critical making and social media.* Cambridge/London, UK: MIT Press.

Ratto, M., and Boler, M. (2014b). Introduction. In M. Ratto and M. Boler (eds.), *DIY citizenship. Critical making and social media* (1–22). Cambridge/London, UK: MIT Press.

Rosner, D. K. (2013). Making citizens, reassembling devices: On gender and the development of contemporary public sites of repair in Northern California. *Public Culture, 26*(1), 51–77.

Rosner, D. K., and Ames, M. G. (2014). *Designing for repair? Infrastructures and materialities of breakdown.* Paper presented at 17th ACM Conference on Computer Supported Cooperative Work and Social Computing, CSCW 2014, Baltimore, MD, February 15–19, 319–331.

Rosner, D., and Turner, F. (2015). Theaters of alternative industry: Hobbyist repair collectives and the legacy of the 1960s American counterculture. In C. Meinel and L. Leifer (eds.), *Design thinking research* (59–69). Heidelberg, Germany: Springer International Publishing.

Serra, P., Camilo, E., and Goncalves, G. (eds.) (2014). *Political participation and web 2.0.* Covilhã, Portugal: Livros Labcom.

Stichting Repair Café (n.d.). *About repair café.* Accessed August 1, 2017. http://repaircafe.org/about-repair-café.

Toffler, A. W. (1980). *The third wave.* London, UK: Random House.

Ullrich, P. (2015). Postdemokratische Empörung. Ein Versuch über Demokratie, soziale Bewegungen und gegenwärtige Protestforschung. *IPB Working Waper.* Berlin, Germany. https://protestinstitut.files.wordpress.com/2015/10/postdemokratischeempoerung_ ipbworking-paper_aufl2.pdf.

Walker, D., and Myrick, F. (2006). Grounded theory: An exploration of process and procedure. *Qualitative Health Research, 16*(4), 547–559.

5 Intimate Citizenship Politics and Digital Media

Teens' Discourses, Sexual Normativities and Popular Social Media

Sander De Ridder and Sofie Van Bauwel

Introduction

Intimate citizenship refers to issues and debates on intimate and sexual politics in society. Such debates on people's intimate personal life are found in numerous public dialogues. They deal with the many areas of social life, such as 'families of choice' and 'designer babies', to name just a few. Over the past decade, however, intimate citizenship debates have increasingly been related to people's widespread participation on all kinds of digital platforms on which 'ordinary' people have a voice to reach out to large audiences. For example, 'YouTube' is well known as a digital space in which lesbian, gay, bisexual and transgender persons (LGBT's) can share coming out experiences and everyday life struggles and so help others (Alexander and Losh 2010; Wuest 2014). Besides using digital platforms for protesting gay marriage, or any kind of civic and democratic engagement, debating intimate citizenship and digital media often refers to everyday intimate and sexual practices that are now being related to the use of media, while they were not before. Because of changing online spaces to experience intimacy and sexuality, governments, academics and largely citizens are dealing with questions such as; what are the possible health risks arising from meeting sexual partners on the internet (Couch and Liamputtong 2008), how should governments protect children against online predators, or why is it that teenage girls are often harshly judged for posing 'too sexy' on profile pictures (Ringrose 2011)?

Lately, online spaces for experiencing intimacies and sexualities have received much attention from government bodies in Europe, such as the Safer Internet Program from the European Commission. This program focuses on a better internet for children. It deals with topics such as online sexually explicit materials and pornography, grooming, young people sharing explicit materials (e.g. 'sexting') and so on; such policy questions are vital intimate citizenship questions. However, research on how young people themselves negotiate intimate citizenships and everyday sexually mediated lives remains scarce, while mainly children's and teenagers' intimate practices are at the heart of debates on intimate citizenships and digital media. Those debates, often becoming media panics, are usually framed in such a way that society believes young people's uses of digital media are 'out of control' (Thiel-Stern 2009; Wuest 2014). Therefore, exploring how young people themselves negotiate intimate citizenship in digital media within their own life-worlds and peer groups seems an important addition to current debates.

Within this chapter, we will introduce a case study in which we explore young people's (14–18 years old) discourses on a variety of intimate practices on popular social networking sites. To make sense of intimate and sexual practices in social media and among peer groups, we focus particularly on the media-related normativities that are currently emerging. We will relate those practices primarily to dynamics of peer group inclusion and exclusion (Warrington and Younger 2010), and to the specific dynamics of social media and broader digital media culture. By so doing, we hope to explore some challenges for intimate citizenships that are particularly related to the intimate and sexual well-being of teenagers online. Central to this chapter is that we see intimate citizenships as broader than only being part of discussions on governance or democratic politics and institutional practices; rather, they are inextricably intertwined with how people make sense of them in everyday lives. Within the everyday lives of people, often indirectly, sexual politics are debated and continuously made sense of. For example, young people may have straightforward ideas about which intimate and sexual practices in social media are bad and which are more socially approved. Thus, to make sense of such negotiations, this chapter focuses on 'the political', rather than 'politics'. According to Chantal Mouffe (2005, 9), the two concepts have different meanings: by the 'political', she means the 'dimensions of antagonism', which she sees as "constitutive of human societies"; 'politics' refer to 'the set of practices and institutions through which an order is created'.

First, we will introduce the notion of intimate citizenship and further relate it specifically to digital media participation. Next, we will introduce our case study to show the relevance of the intimate citizenship framework while exploring young people's sense making practices and discourses on mediated intimacy in social media. We will end this chapter with a concluding reflection on the capacity (or lack of it) of (young) people to freely express their intimacies in their own voices in digital media.

Intimate Citizenship

Intimate citizenship is difficult to define, mainly because of the concept's 'multi-faceted' nature ever since its emergence in the early 1990s

(Richardson 2017, 208–209). Intimate citizenship explores the spaces of people's sexual lives which often used to be exclusively private, but now have become subject of public discussion and societal concerns; intimate citizenship often refers to a public discourse on the personal life and a 'cluster of emerging concerns over the rights to choose what we do with our genders, eroticisms, bodies, feelings, identities and our representations' (Plummer 2003). The work on intimate citizenship has mainly been developed by prominent sociologists of sexuality such as Ken Plummer (1995, 2003) and Jeffrey Weeks (1998), but also queer literary critics such as Lauren Berlant and Michael Warner have written about intimate citizenship as a project that should 'support forms of affective, erotic, and personal living that are public in the sense of accessible, available to memory, and sustained through collective activity' (Berlant and Warner 1998, 203). In a recent literature review on the notion 'intimate citizenship', Diane Richardson (2017, 211) summarises how the majority of research on intimate citizenship has focused primarily on advancing the positions of non-normative sexualities in societies – think about 'lesbian and gay citizenship' (e.g. gay marriage) – but also intimate citizenship as the right to 'participation in consumer society' (e.g. queer lifestyle as citizenship through consumption) and, last, research that critically assesses the normative assumptions vested historically in sexual policies: a queering of citizenship or what is often referred to as 'queer world making' (Berlant and Warner 1998, 199).

Although reflections on intimate citizenship come in many forms, they usually refer to *debates on sexual politics* and a *reconfiguration of citizenship*. Within this chapter, we will not so much talk about intimate citizenship and how it is debated related to societal institutions and the law (e.g. marriage), or claims for rights (such as the sexual rights initiative from the United Nations), but rather how intimate citizenship is negotiated into everyday discourse (chat, literature, media representations) by citizens *themselves*. To study these intimate citizenship negotiations, Plummer (1995) refers to them as practices of 'intimate storytelling'. Spaces for such intimate stories can be found everywhere (public spaces, online, etc.) and across different interpretative communities. As a sociologist of symbolic interactionism, Plummer elaborates on how people use intimate stories, their own stories and other people's stories, as recourses to construct their own intimate sexualities. Plummer's central argument refers to the idea that these stories become meaningful in 'flows of power', which is how sexual politics come into being. Sexual politics are a system of 'sexual stratification', which is 'about the making and contesting of sexual hierarchies'; such hierarchies refer to how certain intimate sexualities are respected and valued, while others are stigmatised (Seidman 2010, 55). Consequently, intimate citizenship could then be understood as the capacity, freedom or choice of people, without being stigmatised or less valued, to tell their intimate stories.

A particular dimension of debates on intimate citizenship, and debates on citizenship more generally, are normative questions. Plummer (2003, 68) formulates this in relation to intimate citizenship as questions that reflect on '*how* (emphasis added) to live a personal life in a modern word'. Dealing with 'cultural citizenship', Nick Stevenson (2003) argues that questions on *how to* are important in order 'to search for a new ethics', especially in contemporary times where intimacy is lived and publicly discussed in formerly unknown spaces; for example, finding a lover on dating sites, or public debates on alternative families in newspapers and on television are all such formerly unknown spaces to give meaning to intimacy. The essence of such a cultural citizenship is, according to Stevenson (2003, 25), an "acceptance of universal principles and the recognition of difference". Although reflections on an intimate citizenship should start with the idea that there are multiple values and not just one truth, finding some universal values for 'ethical sexualities' and a 'good intimate and sexual life' is important. Such values could be 'caring and loving sexualities, emphatic and compassionate sexualities, a respectful and dignified sexualities based on rights, a flourishing sexualities with sexual wellbeing, as well as sexual and gender justice: a fair and just sexualities' (Plummer 2015, 36).

Intimate Citizenship and Digital Media Participation

We want to continue by arguing how intimate citizenship is useful to frame debates on sexual politics related to participation in digital media. Intimate citizenships can help us to reflect on how online spaces are creating new kinds of intimate and sexual experiences. Online spaces could be seen as online mediated spaces where a lot of intimate stories are told and read; such spaces have affective dimensions; some stories will be 'liked', while others will be judged or some will maybe have the power to be transformative. Online mediated spaces have specific power dynamics as they connect the public and the private in specific ways, but also because people attribute meanings to particular mediated places. For example, asking someone you do not know on a date is perhaps the social norm on a flirtatious mobile app like 'Tinder', but not on a professional social networking site such as 'LinkedIn'. Most importantly, framing such practices as being related to questions of intimate citizenship gives rise to questions about how to lead a good intimate and sexual life in digital mediated spaces where the private/public dichotomy is blurred. Further, this also emphasises the vital role of societal debates on intimate storytelling practices related to digital media, as intimate citizenship often refers to public discourses on the personal life. For example, recently there has been much debate on the popularity of 'sexting' in youth cultures (sexting refers to using a mobile phone to send naked or semi-naked pictures). There is frequent media coverage on how sexting went (or could go) wrong, usually stories about young girls losing their sexual reputations because their pictures were distributed without consent. This creates moral panics among parents, educators, pundits and young people's own peer groups (Ringrose et al. 2013; Hasinoff 2014). Such public discourses on the personal relate to how intimacies are socially and culturally organised in people's everyday lives. At such moments the private, the public and popular digital media culture are clearly interconnected.

Within this chapter, we will continue to focus on what is usually seen as being central to participatory practices in popular digital media culture; the act of self-representation referring to 'activities of participating audiences in digital culture' (Thumim 2012, 6). Although in every social interaction people are performing 'the self' (Goffman 1959), self-representation is specific as it 'raises question about the mediation of a textual object' (ibid.). When people use self-representation tools to tell intimate stories, they are using specific tools that social media provide, often playing a particular role in shaping or co-constructing the meanings of such stories (De Ridder 2015). Although social media can be seen as opportunity structures for participation in which people are empowered to tell intimate stories with their own voices, there is still a continuous ideological and democratic struggle to do so 'freely' (De Ridder and Van Bauwel 2015b); such struggles are at the heart of intimate citizenship in current digital culture.

In communication and media studies, 'affordances' have been high on the agenda to study how digital media audiences' practices and socialities online are shaped or constrained by digital technologies. At the same time, affordances also refer to the ways in which people are not completely determined by technologies (Hutchby 2001). For example, to fill in a bibliographical description on a social networking site, you are supposed to use drop down menus, choosing between fixed options, such as when communicating sexual identities (e.g. I like men/women/both). However, in practice, people do have agency here, when, for example, not completing this form and communicating their sexual identities in other ways (by uploading pictures, writing a more elaborate text, etc.). Affordances should be seen as more than 'technological features' that function in rational ways. They are meaningful constructs that 'emerge between users' perceptions, attitudes and expectations; between the materiality and functionality of technologies; and between the intentions and perceptions of designers (Nagy and Neff 2015, 5). Affordances are essential to understand the complex struggles of intimate citizenship related to participation in digital media. First, technology has the power to shape intimate stories in particular ways because of its material and functional dimensions. Second, designers and social media companies are powerful, as they are creating those platforms, its marketing, its terms of services, etc. Third, digital media platforms' 'functions' and meanings are continuously being (re-)negotiated by people's specific sense-making practices; affordances are thus far from being only rational features, but are rather continuously (re-)imagined.

As digital media have become important for intimate stories to thrive, they should be seen as spaces where reflections on sexual ethics are acute. As shown in the above paragraph, sexual ethics in digital media are intertwined with the affordances of social media; people's complex struggles with all kinds of communication on platforms. Such struggles depend not only on how to use the platform as a material object, but also on finding out the specific normative organisations of sociality in a digital mediated place.

Case Study: Exploring Intimate Citizenships in Youth Culture and Social Media

To explore the relevance of the notion of intimate citizenship, we will now introduce one particular case which relies on qualitative and interpretative research done among young people in Northern Belgium, exploring discourses on a variety of intimate practices (gendered, sexual and relationships) related to the use social media.[1] This particular case study is based on data collected in eight focus groups (N = 51) with young people between 14 and 18 years old, conducted between November 2011 and February 2012. Participants were recruited in daily offline contexts such as schools, youth movements and peer groups. The interviews were recorded and transcribed verbatim. An explorative coding was done using the qualitative data analysis software NVivo 10. Using a grounded theory approach, several themes were defined systematically; themes like social media as a place, social media practices in everyday life, intimacy and media cultural complexities in social media life. Further down, we will elaborate on some specific themes in the thematic analysis: authenticity, the self and social control.

In this case study based on the data gathered in focus groups, we talked with young people about general social media use, daily online interactions, representations and self-representations. The talks focused mainly on their reflections on intimate storytelling practices of their peers, and their own intimate storytelling practices. The talks exposed discourses on the experiences of intimacy related to social media use, which means that the results presented here do not say anything about the actual experiences of these young people's social media use in everyday life – especially because we observed how peer pressure dynamics unfolded in the groups of participants.

While exposing discourses on intimacy inductively, we observed how they became meaningful around particular notions of authenticity, the self and ideas on social control. These themes are discussed here as they negotiate the flows of power in which sexual politics in social media operate and thereby embody struggles of intimate citizenship.

Authenticity

When referring to peers' intimate stories, we observed how our participants continuously emphasised the importance of authenticity; referred
to as being 'real', being your 'true self' and being 'natural' and 'normal'
in stories on social media. For example, you should not post too many
status updates on Facebook or post over-performed pictures; in the
words of participant Ella[2] (girl, 18 years old): 'Yes, like a very spontaneous picture. As if you are a normal person'. This craving for authenticity was usually seen as an 'inherent quality' (Vannini and Williams
2009) of a particular intimate storytelling practice on social media;
some stories were seen as 'good' and thus 'authentic', while others were
seen as 'bad', meaning 'inauthentic'. Authenticity was used as a social
construct, in which the participants evaluated *other* people and peers'
stories; authenticity links to specific moral codes that police people how
to behave. The social value of authenticity operates as a cultural myth
that can be deconstructed as 'tradition bound, pretentious, and essentialist' (Grazian 2010, 191).

In our case study, meaning-making on 'authentic intimate stories'
was usually related to talking about pictures on Facebook profiles, referring to and judging particular elements of visual culture, such as the
use of close-ups, posing, 'photo shopping' and also self-portraits in social media (e.g. self-portraits by using a mirror or taking a selfie with a
front-facing camera on a smartphone); all such exceedingly performed
pictures were referred to in a very negative sense, particularly those with
a sexual connotation, such as a gendered stereotypical gaze (e.g. lovingly
for girls and tough for boys) and seductive poses (e.g. using close-ups,
gazing into the camera); 'sexiness' was usually read as inauthentic and
therefore morally disapproved of: "Getting all dressed up to pose on
Facebook. I don't know, You can also (...) I think this is all nonsense to
dress up and then take a picture in front of the mirror" (Bart, boy, 18
years old). Such judgments, often harshly formulated (by referring to
"sluts" and "playboys"), were made continuously through the different
focus groups.

Although too much performance and 'sexiness' is judged as it is seen
not to represent an 'authentic self', at the same time, performing highly
idealised selves and being attractive/entertaining to your audience plays
a crucial role in young people's social media self-representations (De
Ridder and Van Bauwel 2015b). What is seen as seemingly authentic (or
not), could be understood as a struggle to be popular in one's peer group.
Emiel (boy, 16 years old) exposes this struggle when thinking out loud
how to choose a profile picture: "Yes, it can be an ordinary picture...
Of course, you don't...You don't post the ugliest picture on your profile,
but, yes ... Anyone can see me as I am". However, these negotiations

particularly apply when they are representations of intimacy and love, as in the following quote by Joran, a 16-year-old boy:

> To be honest, actually I think people do not need to know that you have a girlfriend or a boyfriend. And, for example, I do not put this on Facebook yet. But yes, now there is still 'single' mentioned, but one time I will change it. HaHa actually, no one can see that I've already put it on my profile. I don't show this to other people, only to myself! And eeum pff, I think it's sometimes funny to have a file labeled as "my love" to "in a relationship with". I think that's funny for once. But not like, continuously posting pictures with heart shapes above. I think that is over the top.

As the above quotes show, intimate storytelling practices are carefully managed in social networking sites. Young people struggle to tell intimate stories in semi-public spaces, regulate and discipline their own self representations as social networking sites afford social control. Such negotiations on 'good' and 'bad' intimate storytelling practices in semi-public spaces are vital to explore sexual politics in contemporary youth culture and discussions on intimate citizenships.

The Self and Social Control

Young people's negotiations on representing sexiness and love in social media could be seen as how they negotiate sexual politics in everyday life. We have shown how, particularly related to the use of social media, intimate self-representations are valued in respect of whether they are seen as authentic or not. In this way, the self can be seen as an arbiter, as pointed out by Liesbet van Zoonen (2012, 61). Young people read intimate stories when they are online, observe and judge; ultimately, they see *themselves* as the authoritative position to speak from when being asked to give meaning to intimate stories in social media. Such judgements usually emphasise that they acknowledge people should express them as *they* like, but at the same time also make clear how they would not *themselves* ("*I* would…") produce such self-representations:

> Yes, I think that… I have no problem with the fact that people do that [referring to posting a picture when kissing], but I think that myself I wouldn't do that, but maybe an ordinary picture – but not when you're kissing, or so – but an ordinary picture of things you do with your friends, this is totally ok, but [pictures of] kissing… That I would not do. But, I don't have a problem if other people do so.
> (Joke, girl, 14 years old)

How do these discourses negotiate intimate citizenship and, moreover, what does this mean for sexual politics? Clearly, debating intimacy in youth culture as a practice related to social media introduces particular regimes for *controlling* intimacy, a way of controlling intimacy that is post-panoptical (Bauman 2000). Usually, young people were aware and agreed on the reflexivity of intimate selves and the existing diversity of intimate stories that are told in social media among their peer groups. However, at the same time, they still argued for essentialist beliefs as if intimate selves had a particular authentic core (a 'real', 'normal', 'biological', etc.). The previously demonstrated intensive peer control over intimate interactions is afforded by social media that allow an intensive lateral surveillance (Andrejevic 2006). Considering that popular social media are (semi-) public spaces in which intimate citizenships are daily and intensively negotiated, we can see how such spaces only allow affective, sexual and personal living in strict and normatively regulated ways.

Intimate Citizenships and Media Ideologies

Our case study showed how negotiations on sexual politics are interconnecting the public, private personal life and popular digital media culture; social media are crucial spaces for intimate citizenship questions to emerge in youth cultures. As such, social media cultures become powerful and interwoven in people's most intimate and personal spheres and media practices (Hepp 2012), which gives new meanings to intimate citizenships. Social media become powerful through their affordances, which are functional technological features (e.g. networked technologies that allow lateral surveillance), but affordances are also imagined; people's perceptions and expectations of technologies become intermingled with people's intimate practices (De Ridder et al. 2016). For example, we noticed how teens were very aware of the pressing peer control in social media; they had expectations and imaginations of the audiences watching what they post online. Likewise, they reflected about what is acceptable to 'share' on the different social media platforms they are using. These power dynamics of digital media culture are referred to by media anthropologist Illana Gershon as media ideologies: "Media ideologies are a set of beliefs about communicative technologies with which users and designers explain perceived media structure and meaning" (Gershon 2010, 3). Interestingly, as social media have become intertwined with every intimate aspect of human life, media ideologies are also becoming interwoven in everyday intimate and sexual lives, hence producing different subjectivities and normativities regarding living a sexual life.

Crucial to how intimate citizenships are negotiated online is to explore what this means for (young) people's capacities to express their intimacies in their own voice, without being stigmatised or less valued. This concern specifically relates to those people who do not identify within the heteronormative borders which society imposes; for example, research has shown how self-representations in popular social media of gay and lesbian youths who express same-sex love or desire are not always well-received by their peers (De Ridder and Van Bauwel 2015a). *Many popular social media are therefore spaces that hardly allow a voicing of sexual difference, especially those in teenagers' life-worlds.* Rather than constituting a political space of antagonism (Mouffe 2005), daily experiences of popular digital media culture are introducing sexual politics in which hierarchical orders are created; many examples show how intimate and sexual stigmatisation has become interwoven with media ideologies. While digital media's participatory possibilities are often celebrated for protesting the stigmatisation of sexual identities, it is often misunderstood how participatory possibilities are deeply rooted within same-age power structures. Therefore, young people's everyday engagements with digital media should be seen as being contextualised within broader social and cultural power dynamics such as peer group exclusion and essentialist beliefs about the organisation of love and intimacy. Debating intimate citizenship can uncover such misunderstandings of young people's online participations, as it transcends common beliefs by actually exploring what people say and their stories. Related to young people's intimate practices on social media, we should transcend popular beliefs about online participatory practices *as if* they were automatically more sexually inclusive. Second, we should transcend popular beliefs *as if* young people's online sexualities were always 'out of control' and therefore need more 'management'.

Our argument is that debates on sexual politics and intimate citizenship from a bottom-up perspective, meaning how people are debating sexuality and social media in their everyday lives, should be seen as being inseparable from questions on governance, democratic and institutional practices in digital life-worlds. Thus, intimate citizenship is a useful concept as it could combine these top-down and bottom-up dynamics. For instance, young people's media ideologies on intimate storytelling seem to be concentrated on carefully managing and controlling authenticity and realness, leading to self-surveillance because they fear to be stigmatised (as a slut, as a playboy, as gay, as ...). Remarkably, institutions that govern media literacy projects and policies, while reaching out to young people, often refer to those same dynamics in which they frame 'managing identities', 'reputations' and being 'real' in social media as 'better'. Thereby, they are reinforcing those media ideologies that do not contribute to any sort of ethical sexualities and sexual wellbeing that we have discussed before (Plummer 2015, 36). Such ways of governing tend to limit rather than maximise democratic participation in digital media.

To end our discussion on the importance of intimate citizenship politics and digital media, we want to briefly address two points of concern. First, it should be evident that people, and especially young people, should be made aware of online risks (which continues to be a challenging topic for policy-making bodies), especially by making people aware of such risks without hampering their opportunities to participate in digital spaces freely. As intimate citizenships are concerned with the opportunities to *choose* what we do with our intimate and sexual identities, self-representations, genders and so on (Plummer 2003), in order to create a fair and just sexualities for all, such 'choices' can never come without individual responsibilities and a moral accountability (Butler 2005). This will continue to be a careful balancing act in the near future, particularly when we have in mind all the parties that could be seen as accountable. Here, we can think of many actors (such as the individual, the social media company, the designer, or perhaps even the state, ...), but this is far from clear at the moment. Second, the idea of an intimate citizenship by choice could be seen as highly Western-centric. Indeed, it does depend on geo-political contexts. Moreover, such 'choices' are 'contingent on social, economic and cultural capital' (Richardson 2017, 217). It may seem unsettling to talk about our freedom to represent our sexual selves in social media, while so much sexual violence and pauperisation can be found around the world and specifically in non-Western societies. We should take this into account. However, at the same time a lot of stories can be found in which social movements for sexual rights and wellbeing have success and improve everyday lives (Plummer 2015, 113); such stories are an important part of intimate citizenship questions.

Acknowledgement

This case is situated within a larger research project entitled "The Online Stage: Youth and Heteronormativity, Self-Representation and Identity Construction in Online Communication" (2010–2014), financed by the Special Research Fund (BOF) at Ghent University Belgium.

Notes

1 The overall aim of this project was to explore the social and cultural organisation of intimate stories, which are young people's sexualities, genders, relationships and desires, as media-related practices in social networking sites. Therefore, the project used a mixed-method approach; a number of qualitative research methodologies such as participatory observation, focus group interviews and a textual analysis of contextual data (e.g. popular press articles on teenagers and social media use).
2 None of the participants' real names are used in this chapter.

References

Alexander, J., and Losh, E. (2010). A Youtube of one's own?: "Coming out" video's and rethorical action. In C. Pullen and M. Cooper (eds.), *LGBT identity and online new media* (37–51). London, UK: Routledge.
Andrejevic, M. (2006). The discipline of watching: Detection, risk, and lateral surveillance. *Critical Studies in Media Communication, 23*(5), 391–407.
Bauman, Z. (2000). *Liquid modernity*. Malden, MA: Polity Press.

Berlant, L., and Warner, M. (1998). Sex in public. *Critical Inquiry, 24*(2), 547–566.

Butler, J. (2005). *Giving an account of oneself.* New York, NY: Fordham University Press.

Couch, D., and Liamputtong, P. (2008). Online dating and mating: The use of the Internet to meet sexual partners. *Qualitative Health Research, 18*(2), 268–279.

De Ridder, S. (2015). Are digital media institutions shaping youth's intimate stories? Strategies and tactics in the social networking site Netlog. *New Media & Society, 17*(3), 356–374.

De Ridder, S., and Van Bauwel, S. (2015a). The discursive construction of gay teenagers in times of mediatization: Youth's reflections on intimate story-telling, queer shame and realness in popular social media places. *Journal of Youth Studies, (18)*6, 777–793.

De Ridder, S., and Van Bauwel, S. (2015b). Youth and intimate media cultures: Gender, sexuality, relationships, and desire as storytelling practices in social networking sites. *Communications. The European Journal of Communication Research, 40*(3), 319–340.

De Ridder, Vesnic-Alujevic, L., and Romic, B. (2016). Challenges when researching digital audiences: Mapping audience research of software, design, interfaces and platforms. *Participations, 13*(1), 374–391.

Gershon, I. (2010). Media ideologies: An introduction. *Journal of Linguistic Anthropology, 20*(2), 283–293.

Goffman, E. (1959). *The presentation of self in everyday life.* New York, NY: Doubleday.

Grazian, D. (2010). Demystifying authenticity in the sociology of culture. In J. R. Hall, L. Grindstaff, and M.-C. Lo (eds.), *Handbook of cultural sociology* (191–200). Oxon, UK: Routledge.

Hasinoff, A. A. (2014). Blaming sexualization for sexting. *Girlhood Studies, 7*(1), 102–120.

Hepp, A. (2012). *Cultures of mediatization.* Malden, MA: Polity Press.

Hutchby, I. (2001). Technologies, texts and affordances. *Sociology, 35*(2), 441–456.

Mouffe, C. (2005). *On the political.* New York, NY: Routledge.

Nagy, P., and Neff, G. (2015). Imagined Affordance: Reconstructing a Keyword for Communication Theory. *Social Media + Society,* July–December 2015, 1–9. doi: 10.1177/2056305115603385.

Plummer, K. (1995). *Telling sexual stories: Power, change, and social worlds.* London: Routledge.

Plummer, K. (2003). *Intimate citizenship: Private decisions and public dialogues.* Seattle: University of Washington Press.

Plummer, K. (2015). *Cosmopolitan sexualities.* Cambridge, UK: Polity.

Richardson, D. (2017). Rethinking sexual citizenship. *Sociology, 51*(2), 208–224.

Ringrose, J. (2011). Are you sexy, flirty, or a slut? Exploring, sexualization' and how teen girls perform/negotiate digital sexual identity on social networking sites. In R. Gill and C. Scharff (eds.), *New femininities. Postfeminism, neoliberalism and subjectivity* (99–116). Basingstoke, UK: Palgrave Macmillan.

Ringrose, J., Harvey, L., Gill, R., and Livingstone, S. (2013). Teen girls, sexual double standards and 'sexting': Gendered value in digital image exchange. *Feminist Theory, 14*(3), 305–323.

Seidman, S. (2010). *The social construction of sexuality.* New York, NY: Norton.

Stevenson, N. (2003). *Cultural citizenship. Cosmopolitan questions.* Maidenhead, UK: Open University Press.

Thiel-Stern, S. (2009). Femininity out of control on the Internet: A critical analysis of media representations of gender, youth, and MySpace.com in international news discourses. *Girlhood Studies, 2*(1), 20–39.

Thumim, N. (2012). *Self-representation and digital culture.* Hampshire, UK: Palgrave Macmillan.

Vannini, P., and Williams, P. J. (2009). Authenticity in culture, self, and society. In P. Vannini, and P. J. Williams (eds.), *Authenticity in culture, self, and society* (1–20). Surrey, UK: Ashgate.

Warrington, M., and Younger, M. (2010). 'Life is a tightrope': Reflections on peer group inclusion and exclusion amongst adolescent girls and boys. *Gender and Education, 23*(2), 153–168.

Weeks, J. (1998). The sexual citizen. *Theory, Culture & Society, 15*(3), 35–52.

Wuest, B. (2014). Stories like mine: Coming out videos and queer identities on YouTube. In C. Pullen (ed.), *Queer youth and media cultures* (19–33). Hampshire, UK: Palgrave Macmillan.

Zoonen, E. A. van (2012). I-pistemology: changing truth claims in popular and political culture. *European Journal of Communication, 27*(3), 56–67.

Part II

Mediated Representations of Participation and Citizenship

6   The Indignados in the European Press

Beyond the Protest Paradigm?[1]

Maria Kyriakidou, José Javier Olivas Osuna and Max Hänska

Introduction

"Indignez-vous!" was the title of the 2010 essay of the French diplomat Stéphane Hessel, who placed the emotion of indignation at the centre of political engagement and called for a non-violent uprising against the failures of finance capitalism (Hessel 2011). It was this call that the disgruntled Spanish citizens responded to when they took to the streets in the spring of 2011 and occupied squares all over Spain in the wake of the global financial crisis in what has been named the 15-M or Indignados movement. Indignados has been the most organized and vocal form of civic resistance to the ways European governments responded to the euro crisis and the austerity measures they implemented (Hyman 2015). Linked to the Arab revolutions of 2011, 15-M has been celebrated as the predecessor of the Occupy movement (Oikonomakis and Roos 2013). More immediately, the Spanish Indignados inspired similar movements across other Southern European countries affected by the Eurozone crisis, such as Portugal, Italy and especially Greece, where the respective Aganaktismenoi occupied the squares of Greek cities over the summer of 2011.

Adopting peaceful means of demonstration and largely coordinated through social media, the Indignados has been a movement unique both in its expressions and in its organisation. It was also unique, we argue here, in the treatment it received from the mainstream European press. Drawing upon a comparative content analysis of the Spanish, Greek and German press, this chapter argues that, in contrast to the dominant paradigm of protest coverage, the protests of the Indignados were not dealt with in a negative way by the European press. Indeed, the reporting of the movement often resembled the celebratory character of a media event, where the citizens were at the forefront of the nation – especially in the cases of the Spanish and Greek coverage. At the same time, however, this focus on the spectacle hardly constructed the movement as an effective political force or presented its voice as a valid alternative to austerity politics.

We understand the protest movement of the Indignados here to be one of the most vociferous examples of political participation and citizen engagement beyond institutional politics within the context of the euro crisis. A movement of mass and international character, the Indignados directly confronted and challenged the malfunctions of domestic and European political institutions and ultimately of liberal democracy (Prentoulis and Thomassen 2013). Enabled by social media, these alternative forms of political participation are still, however, subjected to the media logic of the mainstream press for its public representation and reach. Our aim in this chapter is to explore these mainstream media representations of the protests of the Indignados and the type of (mis) understandings of the movement to which mass media have contributed.

Indignant Citizens against Austerity

Caused by the financial crisis that hit global markets in the second half of 2007 and the beginning of 2008, the crisis of the Eurozone has had an unprecedented and largely unexpected impact on European governments and populations since 2009. After it became apparent that a number of European countries would not be able to repay their public debt, financial and lending agreements took place between national governments, the International Monetary Fund, the European Central Bank and the European Commission. As a first step towards the reduction of public debt, these agreements included a series of austerity policies, such as salary cuts, pension reforms and reduction of the public sector and welfare. The European South, the context of most of these policies, was hit the hardest by the crisis and its concomitant measures. Unemployment rates have been the highest in Greece at 27.0% and Spain at 24.4% – as of June 2014 (Eurostat 2014). With welfare provisions becoming scarcer, Greek and Spanish citizens have been faced with increasing hardship.

Public disappointment and disenchantment with Europe and rage against national governments found its most vocal and organised expression in the protest movement of the Indignados, or 15-M movement, which made its first appearance on the streets of Madrid and Barcelona on 15 May 2011. Puerta del Sol in Madrid and Placa de Catalunya in Barcelona became the protest sites of thousands, as did the squares of all major cities in Spain. Ten days later, on 25 May 2011, and as it was becoming evident that the Spanish protesters were here to stay, demonstrators took over Syntagma square in Athens as well as other central squares in Greek cities. Borrowing their name from their Spanish predecessors, the Greek protesters self-described themselves as 'Aganaktismenoi' (the Greek translation of *indignados*). The occupation of the squares lasted for months until it came to an end towards the end of the summer 2011. In both countries, the movement of the Indignados/ Aganaktismenoi has given rise to solidarity networks that continue to operate as networks of support for the people mostly hit by the crisis (Taibo 2013; Arampatzi 2016).

There are two remarkable characteristics of the movement addressed by the relevant literature. First, its nature as a pluralistic, horizontal movement has been the basis of its unprecedented mass character (Taibo 2013). The movement appealed not only to established activist networks but also to people who had hitherto not actively engaged with political processes, forming a base which was broadly mid-stream and to a lesser degree working class (Casero-Ripollés and Feenstra 2012; Taibo 2013). It became an expression of the crisis of political representation, with its demands mostly focusing on four main issues: (a) rejection of the political establishment and political parties, (b) denouncement of the financial markets, (c) rejection of austerity policies and concomitant welfare cuts and (d) implementation of mechanisms for citizen participation (Casero-Ripollés and Feenstra 2012). At the same time, the movement, both in Spain and Greece, was illustrative of new forms of political mobilisation through online and social media (Gerbaudo, 2012; Anduiza et al. 2014). Facebook, Twitter and mobile phones have been identified as central to processes of mobilisation and organisation of the protests, and one of the reasons of the expansive nature of the group of protesters.

In that respect, the Indignados can be approached not as a social movement as such but as an example of 'personalized politics', an 'expression of large-scale individualised action coordinated through digital media technologies' (Bennett 2012, 20). A major characteristic of such forms of action, according to Bennett, is the emergence of the individual as an important catalyst of collective action through the mobilisation of social networks, itself enabled through the use of social media (Bennett 2012, 22). Such networked action, examples of which include the Occupy movement and the Arab Spring(s), as well as smaller-scale mobilisations, such as campaigns against corporations, are conducted across personal action frames, as opposed to the narrower collective action frames more commonly adopted by social movements. Personal action frames embrace diversity and inclusion, lower the barriers of identification with the cause and validate personal emotion (Bennett 2012, 22f.).

Protest Movements and the Mainstream Media

In contrast to its preoccupation with digital media as a platform for the mobilisation and realisation of the movement, current literature has largely ignored the way the Indignados have been covered in the European press. Research on the dynamics between media and protest movements has repeatedly highlighted the use of established templates (McLeod and Hertog 1999) or frames (Gitlin 1980) in the reporting of protests (see McCurdy 2012 for a comprehensive review). Chan and Lee (1984) have described this template mode of reporting the 'protest paradigm'. They found that the coverage of protests differs in terms of whether they are (a) supported, (b) politicised and (c) moralised within cultural boundaries. These frames differed according to the newspapers' ideological leanings, with right-wing newspapers focusing on social order and safeguarding the status quo, and left-leaning papers privileging the perspective of the protesters (Chan and Lee 1984).

One of the main characteristics of the protest paradigm is the focus on the spectacle, especially formulaic, sensational images of aggression, which highlight the controversial and violent aspects of the protests at the expense of their causes (Gitlin 1980; McLeod and Hertog 1999). At the same time, mainstream media heavily rely on official sources for information about the protests (McLeod and Hertog 1999). Other journalistic tools for the marginalisation of the protesters include, according to Dardis (2006), a focus on the appearance or mental abilities of the protesters, calls on public opinion and judgement, statistics, generalisations, eyewitness accounts to counter the demonstrators' claims and counterdemonstrations. The ultimate consequence of these media template processes is the de-legitimisation of the protesters' claims and ultimately their demonization (McLeod and Hertog 1999). These media 'frames' are not restricted to the news coverage of protests but also media representations of social movements and radical political voices (Gitlin 1980; McCurdy 2012).

The relevant literature draws its assumptions from framing theory, studying the ways media choose to discuss political phenomena. According to Entman (1993, 52), "to frame is to select some aspects of a perceived reality and make them more salient". This process is important not only for the way an issue is described but also because it implicitly suggests how this issue should be thought about or dealt with (Nelson and Oxley 1999). The framing of the protests, therefore, is important as it significantly impacts on public discourse and understanding, and support for the protesters (Gamson 1989, 2005). Mainstream media can serve social movements by (a) mobilising political support, (b) legitimising and validating the protesters claims in mainstream discourse and (c) broadening the scope of conflicts (Gamson and Wolfsfeld 1993).

The case of the Indignados movement provides an interesting case for exploring the 'protest paradigm'. On the one hand, the Indignados have explicitly defined themselves as being in opposition to the political status quo; as such, and based on patterns of reporting observed in existing literature, we expected the Indignados to be marginalised in mainstream media. On the other hand, unlike other protests, the participants did not seem to include a distinct minority of the population (Harris and Gillion 2010), but largely, if not mostly, included lay citizens; namely people that did not actively identify themselves as members of a political movement and, in many cases, had never been mobilised politically before (Taibo 2013). Such wider appeal and obvious public acceptance of the movement poses questions as to how the media might deal with demonstrations that "do not easily fit within the traditional left-right political continuum" (Cottle 2008, 857). Given the Indignados' idiosyncrasies, it is interesting to explore how such a movement with mass appeal was represented in Europe's mainstream media.

Content Analysis of Six Newspapers

We focus here on the press coverage of the Indignados in three countries, namely Spain and Greece, where the protests of the Indignados and Aganaktismenoi took place, and Germany. There are two interrelated reasons for adopting this comparative perspective. First, the Indignados and Aganaktismenoi are two expressions of the same European protest movement, mobilised against austerity policies implemented in the Eurozone. In this sense, it is reasonable to expect that the media coverage of these two movements may share a clear connection to one another. Second, a comparative portrayal of the coverage of European protests against Eurozone policies can shed light onto broader questions about the framing, definitions and interpretations of the euro crisis by the national press. Relevant research has shown that despite discrepancies in the ways the crisis has been covered in the press of different countries (Mazzoni and Barbieri 2014; Picard 2015), anti-austerity voices are generally silenced in mainstream newspapers (Doudaki 2015; Picard 2015).

Our sample comprises six newspapers: *El Pais* and *El Mundo* were the choices of the Spanish press; *Eleftherotypia* and *Kathimerini* were chosen for Greece; and *Süddeutsche Zeitung* and *Frankfurter Allgemeine Zeitung* for Germany. This choice was based on the assumption that the ideological leanings of a newspaper influence the way political phenomena are covered (Chan and Lee 1984), and thus allows to explore diverging representations of the protests. Therefore, three centre-right (*El Mundo*, *Kathimerini* and *Frankfurter Allgemeine Zeitung*) and three centre-left (*El Pais*, *Eleftherotypia* and *Süddeutsche Zeitung*) newspapers were chosen.

Our study covers the period from 15 May 2011, when the first Indignados made their appearance in the squares of major Spanish cities, until the end of June, therefore covering the first 45 days of the movement. We employed systematic sampling to gather relevant material. We did not differentiate between news reports and opinion articles, as the framing of news is important not only in opinion pieces but also in allegedly neutral accounts of events (Doudaki 2015). Newspaper articles were retrieved from Factiva, Nexis and the online archives of the newspapers, using the following search terms: 'Indignados' and 'Aganaktismenoi' ('Αγανακτισμένοι') adding (Spanien & Protest*), (Griechenland & Protest*) to the search for German articles. The Greek and Spanish search returned a large population of relevant articles, from which we sampled by coding every eighth article, yielding a total of 105 articles from the Spanish press (55 articles from *El Pais* and 50 articles from *El Mundo*) and 107 articles from the Greek press (77 articles from *Eleftherotypia* and 30 articles from *Kathimerini*). As the population of relevant German articles (after initial retrieval) was much smaller (28 articles from *Süddeutsche Zeitung* and 39 from *Frankfurter Allgemeine Zeitung*), the entire population of German articles was coded. A pilot study of 10 articles per newspaper allowed us to identify the main frames and consolidate the coding guide. In the case of multiple voices or perspectives within the article, we only coded for the dominant frame adopted by the journalist(s) writing the article, ignoring the different sources.

We identified the frames employed here largely deductively, adapting existing analytical categories that have been highlighted in previous research. One of the ways the protest paradigm marginalises protesters is, according to McLeod and Hertog (1999), through the *type of sources* and voices included in the media reports, which tend to be officials and, therefore, reproduce official definitions of the events. Another prominent marginalisation frame is the *focus on violence*, especially between protesters and the police or non-protesting citizens, which constructs protesters as socially deviant (McLeod and Detenber 1999). We also took into account explicit criticisms or praise of the protests, thus coding for the *overall tone of coverage* (Cammaerts 2013). Further marginalisation frames acknowledged in the literature and explored here include the lack of acknowledgement of the *causes* of the protests and motives of the protesters (Weaver and Scacco 2012), as well as the focus on the *spectacle* of the protests (Gitlin 1980; McLeod and Hertog 1999; Dardis 2006). Regarding the latter, we coded for references to the performative acts of the protesters, their banners and slogans, the diversity of the crowd and the numbers of protesters. We were also interested in the coverage of the tactics of the protesters and their organisation practices and internal conflicts (Cammaerts 2013), in what we named the *organisational frame*. We explored three further frames that were deemed important following the initial thematic analysis. Regarding the *media technology* frame, as a factor instrumental to the movement we explored whether newspaper coverage explicitly engaged with social media. We also coded for the *international frame* of the protest coverage, making connections between protests in different countries. Finally, we looked into what we call here the political frame. Our interest in this was twofold: we investigated whether the movement was explicitly described as political, apolitical or independent from political parties; we also explored whether its political claims were constructed as propositional or merely oppositional. We take claims to mean acts of political communication in the public sphere, consisting of the 'expression of political opinion through some form of physical or verbal action' (Koopmans and Erbe 2004, 98). We coded for all political statements made by protesters as a reaction to the status quo and those providing alternatives, such as policy suggestions, or plans for the development of solidarity networks.

The Focus on the Spectacle

At the first level of analysis, the coverage of the Indignados movement was predominantly neutral across the different newspapers in the three countries (see Figure 6.1). The exception to this was the left-leaning Greek *Eleftherotypia*, which mostly covered the protests in a positive light. The largest amount of negative coverage was found, unsurprisingly, in the centre-right *El Mundo* and *Kathimerini*. The German press adopted an overwhelmingly neutral tone in its coverage of the protest movement.

Part of this overall neutral tone of reporting the protest movement was the limited adoption of the violence frame, unlike the usual coverage of protests as described by the protest paradigm. Incidents of violence between protesters and the police were reported by 15% of the stories in all newspapers. Similar proportions of stories in Spanish and Greek newspapers noted violent reactions of the crowds against specific politicians. The paper with the most stories addressing this issue was the German *Frankfurter Allgemeine Zeitung*, with 23% of its stories mentioning confrontations between the police and protesters.

As in other cases of protests, issues pertaining to the spectacle aspects of the protests were discussed in the majority of the news stories in all countries (see Table 6.1). The number of stories adopting the spectacle frame ranged from 62% in the conservative *El Mundo* to a whopping 89% in the left-leaning *El Pais*. What distinguishes the coverage of the Indignados, though, in comparison to the dominant protest frame is the construction of this spectacle as virtually celebratory, rather than as controversial or dramatic. The images reported were not of aggression or

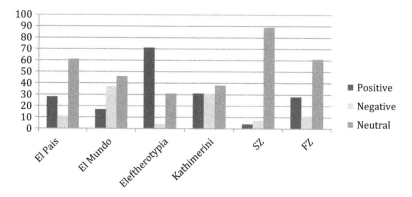

Figure 6.1 Tone of coverage.

Table 6.1 Focus on the Spectacle of the Protests

Spain	El Pais (n = 55)	48 (89%)
	El Mundo (n = 50)	31 (62%)
Greece	Eleftherotypia (n = 77)	51 (66%)
	Kathimerini (n = 30)	20 (66%)
Germany	SüddeutscheZeitung (n = 27)	19 (70%)
	Frankfurter Allgemeine Zeitung (n = 39)	30 (77%)

violence but focused on the theatricality of the protests, the diversity of the gathered crowd, the numbers of the protesters and the days of protests, which highlighted the continuity and mass character of the movement.

The Spanish and Greek coverage in particular focused on the heterogeneity of the protesting crowd, inclusive of people from different social strata and age groups, ranging from unemployed youth to pensioners and disenchanted professionals. Constant press references to this heterogeneity, describing the crowd as *'couples'*, *'groups of friends'*, *'small children with their parents'*, *'disabled on wheel chairs'* or *'old people and pensioners'* constructed a colourful pastiche of protesters in stark contrast to the negative images of them as destructors observed in other demonstrations (McLeod and Detenber 1999). This focus on the carnivalesque element of the protests (Tsaliki 2012) has been pointed out by previous research on the protest paradigm as one of the frequently employed journalistic tools for the marginalisation of protests (Gitlin 1980; McLeod and Hertog 1999; Dardis 2006). However, in the case of the Indignados, the spectacle of the protests was reported in positive terms rather than as a means of trivialising the movement's claims. Daily references to the increasing number of protesters during the first days of the movements in different cities further strengthened the construction of the protests as nationwide events and legitimate democratic expressions of unrest.

Combined with the positive tone of coverage in part of the Greek and Spanish press, this spectacle composed of a diverse pastiche of citizens was often accompanied by an emotional and celebratory mode of reporting. Expressions such as *'magical'*, *'a miracle'*, *'something new'* and *'something that cannot be defined'* were used by the Spanish and Greek press of both ideological allegiances, especially in the first days of the protests, to describe the spectacle of the protesters coming together to occupy the squares. The following is a characteristic illustration from *Eleftherotypia*:

> The whistles and the pots and pans are there again, amidst a colorful crowd expanding on the surrounding streets, where you can find from babies to priests.
>
> (Ξεχείλισε αγανάκτηση το Σύνταγμα 2011)

In stark contrast to the established protest paradigm, the protests of the Indignados were covered as national celebrations or even media events, namely ceremonial events that interrupted the routines of daily media flow and brought together national audiences, triggering a sense of media-induced solidarity (Dayan and Katz 1992).

Significant in the construction of this celebratory spectacle was the focus on the 'aesthetics of nonviolence' (Postill 2013) the movement represented. The peaceful character of the demonstrations was highlighted in the press, which constructed the protests as distinct from previous ones and unique in their adoption of peaceful tools of resistance such as occupying public squares. Numerous articles, especially in the Spanish press, were devoted to the description of the organisation of the movement, the multiplicity of small assemblies and their transverse way of collaboration across different sociodemographic groups.

The Individual at Centre Stage

Another element that clearly distinguishes the coverage of the Indignados from that of other protests was the use of sources. We coded our sample for a number of different sources, such as government officials, opposition representatives, the protesters, public figures other than politicians, such as academics or artists, and citizens that did not participate in the protests. Relevant research has often highlighted the bias exhibited by mainstream media in their reliance on statements from authorities and official sources when reporting stories of social problems and civil unrest (McLeod and Hertog 1999). In sharp contrast, our research shows that when sources were cited, directly and indirectly, they were more likely to be protesters (see Figure 6.2). This was particularly

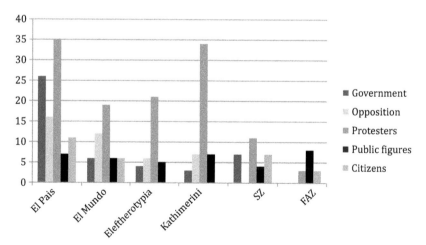

Figure 6.2 Sources mentioned in media.

evident in the first days of the coverage, and did not differ considerably across the newspapers of different ideological leanings. This was also the case for the German *Süddeutsche Zeitung*, which often relied on protesters themselves as news-sources. The only exception in the sample was the German conservative *Frankfurter Allgemeine Zeitung*, which mostly resorted on comments from public figures.

These stories were reported as illustrative of the heterogeneity of the protesting crowd and the apolitical character of the movement, as they focused on the particular circumstances and motives of the participants. A common structure of these reports would be to start by naming the protesters and describing their status, also highlighting the reasons for their 'indignation'. Phrases such as *'Ana, writer and librarian[...]'*, *'Ramon, a civil-servant[...]'*, *'Maria, a secretary until last year, and currently unemployed[...]'*, were very common in the Greek and Spanish coverage of the protests. These stories humanized the movement participants, creating empathetic links between them and the public. At the same time, they legitimised the protestors' claims, contextualising them within an environment of high unemployment and acute economic crisis. The following is an illustration from *El Pais*:

> 'I have two gigs and all they offer me is 5, 000 euro gross per year,' explained Ana Sierra, 26, with a degree in History and Documentation, who also came to show her anger. 'It's a feeling of indignation. We grow up, we strive, and now our only chance is to emigrate. We are doomed to live precariously' she added.
>
> (*El Pais* 2011)

For Bennett (2012, 31), such favourable press coverage can be partly explained by the inclusive character of the personal action frames adopted by the Indignados, as these 'every person' frames are easier to be positively reported and publicly accepted than the exclusive 'collective action frames' which define social movements more narrowly against the established order (ibid.). Along with their lack of explicit political or ideological affiliations and their heterogeneity of composition, the Indignados became representative of the public, the citizens, the ones hit the hardest by the economic crisis.

The Movement and Its Political Claims

What further enabled this coverage of the protesters as representative of the general public voice was the independence of the movement from official party lines and political alliances. In a reaction against the established political model and disenchantment with traditional processes, the Indignados defined themselves as opposed to the political system and its established parties and claimed to offer a democratic alternative to the political status quo.

This independence of the movement from formal political allegiances was the aspect most mentioned when there was any reference of the movement as a political actor. This was the case in all newspapers at a rate of about 20% of all stories. The failure of left-wing parties (such as the IU, ERC or PSOE in Spain and KKE in Greece) to capitalise on the movement was reported as a triumph of the movement to safeguard its independence. The Greek conservative *Kathimerini* also often described the movement as 'apolitical' (*apolitik*), a reference made in 38% of its stories. This was an aspect mentioned both in relation to the diversity of citizen participation discussed above, as press reports made a point to mention examples of individuals that had never before participated in protests, and, more rarely, in order to explicitly attack the protests as lacking any clear political vision. In both cases, however, the coverage ultimately undermined the role of the movement as a coherent alternative political force in the public space.

Further contributing to that was the coverage of the political claims made by the movement. Newspapers made frequent and explicit references to the political slogans and claims of the protesters, such as *'No los votes'* (*'Don't vote for them'*), *'we are not puppets of politicians and bankers'*, *'get out of here!'* (directed at politicians), especially in the first day of the protest. However, the coverage of more proactive political claims was minimal (see Figure 6.3). We observed small differences between left- and right-centred newspapers in Greece and Spain, with the latter being more likely to ignore any proactive or constructive claims of the protesters, however, this difference was rather insignificant. This overall tendency can be explained in the broader context of the coverage, which, as mentioned above, tended to favour the protests as a spectacle in comparison to other themes.

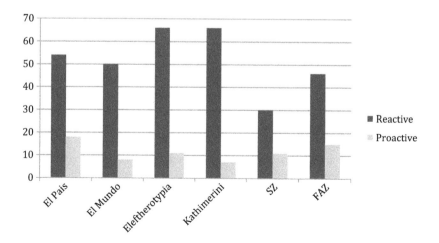

Figure 6.3 Political claims in the selected newspapers.

Networked Indignation

Regarding the media technology frame, we found that all newspapers made references to the role of social media in the organisation and conduct of the protests. The internet and social media became important tools and platforms: both for the protests themselves, and in how they were covered. What in the relevant literature has been described as the social media revolutions (Christensen 2011) was acknowledged in the press as another element of the 'novel' character of the movement. This was especially the case in Greece, a country where internet penetration was at 53% in 2011 (World Bank 2014)[2] and social media were only used by a young educated minority. In this context, the use of new media for the coordination of citizens and organisation of the protests was newsworthy in itself.

Two aspects of how the news reported on the role of media in the Indignados protests are particularly noteworthy. The news made regular references to the websites, Facebook pages and Twitter accounts protesters used to communicate with each other and to mobilise the public. This is partly explained by the fact that the reporting of these protests did not appear to follow the established patterns and routines of protest reporting, and did not rely on conventional primary definers with journalists turning to demonstrators' websites and social networks in order to obtain further information (Micó and Casero-Ripollés 2014). At the same time, reports from the field would describe how protesters made use of their mobile phones and laptops to capture the protests and share them on social networks. Interestingly, by describing the role of Facebook and Twitter as tools for the coordination of the protesters, the press itself became part of this coordination process it was describing. By repeating the names of blogs and Facebook groups, as well as hashtags used by the protesters, such as *#nolesvotes* and *#acampadasol*, the press effectively amplified the movement's visibility.

National Perspectives

To be sure, there were of course differences in the ways the movement was reported in the two countries. As the occurrence and character of the protests varied, so did the coverage: not so much in terms of its content, which was overall positively predisposed to the protesters, but mostly in terms of its magnitude. The press coverage of the Indignados was much more extensive and persistent in Spain, where the movement originated. Although the initial coverage did not draw links between the different demonstrations across the country, considering them as more or less spontaneous and idiosyncratic groups, the protests quickly gained popularity among the public and attracted extensive press coverage. They began to be referred to as the 'Indignados' or '15-M' movement (and occasionally as the *Empörten* in the German press), positioned against the political class (*'politicos'*) and financial elites (*'banqueros'*), through slogans such as *'¡Democracia Real Ya!'* (Real Democracy Now!) and *'¡No los votes!'* ('Don't vote for them!'). The articles covering the movement varied, including not only correspondence from the protest sites but also extensive analyses, reflections on the causes of the demonstrations, their endorsement by public figures and the reactions of politicians. The coverage was significantly more extensive in the centre-left *El Pais*. Despite its initial focus on clashes, *El Mundo*'s coverage also evolved to be more favourable and extensive after the first couple of days of the protests.

The Greek Aganaktismenoi, born as a direct response to the Spanish Indignados but with equally urgent claims and agenda, had admittedly a shorter lifespan: both as a protest movement and in terms of its coverage by the mainstream media. The links to the Spanish movement were prominent in the Greek newspapers, especially during the first days of the Aganaktismenoi occupying public squares across the country. According to rumours triggered in social media and reported by the mainstream media as a fact, Greeks took to the streets after Spanish protesters were seen holding a banner with the phrase *'¡Silencio, que los griegosestán-durmiendo!'* (Silence, because the Greeks are sleeping!) (Oikonomakis and Roos 2013). This added a further dimension to the Greek movement and its coverage, as proving to the Spanish Indignados that the Greeks were not asleep became an issue of national pride. In the protests, this was illustrated through a banner that responded those the Spanish protestors had allegedly held, saying in Spanish, *'Estamosdespiertos! Quehora es? Ya es hora de que se vayan!'* (We are awake! What time is it? Time for them to leave!). This banner figured in the media reports, along with comparisons to the Spanish movement and constant references to the increased numbers of Greek protesters. The political status quo, encapsulated in the concept of 'the Parliament', and the austerity policies imposed by the Troika and the Greek government were identified by the press as the targets of the rage and indignation being shown by the Greek protesters. Another prevalent theme in the Greek press was the politics of the protest space. After the first days of peaceful demonstrations, divisions among the protesters became apparent. While the upper part of Syntagma Square, the square in front of the Greek parliament, was occupied by the diverse 'apolitical' crowd, a large part of which was participating in protests for the first time, action-driven protesters with more evident political orientation, the hardcore part of the movement, congregated in the lower part of the Square (Tsaliki 2012).

The German press coverage was not considerably different from that in Greece and Spain. It adopted an overall neutral tone in presenting the protests in both countries. The focus of the coverage was mostly on Spain, and in particular on the prolonged occupation of Puerta del

Sol in Madrid and other central squares in the country. There was a greater tendency to discuss the causes of the protests in Spain, rather than Greece. The violence frame was mostly discussed in relation to the Greek Aganaktismenoi. The protest movement was often discussed within the context of high youth unemployment and the Greek and Spanish governments' implementation of austerity measures and political reforms. Despite the justification of the Indignados and their actions that such a coverage provided, the German newspapers often noted that the protests were critical of the system but without a concrete alternative plan to articulate. A few reports discussed the protests in Spain along with the E. coli outbreak in Germany, caused by cucumbers allegedly imported from Spain, something that was denied by Spanish officials and generated tension among the two countries.

Discussion: Overthrowing the Protest Paradigm?

We have so far argued that the coverage of the Indignados challenged in a variety of ways the dominant 'protest paradigm' on the basis of which mainstream media tend to report social movements and demonstrations. An explanation of this mostly positive media coverage should be approached within the context of the euro crisis. A European problem with international dimensions, the crisis has complicated questions of national sovereignty in Europe. The austerity measures, unemployment, lack of regulation in the banking sector and many of the other targets of the Indignados' demonstrations have generally been approached as problems caused by invisible international forces. Similarly, the framing of the movement as a reaction against the overall political system, as an impersonal and general force, arguably makes for a representation of the Indignados in public discourse as an expression of citizens' generalised discontent and frustration, rather than an acute threat to the existing establishment. This representation was further reified by the coverage of the protest movement as consciously and determinately detached from political parties, including those on the left that have hitherto been at the forefront of social movements. At the same time, the press rarely placed the movement in direct dialogue with mainstream political processes and decision-making. In this context, the reporting of the Indignados movement acknowledged the presence of a new political subject in the arena of European politics, that of the 'ordinary citizens', the 'people'; but the way this voice was framed it was ultimately rendered unthreatening to the political establishment. The reductionist way in which the movement was portrayed ultimately detracted from its potential as a constructive political interlocutor that the establishment would need to engage with.

Furthermore, the international character of the movement played a significant role in the way Indignados was reported in the mainstream press. Emerging almost simultaneously in different European countries that faced similar economic and social problems, the movement was seen as a powerful expression of citizens' voices from across Europe, defying attempts to frame the protests as a purely domestic matter or by falling-back onto traditional media templates, such as the protest paradigm. Furthermore, press coverage in Greece and Spain was also underlined by a sense of civic or national pride; pride in the way citizens were pioneers in establishing new political formations in the case of the Spanish press, and the way the Greek people responded to the Spanish jibes in the Greek press. The German press made frequent references to the orderly and amicable nature of the Indignados, and discussed the plight of young people in Spain and Greece at length so that it would be hard for German audiences to be unaware of how disproportionally the crisis had affected young people. This sense of intra-national and international competition (between cities and countries), attention and sympathy contributed to the celebratory and emotional coverage of the protests by mainstream newspapers.

At the same time, the positive media reporting of the Indignados should not be overestimated. Despite the early enthusiasm, coverage of the protests and the movement had faded away by the end of summer 2011. In the Greek case, this change was also illustrated by the declining visibility of voices of individual protesters that had dominated the coverage in its initial stages. Furthermore, clashes between the protesters and the police on 28 and 29 June, while new austerity measures were being voted in the Parliament, were seen as an all too familiar scenery and marked the end of the peaceful protests of Aganaktismenoi. In Spain, despite a resurgence of interest in the last week of July, when the Indignados once more occupied the Plaza de El Sol in Madrid, the coverage diminished gradually. This was not necessarily reflective of the movement itself. Although the protesters did gradually leave the squares they had occupied in May–June 2011, the Indignados remained active in many cities and towns in Spain. Even before the dismantling of the camps, the Spanish Indignados in particular had taken strategic actions to strengthen the grassroots movement through neighbourhood assemblies and alternative political platforms (Dhaliwal 2012). These practices and projects, some of which remain strong in the present, have not attracted equal attention from the press. An inherent preference of news media to focus on newsworthy events, rather than processes, means that continuous alternative political engagement and civil resilience are bound to go unnoticed. If the Indignados in the squares made for a great spectacle, their follow-up actions have not and are therefore hardly reported. In this context, the coverage of the Indignados can even be seen as disempowering the movement, in so far as it fails to illustrate citizen action as capable of producing alternative political solutions.

126   *Maria Kyriakidou et al.*

Despite the protest paradigm's breakdown in the reporting of the Indignados, as observed by our study, this is not to be seen as a complete defenestration of established conventions of reporting protests and civil unrest. Though the pro-establishment media bias observed in protest reporting by foregoing research was not as apparent here as it was in the media coverage of previous protests, it was the inherent preference of news media for the spectacular that contributed to the framing of the Indignados in a way that celebrated the peaceful spectacle of the protests but failed to illustrate the relevance of the movement beyond the expression of indignation and the occupation of public spaces. An expression of 'personalised politics' (Bennett 2012), the Indignados is an illustration of the more complex face of modern protest movements, with a wider base and public support (Cottle 2008). To this complexity, the mainstream media seem to respond with equally diverse ways, without, however, utterly abandoning established ways of reporting.

Notes

1 A version of this paper has been published at the European Journal of Communication: Kyriakidou, M., and Olivas Osuna, J. J. (2017). The Indignados protests in the Spanish and Greek press: Moving beyond the 'protest paradigm'? European Journal of Communication, 32(5), 457–472.
2 In Spain internet penetration was considerably higher, at 67.7% (World Bank 2014).

References

Anduiza, E., Cristancho, C., and Sabucedo, J. M. (2014). Mobilization through online social networks: The political protest of the indignados in Spain. *Information, Communication & Society*, 17(6), 750–764.
Arampatzi, A. (2016). The spatiality of counter-austerity politics in Athens, Greece: Emergent "urban solidarity spaces." *Urban Studies*, 1–16. doi:10.1177/0042098016629311.
Bennett, W. L. (2012). The Personalization of politics political identity, social media, and changing patterns of participation. *The ANNALS of the American Academy of Political and Social Science*, 644(1), 20–39.
Cammaerts, B. (2013). The mediation of insurrectionary symbolic damage. The 2010 U.K. student protests. *The International Journal of Press/Politics*, 18(4), 525–548.
Casero-Ripollés, A., and Feenstra, R. A. (2012). The 15-M movement and the new media: A case study of how new themes were introduced into Spanish political discourse. *Media International Australia*, 144(1), 68–76.
Chan, J. M., and Lee, C. C. (1984). Journalistic paradigm and civil protests: A case study in Hong Kong. In A. Andro, and W. Dissanayake (eds.), *The news media in national and international conflict* (183–202). Boulder, CO: Westview Press.
Christensen, C. (2011). Twitter revolutions? Addressing social media and dissent. *The Communication Review*, 14(3), 155–157.

Cottle, S. (2008). Reporting demonstrations: The changing media politics of dissent. *Media, Culture & Society*, *30*(6), 853–872.

Dardis, F. E. (2006). Marginalization devices in U.S. press coverage of Iraq war protest: A content analysis. *Mass Communication and Society*, *9*(2), 117–135.

Dhaliwal, P. (2012). Public squares and resistance: The politics of space in the Indignados movement. *Interface: A Journal for and About Social Movements*, *4*(1), 251–273.

Doudaki, V. (2015). Legitimation mechanisms in the bailout discourse. *Javnost – The Public*, *22*(1), 1–17.

El País, E. E. (2011, May 15). La manifestación de "indignados" reúne a varios miles de personas en toda España. Accessed August 1, 2017. http://elpais.com/elpais/2011/05/15/actualidad/1305447428_850215.html.

Entman, R. M. (1993). Framing: Toward clarification of a fractured paradigm. *Journal of Communication*, *43*(4), 51–58.

Eurostat. (2014). *Unemployment statistics*. Accessed August 1, 2017. http://epp.eurostat.ec.europa.eu/cache/ITY_PUBLIC/3-30092014-BP/EN/3-30092014-BP-EN.PDF.

Gamson, W. A. (1989). News as framing: Comments on Graber. *American Behavioral Scientist*, *33*(2), 157–161.

Gamson, W. (2005). Movement impact on cultural change. In S. J. Pfohl et al. (eds.), *Culture, power, and history* (103–125). Boston, MA: Brill Publishers.

Gamson, W. A., and Wolfsfeld, G. (1993). Movements and media as interacting systems. *The Annals of the American Academy of Political and Social Science*, *528*, 114–125.

Gerbaudo, P. (2012). *Tweets and the streets: Social media and contemporary activism*. London: Pluto Press.

Gitlin, T. (1980). *The whole world is watching: Mass media in the making & unmaking of the new left*. Oakland: University of California Press.

Harris, F., and Gillion, D. (2010). Expanding the possibilities – Reconceptualizing political participation as a toolbox. In J. E. Leighly (ed.), *Oxford Handbook of American Elections and Behavior* (144–161). New York, NY: Oxford University Press.

Hessel, S. (2011). *Time for outrage: Indignez-vous!* (First Edition edition). New York, NY: Twelve.

Hyman, R. (2015). Austeritarianism in Europe: What options for resistance? In D. Natali, and B. Vanhercke (eds.), *Social policy in the European Union: State of play 2015* (97–126). Brussels, Belgium: ETUI aisbl, Brussels.

Koopmans, R., and Erbe, J. (2004). Towards a European public sphere? *Innovation: The European Journal of Social Science Research*, *17*(2), 97–118.

Mazzoni, M., and Barbieri, G. (2014). Grasshoppers against ants or malfunctions of capitalism? The representation of the European economic crisis in the main Italian newspapers. *Perspectives on European Politics and Society*, *15*(2), 238–253.

McCurdy, P. (2012). Social movements, protest and mainstream media. *Sociology Compass*, *6*(3), 244–255.

McLeod, D., and Detenber, B. (1999). Framing effects of television news coverage of social protest. *Journal of Communication*, *49*(3), 3–23.

McLeod, D., and Hertog, J. K. (1999). Social change and the mass media's role in the regulation of protest groups. In D. Demers, and K. Viswanath (eds.),

Mass media, social control and social change: A macrosocial perspective (305–330). Ames: Iowa State University Press.

Micó, J.-L., and Casero-Ripollés, A. (2014). Political activism online: Organization and media relations in the case of 15M in Spain. *Information, Communication & Society, 17*(7), 858–871.

Nelson, T. E., and Oxley, Z. M. (1999). Issue framing effects on belief importance and opinion. *The Journal of Politics, 61*(4), 1040–1067.

Oikonomakis, L., and Roos, J. E. (2013). *"Que No Nos Representan". The crisis of representation and the resonance of the real democracy movement from the Indignados to Occupy.* Accessed August 1, 2017. https://roarmag. org/.../Resonance-Real-Democracy-Movement-Indignad....

Picard, R. G. (ed.) (2015). *The Euro crisis in the media: Journalistic coverage of economic crisis and European institutions.* London, UK; New York, NY: I.B.Tauris.

Postill, J. (2013, July 14). Spain's indignados and the mediated aesthetics of nonviolence. Accessed August 1, 2017. http://johnpostill.com/2013/07/14/spains-indignados-and-the-mediated-aesthetics-of-nonviolence/.

Prentoulis, M., and Thomassen, L. (2013). Political theory in the square: Protest, representation and subjectification. *Contemporary Political Theory, 12*(3), 166–184.

Taibo, C. (2013). The Spanish indignados: A movement with two souls. *European Urban and Regional Studies, 20*(1), 155–158.

Tsaliki, L. (2012). *The Greek "Indignados": the Aganaktismeni as a case study of the "new repertoire of collective action".* Paper presented at the Transmediale Media Art Festival, Berlin.

Weaver, D. A., and Scacco, J. M. (2012). Revisiting the protest paradigm: The Tea Party as filtered through prime-time cable news. *The International Journal of Press/Politics, 18*(1), 61–84.

World Bank. (2014). *Data: Internet users (per 100 people).* Accessed August 1, 2017. http://data.worldbank.org/indicator/IT.NET.USER.P2.

Ξεχείλισε αγανάκτηση το Σύνταγμα. (2011, May 29). [newspaper]. Accessed August 1, 2017. www.enet.gr/?i=news.el.article&id=279683.

7 Speak Your Mind

Mediatised Political Participation Through Second Screens

Udo Göttlich and Martin R. Herbers

Introduction: Mediatised Political Participation

The term 'political participation' is often misunderstood as an active endeavour of citizens, connected to visible, public performances of political engagement. Nevertheless, political participation is not bound to out-on-the street activism, protesting or voting. The seemingly passive activities of gathering information through media in order to form a political opinion needs to be seen as political participation as well, as it prepares citizens to live out their public role and participate in societal and political life. Thinking of political media, newspapers, television news and radio news come to mind. In a 'classical' understanding, these media build the prerequisite for different forms of political participation such as polling and voting or participating in political protests. This holds true, even when these assumptions are based on a unilateral understanding of mass communication, which is in itself restrictive concerning the possibilities to take over an active role as speaker in the public sphere. The audiences of these media have limited chances to talk back, getting no opportunity to voice their opinion on the presented issues directly. Participation is pre-organised, e.g. by the editorial side of newspapers, letters to the editor are pre-selected and callers on radio shows can be taken of the air easily. Thus, the audience misses the chance of active participation.

Currently, this framework is changing: With the advent of the digitalisation of media and the participatory features of the so-called Web 2.0, many new platforms and networks colonise the public sphere and create new possibilities to talk back. But the 'old' media do not capitulate easily – on the one hand, they open themselves up to these new forms of communication; on the other hand, they maintain control over these input channels. Especially established television formats like political talk shows present themselves nowadays on the internet with elaborate homepages, offering further information on the current themes and topics dealt with on the shows as well as the opportunity for the audience to give their opinion through new channels of communication, such as email, message boards or accompanying web chats during the course of the show. These features should allow the users not only to participate on the show, but also to follow the aim of offering an opportunity to participate in the public discourse on the given issue. These new options for participation are even advanced by the use of second screens and social network sites such as Facebook, as they allow the audience to voice their opinion during the course of the show in a casual way – using tools for otherwise private communication and thus bypassing the producer-controlled channels of communication.

This chapter gives a theoretical account of mediatised political participation. Following Jürgen Habermas' theory of the *public sphere* (Habermas 1989, 1997), it contextualises the processes of communication and participation against the backdrop of the theory of democracy. We place special emphasis on the role of social interaction and mass-mediated communication. As these undergo changes through recent processes of digitalisation, we turn to Axel Bruns' (2008) theory of *produsage* in order to describe the current relation between media producers and audience members with regard to the use of participatory media such as social network sites, often used as second screen applications in the course of watching television. After analysing the classical forms of audience participation in television talk shows, we turn to the new forms of *mediatised participation*. Comparing secondary sources and original research, we present preliminary insights by analysing audience participations and public participations through second screens. Drawing conclusions on the theories of Habermas' (1989, 1997) public communication and Axel Bruns' (2008) produsage, the chapter presents suggestions for future work in this field.

Political Participation Through Communication

Although the various theoretical approaches to democracy may vary on many different levels, they all agree on the normative presupposition that it works best when citizens are enabled to participate (Delli Carpini 2000). Nevertheless, democratic participation comes in many forms as well – from rather complex actions, such as running for office, or assumedly simple forms, such as keeping up with the news. Thus, political participation is always a process of communication (Carpentier 2011). This affects citizens in at least two ways: They are members of various audiences, subject to political communication, and as they voice their opinion on certain political issues they are also producers of political content. These communications usually take place in the public sphere (Habermas 1989, 1997), which consists of thematically bundled communications on various political issues. The rational exchange of arguments, as Habermas envisions it, serves as a backdrop for democratic reasoning. Through deliberation of equal citizens, a consensus is derived and employed politically. The all-encompassing process of public communication can be subdivided into different forms. As Jürgen Gerhards and Friedhelm Neidhart (1990) point out in addition to Habermas' thoughts, public communication – and thus political participation – can take place in *social interactions* and in *mass media.* In the case of social interactions, the basic idea of democratic communication among citizens is brought forth. The authors sketch a form of communication which takes place in public and is conducted by two equal citizens exchanging arguments about a political issue. These interactions are self-organised, as the citizens take turns in order to discuss the issue at hand. Other citizens can approach and join in the conversation, but can also leave it without any restrictions. As soon as the conversation stops and the citizens disperse, this form of public deliberation ends. Thus, through social interactions, a highly unconditionally assembled, but also fleeting form of communication and political participation is established. As Habermas (2006) points out, this form of public deliberation is contextualised by the group size, as smaller groups might gather in this way to discuss the issues of the day. But with regard to a state-wide discussion, a different form of public communication has to be put into action. *Mass-mediated public communication* plays a vital part for public deliberation and civic participation, as most citizens turn to media outlets such as newscasts on television or in newspapers in order to keep up with current events and the issues of the day. Nevertheless, these are organised forms of communication, which enable a different kind of public communication as social interactions. Taking television as an example, this form of mediated communication is highly efficient in distributing information, as specialised journalists broadcast the news to a wide, yet undefined audience. Nevertheless, this distribution of communication is unilateral and producer-driven. Following the post-Marxist line of argumentation it can be said that the television producers hold the means of production, which places them in a powerful situation in which they are able to produce television content – on political issues – which do not necessarily follow democratic, but rather economic interests (Gitlin 1979). Thus, the production side holds the power over the selection of political issues and their framing, which serve as the cornerstone for public deliberation. Furthermore, the audience does not necessarily have the option to talk back and establish a dialogue, as it is possible in social interactions. Deliberation as a part of the show has to be established through the production side, as audience members have to be invited to join the show and need to adhere to the 'rules of the medium' in order to make themselves heard (Neumann-Braun 1993). Thus, mass-mediated communication serves a problematic role for the public deliberation of political issues and for political participation as well (Habermas 1989).

Nonetheless, with the advent of the internet and widely available forms of digital communication and participatory media, such as blogs or social network sites, these assumptions have to be re-evaluated. Through the use of the latter, individual audience members and citizens alike are enabled to become content producers or even publishers, as they could make use of digital content production systems, such as blog hosting services, to voice their opinion on all kinds of issues. Thus, they are entitled to the means of production as well, without giving up on their roles as citizens and audiences members. As Bruns (2008) points out, the formerly fixed roles of producer and audience, as well as the forms of communication which tie them together undergo changes and merge, forming produsers who create content and engage with it at one and the same time. This leads to new forms of media production and engagement with media content. Participatory media, such as social network sites, play a vital role in this newly found "convergence culture" (Jenkins 2006). With regard to television, this has wide-spread consequences. The Brunsian produser engages in a form of neoliberal participation with the classical producers and adds to, or critiques the televised content, and thus overcomes the post-Marxian power relations inscribed in the media content (Fish 2013). Using social network sites, such as Facebook or Twitter, as publishing tools, the produsers make themselves visible to the producers and become an integral part of the production side. Although this form of participation is in itself grounded in the use of websites thriving to sell ad space to marketers, thus commodifying the audiences (Fuchs 2014), these new forms of communication and participation still serve as an addition to mediated public communication. They add the element of social interaction and its unruliness to the established and rigid forms of organised televised communication, thus allowing dialogue and participation. As the audience starts tweeting during the course of a show, they add a layer of opinions and arguments to the show's content which would otherwise have been left unseen.

Television Talk Shows as a Mediated Public Sphere

Regarding the transformation of communication and participation in the public sphere, political television talk shows serve as a prime example for audience engagement opportunities in a mediated setting. The idea of the genre is inherently democratic, as it can be regarded as a simulated form of public debate on a certain topic. Just like Habermas (1997) would describe his notion of the public sphere, communication in talk shows is centred around a certain political issue and presents facts and opinions on the issue at hand. A variety of guests, usually experts on that topic, are invited and given the opportunity to present their ideas regarding the issue. As the debate becomes heated, a professional host serves as the moderator for the discussion, thus catering to the idea of a rational discourse, which follows certain rules of argument and civility (Schultz

2004). However, there are certain differences between Habermas' ideas on the public sphere and the notion of talk shows. Most strikingly, these shows take place in a mediatised context – they are professionally produced and thus adhere to the problems of a mass-mediated public sphere. As the rules of television favour any communication which draws the audience in and keeps them bound to the screen (in order to commodify them), television talk show communication is seldom consensus oriented. Thus, an emphasis is placed on the production and presentation of conflict. This is brought forth through the selection of controversial topics and guests who have highly polarised opinions on the issue at hand (Lunt and Stenner 2005). Democratically speaking, the show's idea is not to reach a consensus, but to foster debate and to present conflicting ideas, which follows Chantal Mouffe's (2005) critique of Habermas' theory of mediated public discourse. Nevertheless, these shows still serve a democratic purpose as they present opinions and positions on a certain issue, which allows opinion formation and thus political participation in the audience.

Television talk shows include audience members in many ways which changed during the course of time. As Francesco Casetti and Roger Odin (2002) point out, the way audience members are included is bound to the underlying media system. The members of the audience become an integral part of these shows over the course of time. The first television talk shows were merely a roundtable of elite experts, catering to educated citizens in front of the television set. Over time, the table of experts was situated before a live audience and the floor was opened to questions from the present audience members, allowing interaction between experts and ordinary citizens. Further development showed the integration of everyday citizens into the table of experts, allowing a 'man-on-the-street'-level view on the issue at hand. Nonetheless, this view was brought forth by the logic of television production and had to adhere to its rules, thus rendering it a mediated form of audience participation.

Through the course of digitalisation, a new form of audience integration and thus participation comes into being. Members of the television audience can engage with talk shows through second screens, e.g. tablet computers or smartphones, which they use while watching the shows. Accessing social network sites such as Facebook or Twitter, members of the audience make themselves visible, comment on the show and engage in discussion with other audience members or even the show's participants. Through this mediated form of communication, an element of social interaction is brought back into the mass-mediated public sphere. Adding a layer of easily accessible and seemingly boundless communication, the inherently paternalistic style of presenting experts' opinions is overcome and audience members become empowered to voice their opinion and be heard on the media.

Second Screen Participation in Television Talk Shows

This theoretical framework is highly normative and follows the assumption that the use of second screens for political participation is widespread and everyday media behaviour. Thus, we must take a closer look at the few empirical sources at hand to further differentiate the actual use of second screens and to evaluate the theoretical background. A short, and by all means incomplete, review of current findings on second screen use and a short report on findings from our original research project can be used to assess the theoretical findings.

A ground-breaking study by Marius Johnen and Birgit Stark (2015) used a quantitative analysis to describe German second screen users' socio-demographically, as well as with regard to their motivations to using such devices. Their results show that the typical second screen users are younger males, aged 20 to 29, with access to mobile computing devices, a high affinity for television and the internet in general, and a mildly neurotic disposition, leading easily to boredom and a constant need for stimulation. Thus, the use of the second screen during the course of watching television is driven by the need for excitement and entertainment. The use of second screen appliances is therefore seldom directed at the television programmes, like the use of Twitter for commentary: Congruent with the findings of Ramona Vonbun and Klaus Schönbach (2014), this proves to be the behaviour of politically sophisticated citizens, whereas the use of second screens is mainly used for reasons of entertainment and not for interaction with the televised content.

This form of silence of the audience is shown on the content level of second screen usage as well. As Fabio Giglietto and Donatello Selva (2014) found in a qualitative content analysis of tweets in the context of Italian television talk shows, the main part of tweets which used the hashtag of the shows were undirected. They remained unanswered and can be seen as personal statements and opinions on various aspects of the show (such as the behaviour of the guests or the host), but were not aimed at fostering dialogue or deliberation.

In our research project "Mediatized Media Reception" we inquire about the use of second screen appliances for user commentary on German entertainment television programmes (Göttlich et al. 2015). Based on the theory of mediatisation (Krotz 2009) we argue that television audiences and their viewing behaviour are recently shaped by the use of second screens. Accessing social networking sites through the second screen in order to comment on television shows such as criminal dramas or live television events is said to be a predominant mode of behaviour (Proulx and Shepatin 2012). We challenge this assumption by analysing the use of second screens in everyday situations of a variety of members of different media generations (Berg et al. 2015). Conducting explorative qualitative interviews with 58 German citizens, we subdivided our sample into three groups separated by age (younger than 29, 29 to 50, and older than 50 years) in order to analyse whether the use of second screens is bound to a certain age group. Furthermore, we were interested in the ways the second screen is used in these social groups. Our study shows that a large portion of our sample has access to multiple screens while watching television, but refrains from using it to comment on the shows. Our participants stated various reasons for remaining silent. Most strikingly, they admitted watching television talk shows on a regular basis, but did not feel the need to comment as these shows were regarded as not being worthy of comment. This reason was mainly given by our older participants (aged 50 and older), who were socialised in a time when audience participation was mainly producer driven. Thus, older participants refrain from commenting through the second screen since they are not used to this form of communication, although they are well aware of it. Younger participants refrain from commenting on these shows as well, despite having been socialised to use the second screen frequently. Here, though, television talk shows are not relevant and thus do not show up in their 'media menu'. This group therefore remains silent as well and does not show any form of active participation (Göttlich and Herbers 2016).

Conclusion

Taking the presented findings and lines of argumentation into account, one can say that political participation through second screens in television talk shows faces difficulties, but does provide opportunities for political discourse as well. Strikingly, it could be shown that the actual use of the technological possibilities to engage with television context through second screens is not widely spread. When audience members turn to second screens during a television show, they use it merely in a passive way. They become *lurkers* (Nonnecke and Preece 2000), who watch the communication of others without engaging with them. If audience members do decide to voice their opinion on a talk show, in the case of Twitter it is usually in the form of a single tweet which remains unanswered, as the studies on the second screen show. The content of the tweets is seldom constructive or aimed at political discourse, but rather disruptive, criticizing the talk show, its host or its guests on a more personal level, rather than engaging with the content. Nevertheless, this rather bleak picture of audience participation on television talk shows still represents a form of democratic engagement. It may not be as normatively rigid as Habermas envisioned it, but it nevertheless serves a democratic purpose. It shows that an easily accessible form of communication leads to (unruly) engagement and participation. This is still a democratic practice, although not consensus oriented in itself. It rather shows that audiences and thus citizens are emotional beings who feel the need to talk and be heard. The arena of television talk shows proves to be a valid form of input into the discussion of public issues. The form of audience engagement shows that at this point it needs to be put into perspective with other forms of mediated political discourse in order to draw further conclusions. As other studies show that the use of second screens for engaging with news shows on television seems to be a more active form of participation (Loosen et al. 2013; de Zúñiga et al. 2015), as well as in political live events (Vaccari et al. 2015), a closer look at the normative presuppositions for mediated political participation has to be undertaken, in order to grasp the extent and forms of this basic democratic practice.

References

Berg, M., Hepp, A., and Roitsch, C. (2015). *Media generations. Mediatized communications across the life span.* Paper presented at the 65th Annual Conference of the International Communication Association, San Juan, Puerto Rico, 21–25 May.

Bruns, A. (2008). *Blogs, Wikipedia, Second Life, and beyond: From production to produsage.* New York, NY: Peter Lang.

Carpentier, N. (2011). *Media and participation. A site of ideological-democratic struggle.* Bristol, UK and Chicago, IL: Intellect.

Casetti, F., and Odin, R. (2002). Vom Paläo- zum Neo-Fernsehen. Ein semio-pragmatischer Ansatz. In R. Adelmann, J. O. Hesse, J. Keilbach, M. Stauff, and M. Thiele (Eds.), *Grundlagentexte zur Fernsehwissenschaft. Theorie – Geschichte – Analyse* (311–334). Konstanz, Germany: UVK.

de Zúñiga, H. G., Garcia-Perdomo, V., and McGregor, S. C. (2015). What is second screening? Exploring motivations of second screen use and its effect on online political participation. *Journal of Communication, 65*(5), 793–815.

Delli Carpini, M. X. (2000). In search of the informed citizen. What Americans know about politics and why it matters. *The Communication Review, 4*(1), 129–164.

Fish, A. (2013). Participatory television: Convergence, crowdsourcing, and neo-liberalism. *Communication, Culture & Critique, 6*(3), 372–395.

Fuchs, C. (2014). *Social media. A critical introduction.* London: SAGE.

Gerhards, J., and Neidhardt, F. (1990). *Strukturen und Funktionen moderner Öffentlichkeit. Fragestellungen und Ansätze.* Berlin, Germany: Wissenschaftszentrum Berlin für Sozialforschung.

Giglietto, F., and Selva, D. (2014). Second screen and participation: A content analysis on a full season dataset of tweets. *Journal of Communication, 64*(2), 260–277.

Gitlin, T. (1979). Prime time ideology: The hegemonic process in television entertainment. *Social Problems, 26*(3), 251–266.

Göttlich, U., and Herbers, M. R. (2016). Remembering television: Changes in audience practices' in the course of mediatisation. Paper presented at the Annual Conference of the IAMCR, Leicester, UK, 27–31 July.

Göttlich, U., Heinz, L., and Herbers, M. R. (2015). *Changes in television audiences' practices. Commentary and co-orientation in the age of second screens*. Paper presented at the Annual Conference of the IAMCR, Montréal, QC, 12–16 July.

Habermas, J. (1989). *The structural transformation of the public sphere. An inquiry into a category of bourgeois society.* Cambridge, UK: Polity.

Habermas, J. (1997). *Between facts and norms. Contributions to a discourse theory of law and democracy.* Cambridge, UK: Polity.

Habermas, J. (2006). Does democracy still enjoy an epistemic dimension? The impact of normative theory on empirical research. *Communication Theory,* 16(4), 411–426.

Jenkins, H. (2006). *Convergence culture. Where old and new media collide.* New Haven, CT and London, UK: New York University Press.

Johnen, M., and Stark, B. (2015). Wenn der Fernseher nicht ausreicht. Eine empirische Analyse der Second Screen-Nutzung. *SC/M. Studies in Communication\Media,* 4(4), 365–406.

Krotz, F. (2009). Mediatization. A concept with which to grasp media and societal change. In K. Lundby (ed.), *Mediatization. Concept, changes, consequences* (19–38). New York, NY: Peter Lang.

Loosen, W., Schmedt, J.-H., Heise, N., Reimer, J., and Scheler, M. (2013). *Publikumsinklusion bei der Tagesschau. Fallstudie aus dem DFG-Projekt "Die (Wieder-)Entdeckung des Publikums."* Arbeitspapiere des Hans-Bredow-Instituts Nr. 26. Hamburg, Germany: Hans-Bredow-Institut.

Lunt, P., and Stenner, P. (2005). The Jerry Springer Show as an emotional public sphere. *Media, Culture & Society,* 27(1), 59–81.

Mouffe, C. (2005). *On the political.* New York, NY and London, UK: Routledge.

Neumann-Braun, K. (1993). *Rundfunkunterhaltung. Zur Inszenierung publikumsnaher Kommunikationsereignisse.* Leipzig, Germany: Gunter Narr.

Nonnecke, B., and Preece, J. (2000). Lurker demographics: Counting the silent. In ACM SIGCHI (Ed.), *Proceedings of CHI 2000.* The Hague, the Netherlands: ACM.

Proulx, M., and Shepatin, S. (2012). *Social TV. How marketers can reach and engage audiences by connecting television to the web, social media and mobile.* Hoboken, NJ: Wiley & Sons.

Schultz, T. (2004). Die Moderation politischer Gesprächsrunden im Fernsehen. Eine Inhaltsanalyse von "Sabine Christiansen", "Berlin Mitte", "Presseclub" und "19:zehn". *Publizistik,* 49(3), 292–318.

Vaccari, C., Chadwick, A., and O'Loughlin, B. (2015). Dual-screening the political. Media events, social media, and citizen engagement. *Journal of Communication,* 65(6), 1041–1061.

Vonbun, R., and Schönbach, K. (2014). Wer ist politisch aktiv im Social Web? Eine Studie zur politischen Online-Kommunikation in Österreich. *Publizistik,* 59(2), 199–212.

8 "My Body, My Decision". The Abortion Debate and Twitter as a Counterpublic Sphere for Women in Turkey

Perrin Öğün Emre and Gülüm Şener

Social Media as an Alternative Space

The evolving structure of social movements after the battle of Seattle has become enmeshed with the dynamics of the cyber environment which influence activism forms. Social movements find the opportunity to rapidly communicate and organise around social events thanks to their spontaneity. Throughout social movements, such as Iran's Green Movement, the Arab Spring, Occupy Wall Street and the 15-M Movement in Spain, social media has provided diffusion of oppositional discourse and activism which were previously limited by power structures and conventional media, thus creating an alternative public sphere.

Social media is an alternative space where digitally literate women are free of daily restrictions within the/a patriarchal social structure, allowing them to express themselves and find opportunities for socialisation. In Turkey, where levels of physical, emotional and digital violence against women are high and where women are underrepresented politically compared to (other) countries with more developed women's rights, social media has come to play an important role in exposing women's voices and transforming them into political subjects. As we see in the abortion debate, women consider social media applications, such as Facebook, Twitter, digital dictionnaries and blogs, as a means of debating public problems to produce alternative discourses and in creating activism. Women who had not been involved in any political struggle proclaimed their opinions for and against the AKP abortion resolution and suggested solutions on Twitter. Social media is an important communication tool for feminist movements. Since it creates an alternative expression and participatory space for socialisation, social media allows digitally literate women to go beyond the scope of their usual bounds and disseminate their ideas and feelings effectively. Social media has become an important tool for reflecting the voices of women who live in countries, such as Turkey, where different forms of violence (physical, sexual, emotional and digital violence) against women are widespread.

'My body, my decision' is one of the campaigns which protest the biopolitics acts of the government. This chapter seeks to examine the role of

social media as a counter public sphere allowing internet users to participate in this discourse. As a research method, all discussions on Twitter
around the 'abortion law' in 2012 and 2013 are examined using content analysis. 'Every abortion is Uludere', a declaration made by Turkish
Prime Minister Recep Tayyip Erdoğan on 25 May 2012, when making
an analogy comparing abortion to the massacre of 34 Kurdish youngsters by a drone strike in southeastern Turkey, provoked a burst of rage
among women and a massive protest in the online and offline worlds. In
the following weeks, Recep Akdağ, Minister of Health, announced that
they were preparing a new bill which would ban abortion after the first
four weeks of pregnancy. Feminist movements, women's organisations,
the mass and alternative media as well as individual women reacted immediately and started to run campaigns against the government's new
policy: 'No Abortion Ban' and 'My body, my decision!' are two of the
main campaign slogans protesting against the government's biopolitics
and regulations regarding women's bodies. Social media, especially
Twitter, was one of the main communication channels for discussion
and the organisation of protests.

(Counter) Public Spheres

The development of a communication medium is welcomed by the pro-
ponents of the techno-deterministic perspective as a signal of a new era
and the democratisation of information. The democratising functions
of communication technologies have been reconsidered with the advent
of the internet. The internet is conceived by many authors as a regener-
ating force for political life and democracies, creating alternative spaces
for free speech (Turkle 1997; Rheingold 2000; Benkler 2006; Shirky
2008; Howard 2010), new public spheres (Dahlgren 2000, 2001, 2005)
or counter publics and counter public spheres (Warner 2002; Downey
and Fenton 2003; Fenton and Downey 2003; Calhoun 2011; Wimmer
2015) enhancing political participation and civic activism (Castells
2005, 2012; Papacharissi 2010) with its potential for more horizontal,
instantenous, cheaper and interactive communication between political
actors and citizens.

Studies dealing with the relationship between the internet and
democracy rely on the notion of a *public sphere* and the deliberative democracy theory developed by German philosopher Jürgen
Habermas. According to his theory, the public sphere is conceptualised as a constituent political principle of modern democracies. Analysing the role of the press in the formation of a bourgeois public
sphere in the seventeenth and eighteenth centuries, Habermas (2009)
believes that citizens' access to information will enrich rational and
critical deliberation about public issues resulting in the creation of a
public sphere and the empowerment of democracy. Similarly, digital

technologies, based on horizontal communication, increase possibilities for mobilising apolitical individuals, where protests in the street and in the digital world intermingle and complete each other. Political participation and civic activism become the main activities for many activists as we witnessed in the Iranian Green Movement, the Arab Spring, the Occupy Wall Street Movement, the Indigñados, Gezi Park protests, etc. In his book *Tweets and Streets* Gerbaudo considers social media as a platform that creates a new feeling of centralisation and a 'choreography of assembly' for activists and social movements (2012, 21–23). Dahlgren (2009, cit. Bessant 2014, 37) believes that digital technology moves us beyond a narrow definition of the 'public sphere' by connecting us to 'civic cultures in subtle, unintended and surprising ways'.

Habermasian's idealised public sphere notion is criticised for being too limited, ignoring *counter* or *oppositional* public spheres created by the *proleteriat* (Negt and Kluge 1993) or women (Fraser 1989) as it is particularly focused on the male bourgeois public sphere. According to Calhoun, those who are excluded or who disagree with the dominant organisation of the public sphere often build their own media and networks of communication and with them their counter publics (2011, 14). Contextualising the notion of counter public sphere in the network society, Fenton and Downey (2003, 22) see the rise of counter public spheres both as a consequence and response to the globalisation of modernity and the crisis of dominant public spheres. They emphasise the competitive and dynamic relationship between dominant and counter public spheres: "Counter public spheres may provide vital sources of information and experience that are contrary to, or at least in addition to, the dominant public sphere thereby offering a vital impulse to democracy." Wimmer, who sees the origins of counter publicity in the fifteenth and sixteenth centuries in Protestant Europe, explains the current scientific and public attention by factors, such as globalisation and its critics, the crisis of the dominant public spheres and new possibilities for progressive protagonists, the internet and the possibilities for connecting (2015, 2):

> Currently, new media and digitalization influence counterpublic spheres on all levels on public communication: On a micro-level, digital media are inseparable from the political everday life of media activists. On a meso-level they are used both in internal and external communication of participants of public spheres, such as in the form of Internet campaigning. The diffusion of online and offline communication and their integration in the everyday life of citizens, also raises serious questions regarding the constitution of counterpublicity on a macro-level.

> (Wimmer 2015, 3)

Moreover, new conceptualisations are made by some authors inspired by Laclau and Mouffe's concept of *radical democracy* or Deleuze and Guattari's concept of *rhizome* in order to explain the political role of the internet. From a postmodern perspective, Poster (1995) explains why the Habermasian approach is in decline:

> For Habermas, the public sphere is a homogeneous space of embodied subjects in symmetrical relations, pursuing consensus through the critique of arguments and the presentation of validity claims. This model, I contend, is systematically denied in the arenas of electronic politics. …But the fact is that political discourse has long been mediated by electronic machines: the issue now is that the machines enable new forms of decentralized dialogue and create new combinations of human-machine assemblages, new individual and collective 'voices', 'specters', 'interactivities' which are the new building blocks of political formations and groupings.

Dahlberg (2007, 129) refers to the *agonistic* position to explain political aspects of the internet: "The agonistic position is important here because it focuses upon discursive power and political practices from 'the margins', deploying the concept of counter-publics to do so." Unlike deliberative considerations, agonistic public sphere theorists conceive the internet as a site of political struggle and conflict, a contested terrain. Agonists see the internet as supporting marginalised discourses to develop their own deliberative spaces, to link up with other excluded voices in developing representative, strategically effective counter discourses and subsequently to contest those meanings and practices dominating mainstream public sphere(s) (2007, 134).

Moreover, this techno-fetishist discourse on the internet and its democratic functions is limited by a number of factors. Dahlberg (2001, 2) summarises these factors limiting the expansion of the public sphere online:

> These factors include the increasing colonisation of cyberspace by state and corporate interests, a deficit of reflexivity, a lack of respectful listening to others, the difficulty of verifying identity claims and information put forward, the exclusion of many from online political fora, and the domination of discourse by certain individuals and groups.

Other limits may be digital surveillance (Morozov 2011) by states and corporations, censorship and control of authoritarian regimes (Kalathil and Boas 2003), monopolisation in new media (Hindman 2009), a digital divide (Norris 2001), clicktivism/slacktivism (Christensen 2011) and dissemination of hate speech through social networks or disinformation, etc.

Internet and the Empowerment of Women

The masculinist potential of the public sphere was criticised by feminist thinkers as the Habermasian public sphere excludes and marginalises women from the public debate and leads to the development of 'alternative routes to representation and participation in the public sphere'. Fraser (1990) identifies 'counter-publics', or subaltern discursive networks in which 'alternative styles of political behaviour and alternative norms of public speech' are elaborated:

> The exclusion of women from the public sphere has been identified as one of its most long-standing and foundational features (...). The codes of appropriate conduct and speech that developed in the public sphere are implicitly masculine although legitimised as gender-neutral and universalist, while the concerns and experiences of women are characterised as partial or private matters that can be marginalised or overlooked in public life (...).
>
> (Salter 2013, 226)

Felski revised the Habermasian notion of the public sphere, separating it from its patriarchal, bourgeois and logocentric attachments and puts the public sphere as central to feminist politics (cit. Poster 1995):

> Unlike the bourgeois public sphere, then, the feminist public sphere does not claim a representative universality but rather offers a critique of cultural values from the standpoint of women as a marginalized group within society. In this sense it constitutes a *partial* or counterpublic sphere... Yet insofar as it is a *public* sphere, its arguments are also directed outward, toward a dissemination of feminist ideas and values throughout society as a whole.

Haraway presented a new perspective to understand women and technology relationships in her 'cyberg manifesto' (1985). Cyberfeminists refer to the possibilities that the new technologies offer to escape from bodily gender definitions and construct new gender identities, or even genderless identities (van Zoonen 2012, 12): "Cyberfeminism is a philosphy which acknowledges, first, that there are differences in power between women and men specifically in the digital discourse; and second, that Cyberfeminism wants to change this situation" (Hawthorne and Klein 1999, cit. Goulding and Spacey 2003, 38). Van Zoonen (2002, 5) claims that the internet and gender are mutlidimensional concepts that are articulated in complex and contradictory ways. There is a mutual shaping, and the use of the internet does not automatically result in male dominaton. She distinguishes four types of articulations constituting traditional, deliberative, reversed and individualised use cultures.

Since the beginning of the 2000s, many scholars have emphasised the possibilities and limits of the internet for women. An optimistic approach seems to dominate this research area as the internet and now social media have been celebrated as technologies of empowerment for women. Sutton and Pollock (2000, 699) believe that women are using the technology as a form of empowerment by creating women's venues, resources and networks for organisation purposes: "Women's participation in decision making and creation of relevant resources is a vital part of developing an inclusive technology, and ensuring that women have the opportunities in education and employment that are becoming associated with use of ICTs" (Sutton and Pollock 2000, 704). According to Schuster's research, young women in New Zealand used new media to connect with other women in order to have political discussions and to organise events in the 'real world'. The young women preferred new media for its low-cost dynamic structure that enables access to large groups of people. She emphasises that "political online work offers many opportunities for feminist participation, but it excludes people not using new media, and thus contributes to the enhancement of a generational divide among women engaging with feminism" (Schuster 2013, 8).

However, the internet is not gender-neutral. Some limits of technology for women are illustrated as follows: pornography, women hating, access (Sutton and Pollock 2000, 702f., Goulding and Spacey 2003, 34), language and culture (Sutton and Pollock 2000, 702f.), time and money, lack of confidence and negative experiences with the internet (Goulding and Spacey 2003, 34f.).

The Abortion Debate in Turkey

For some feminists, body politics is 'the principal site for power in modern societies' reducing social agents into docile bodies (Armstrong 2003). Women especially struggle against objectification of the female body and violence against women, and campaign for reproductive rights for women. 'The personal is the political' shows, as Butler (1990) argues, that feminist politics should have an identity politics to allow women to publicly visualise their struggle. To convert docile bodies into subjects, women should express themselves effectively to the power. The struggles around body politics are crucial to the struggle for equal rights in public. This form of body politics emphasises a woman's power and authority over her own body. On the other hand, Foucault uses biopower to describe how the various institutions and disciplines arising in the eighteenth century controlled the productive capacities of individuals and the population at large. The state through institutions (army, family, police, schools, etc.) fosters 'the optimization and intensification of the life *force*'. The force of life can be maintained especially by governmental policies and protections, such as welfare, healthcare and safe working conditions (Sharma 2011, 441). Therefore, the creation of a democratic space which allows the contact of different perspectives is necessary and common sense. Armstrong (2003, s.p.) refers to Brown in this context:

> In light of these inadequacies, Brown calls for the politics of resistance to be supplemented by political practices aimed at cultivating "political spaces for posing and questioning political norms [and] for discussing the nature of 'the good' for women" (Brown 1995, 49). The creation of such democratic spaces for discussion will, Brown argues, contribute to teaching us how to have public conversations with each other and enable us to argue from our diverse perspectives about a vision of the common good ("what I want for us") rather than from some assumed common identity ("who I am").

Abortion, literally defined as the ending of pregnancy, has long been debated by many cultures and religions around the world; it has led to many ethical, philosophical and legal discussions, even 'pro-choice' and 'pro-life' activism. According to the UN's report entitled 'Abortion Policies and Reproductive Health around the World', the percentage of governments permitting abortion increased gradually for all legal grounds between 1996 and 2013, except to save a woman's life which remained at 97%. Out of 145 countries, 87 governments (60%) had implemented concrete measures to improve access to safe abortion services in the past five years (2014, 1). In modern Turkey, abortion was outlawed until 1983. In the post-First World War era, the Republican Popular Party launched the first family planning policies and an anti-abortion campaign in order to increase fertility and population. In the 60s and 70s, industrialisation, population growth and development of civic rights led to public discussions on birth control and abortion laws. Even though abortion was illegal, it was widespread among women living in urban and rural areas. In 1979, there were approximately 500,000 miscarriages and 25,000 women who lost their lives in one year only (Karaömerlioğlu 2016). Abortion became legal in Turkey when the 'Population Planning Law' (No. 2827) was passed on 27 May 1983. Article 5 says that abortion is an arbitrary choice for women and uterine evacuation is allowed until the end of the 10th week of pregnancy, except for mothers who have health problems. Between 1983 and 2008, abortion cases decreased by 60%, the rate of maternal mortality decreased sixfold, length of life for women increased fourteenfold.[1] However, the Justice and Democracy Party, the conservative ruling party since 2002, has developed policies and discourses aimed at restricting abortion. On the one hand, the Islamist government reproduces patriarchal discourses in order to control women's bodies using the media; on the other hand, they use economic arguments pretending that Turkey needs a population growth to become a power in the world economy. The solution is quite simple for government representatives: Every woman has to have at least three children. From this point of view, women are only defined by their physical capacities for reproduction and motherhood. In 2008, former Prime Minister Recep Tayyip Erdoğan addressed women in a panel on International Women's Day: "To keep our young population increasing, give birth to at least three children. I consider abortion to be a crime", he said, then continued, "I'm asking you: What is the difference between killing a little one in the womb of his mother and killing it after birth?" By emphasising the high rate of C-secton births in Turkey, he affirmed that there was an "insidious plan" to keep Turkey from becoming a major international power by reducing population growth (Seibert 2012). In 2012, the bill on reproductive health was presented in the parliament, proposing that abortion could only be performed if the pregnancy was at no more than four weeks. In May, another argument on women hit the headlines: 'Every abortion is Uludere'. This declaration by former Turkish Prime Minister Recep Tayyip Erdoğan on 25 May 2012, making an analogy between abortion and the massacre of 34 Kurdish young people by a drone in southeastern Turkey, provoked a burst of rage among women and massive protestation in online and offline worlds. But this was not the only shocking speech about women. A few days later, the Minister of Health Recep Akdağ talked about banning abortion: "They are asking what will happen to a woman if she is raped and she gets pregnant? If something like that happens, she should give birth to the child, and, if necessary, the government can raise the child" (Mavzer 2013).

In reaction to these conservative approaches of AKP's representatives, the alternative news website Bianet launched a campaign called 'Benim Kararım' or 'my decision'. The campaign aimed to construct solidarity on social networks by motivating people to send their pictures on which they either hold signs or (they) write slogans on their bodies saying that abortion is none of the government's business. Some of these slogans are: (for women) 'My Body, My Decision', 'This Is My Issue', (for men) 'Woman's Body, Woman's Decision', 'My Wife's Body, My Wife's Decision', 'My Daughter's Body, My Daughter's Decision', 'My Girlfriend's Body, My Girlfriend's Decision', 'This is a Women's Issue', 'My Sister's Decision', 'My Mother's Decision' and so on. Scores were posted online on the website benimkararim.org (Gharib 2012).

The Abortion Debate on Twitter

The abortion debate fell like a bombshell on the Twitter agenda as thousands of women shared millions of tweets and took to the streets to protest government policies regarding women's bodies. Twitter has a central role in the formation of new social movements as we witness in many protests around the world. Twitter's interface allows users to communicate more directly, instantanously, briefly and personally. On Twitter, the formal communication style of politicians and the communicational distance between politicians and citizens change radically compared to face-to-face communication and mass media. By using hashtags (#), users open public debates on any issue, they show their reactions against government policies and similar or opposing ideas become visible on the same column. Unlike the Habermasian idealised public sphere, in which citizens spark rational debate around political issues in the same physical space and in a shared period of time, Twitter gathers together people with anonymous or real identities, who can send 140 characters in length and provides a limited space and time for a long and dialogical discussion. Twitter can be considered as a site for confrontation of hegemonic as well as counter ideologies and an alternative or counter public sphere challenging dominant public sphere constructed by the mainstream mass media. Citizens debate political issues on micro, instantenous and flexible public spaces on Twitter (Şener et al. 2013). A considerable amount of research has been devoted to question the political potential of Twitter; some arguing that the platform facilitates public discussion and debates (Bruns and Burgess 2011), others criticising Twitter as a monitoring tool serving authoritarian regimes (Christensen 2011, 156), a platform for causing group polarising instead of enhancing public conversation (Yardi and Boyd 2010, 316; Himelboim et al. 2013), or for circulating hate speech (Christoforou 2014). Segerberg and Bennett (2011, 201) posit Twitter in protest ecology as one of the potentially digital mechanisms that co-constitute and co-configure the protest space: "Twitter is interesting as an organizing mechanism within the specific protest ecology. As well as transmitting information, networked protest spaces constitute negotiated spheres of individual and collective agency".

Political discourses enter Twitter, they have their own life and become part of the networked public sphere according to Maireder and Ausserhofer (2016, 404). They analyse the journey of political tweets from three different perspectives: networking issues, networking media objects and networking actors. Schmidt (2016, 48) suggests a new concept for understanding the publicness on Twitter: personal publics. He considers personal publics as an ideal communicative space in which the information is retrieved and exposed if it is valid for users; it is sent to a specific audience and the communication is interactive. However, Fuchs criticises Twitter for not being a real public sphere:

> It should neither be the subject of hope for the renewal of democracy and publication, nor the cause of concerns about violence and riots. What should first and foremost concern us is inequality in society and how to alleviate inequality.
>
> (Fuchs 2014, 207)

Content Analysis of the Topic Abortion on Twitter

The fieldwork covers two periods. The first period was between 23 May and 15 July 2012, when the abortion debate was at its peak and women protestors poured onto the streets; the second period was between 18 December 2012, and 31 January 2013, in which the debate blazed up again. During this time, the abortion debate was seen most on Twitter. Computerised content analysis software developed by TTBoom Social Media Agency is employed to analyse the volume and (the) content of Twitter posts. A sample of 6,000 tweets was drawn on the abortion debate from a total of 600,000 tweets on Twitter using random systematic sampling to generate a representative sample. The two keywords 'kürtaj' (abortion in Turkish) and 'kurtaj' (abortion written without using Turkish letters) were analysed in association with other words, such as women, religion, civic rights, health, politics, AKP, freedom, equality, etc.

The cast study consists of a content analysis which includes particular terms used most in the abortion debate. Basically, the keywords and their related words are chosen and followed on Twitter depending on the agenda. Then, the density of these keywords is evaluated and the users are also taken into account. The analysis revealed the major actors accentuated in the abortion debate. It is important to see the male and female leading actors in this (abortion) debate. The most popular part of the debate could be identified by retweet analysis as well as hashtag analysis, which allow exposing the density of the abortion debate on the Twitter agenda.

The main objective of this project is to measure the potential of social media for creating alternative public sphere(s) and discourse(s) around public issues. Focusing on the abortion debate on Twitter in Turkish, we are seeking to map online discussions and messages around Turkish government policies pertaining to women's health issues. First, we revealed the volume of tweets concerning the abortion debate, the principal actors (NGOs, feminist movements, the most influential users, journalists, etc.) who publicly stated an opinion on Twitter against the government's bill, and the most influential tweets and hashtags which motivated women to protest on the streets. Second, we analysed the opinion of Twitter users (whether they are pro-life, pro-choice or neutral) about the right to abortion in order to understand in which contexts people discuss and form opinions. We especially aimed to measure Twitter activities of women's organisations which were supporters of the campaign.

Chronology and Sources of the Abortion Debate

The abortion debate on Twitter was not limited to the proposed bill, but instead created a large public sphere in which all women's policies and problems, such as former political decisions and crimes, were discussed.

According to Monitera, Turkish Twitter users number 7.2 millon, 5.3 million being active Twitter users. Fifty-three per cent of Twitter users were men and 47% were women. In 2013, Twitter users increased by 33% and reached 9.6 million. The daily tweet number rate rose by over four times (470%) (Webrazzi 2013).

The chronology of the debate is important in order to understand the debate process and the peak point of the opposition.

May 26: The debate began after claims of the Prime Minister. Prime Minister Recep Tayyip Erdogan called abortion 'murder', and his government was reported to be working on legislation to ban the operation for those past four weeks from conception, except for emergency cases. When Minister of Health Recep Akdag emphasised a total ban on abortion in his speech, critical thoughts surrounding this news were shared on Twitter.

May 29: The second critical debate emerging on Twitter was regarding the Uludere case (5,750 tweets are shared). General attention was focusing around the article of the famous woman journalist and Hürriyet columnist Ayşe Arman: 'Both abortion and caesareans are women's business, not politicians'.

May 30: Abortion was most frequently spoken of on this day and a total of 5,750 files were shared. Erdogan's perspective repeatedly came under strong criticism and women's call for action was the second most shared tweet. Moreover, journalists' articles were also shared during this day.

May 31: This was the second day when the abortion debate was most spoken of (5,657 tweets). Also, rape was the most used theme due to a deputy's speech claiming that 'A rapist is more innocent than someone who has an abortion'. In a reference to babies born as a result of rape, Mr. Akdağ said that the state would look after the babies if 'the mother has been through something bad'. Tweets about contraception methods were shared and people argued that the abortion law had been produced in favour of the medical sector! On the other hand, 'ban' was a commonly used word, and the relationship between abortion rights and headscarf rights was expressed under this keyword. Rape, ban and method of contraception were themes which were articulated sequentially (Figure 8.1).

June 04: The abortion debate grew in intensity following the speeches of a Minister: The Director of Turkey's Department of Religious Affairs, Mehmet Görmez, spoke out on the directorate's view of abortion: "If there is no legitimate reason then abortion is murder and is forbidden by religion." Some women activists, such as Safak Pavey and Hidayet Şefkat Uysal, responded to him immediately. The debate lasted until June 20.

June 21: Nurettin Canikli, a lawmaker belonging to the Justice and Development Party, said: "The abortion issue is off the agenda. No

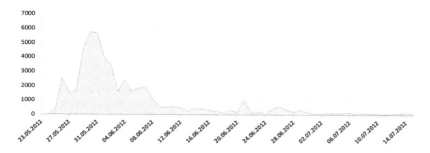

Figure 8.1 Amount of abortion tweets between May and August 2012.

legislation will be introduced to the parliament on this issue." However, Health Minister Recep Akdağ said on Monday the ministry will submit a report to the cabinet on abortion rights. The debate about abortion was scaled down throughout the summer, but it had heated up again by January 2013. Tweet numbers increased during January.

January 8–9: In Ayşe Arman's column on Tuesday a letter was published from a reader with the title "They conducted an abortion without anesthetics". The Twitter public responded to this action by sharing 1,053 tweets which were almost all against abortion.

January 11: The Minister of Health reacted to her article and Arman's response was appreciated by Twitter users: "Here is my response to the Minister of Health: Was everything great on the abortion issue? Did I invent it all?"

January 13: Tweets showed a decline and mostly mainstream media articles were shared on Twitter.

Out of 6,000 tweets as a random sample, 41% of tweets had a link. All tweets without user comments were accepted as neutral; 52% of the messages were neutral. Tweets against the abortion ban amounted to 44%, contrary to those supporting abortion were 4%. Usually, the Twitter agenda was shaped and referenced by mainstream media. News from the daily newspapers Hürriyet, Habertürk and Radikal were shared the most. Due to the shared tweets, mainstream media played a key role in the abortion debate, both in the offline and online worlds. Especially news sourcing from Hurriyet were retweeted 239 times and mentioned or linked to the tweet 417 times.

According to the user analysis, 40,751 users shared 60,000 different messages within two different periods: 23 May 2012–15 July 2012 and 18 December 2012–31 January 2013. The ten users with the most number of tweets were campaign account 'abortion is a right' (kurtaj_haktir) with 652 tweets was top of the list, the blogsphere of the daily national newspaper, Milliyet (Milliyet_blog), and a woman actress (DilaSipahi). The majority of the accounts which had increased tweet numbers were

Table 8.1 Tweet News Sources (n = 6000)

Source	Retweet	Other (Mentioned-Linked)	Total
Hürriyet	239	417	656
Haberturk	44	91	135
Radikal	40	94	134
NTV	88	37	125
Cnntürk	53	41	94
Cumhuriyet	28	8	36
Dipnot TV	28	4	32
Milliyet	2	28	30
Bianet	12	15	27
Enhizlihaber	5	16	21

informational media resources accounts. Mainstream media Twitter accounts were apparently popular (see Table 8.1). NTV (one of national news broadcasting channel) (607), acımasıztweet – Ministry of Health (498) and journalist cuneytozdemir (348) were the users whose messages were most frequently retweeted. With 325 tweets, Ayşe Arman was ranked fifth after Hürriyet.

A list of the countries with abortion bans was the most retweeted content. It was retweeted 607 times. A statement by the Minister of Health, proclaming the pregnancy of a woman to her family without her consent, was ranked second. This was retweeted 498 times. In addition, journalist Cuneyt Ozdemir accused Ayşe Arman of using photos of herself in the nude to abuse the campaign. Retweeted 348 times, the dispute between two journalists was highly retweeted and took the third place (see Table 8.2). AK Party was the most vociferous party during the abortion debate (611 tweets). The Republican People's Party (CHP) was the second (125 tweets) and the Nationalist Movement Party (MHP) and the BDP played a passive role in the debate (19 and 31 tweets). Of the tweets about abortion, 73% were referenced by the Minister of Health were opposed to the abortion ban. Comments which supported the abortion

Table 8.2 Most Retweeted Content

Content Retweeted	Retweet Number
68,000 women lose their lives every year in countries that banned abortion (@ntv)	607
If you want to know baby's father, please press 1. If you say, that you don't have this kind of daughter, please press 2. For abortion, please press 3! (@acimasiztweet)	498
There is a serious abortion debate, as soon as, catching a chance to undress herself by saying 'my body, my decision'. What does it mean? (@cuneytozdemir)	348

ban were linked to the Minister of Family and Social Policy. Moreover, the conservative argument about the sanctity of the 'family' was used against abortion.

Nursuna Memecan, Minister of Family, Social Policy and the AK Party's women's deputy, could not play a major role in the debate. She was particularly criticised for supporting the Prime Minister's speeches. Amongst non-political people, Ayşe Arman and her articles were the most referenced during the abortion debate on Twitter. Users who opposed the abortion ban referred to Ayşe Arman's articles. Due to his oppositon to the body protest, another journalist, Cuneyt Ozdemir, received a reaction from the Twitter public. Ayşe Arman is the person who is more in touch with women's issues than Memecan. Although CHP had the opportunity to create an agenda against the AK Party as the main opposition party, it was referenced only 11% in the debate.

The Role of Women

Tweets about women were mostly related to the ban; 23% of the tweets which included 'women' as a keyword were related to the ban. The second relation was with 'right' and 'action' due to the protest claims of woman organisations on Twitter. 'Politics' was another intensely used keyword used in connection with 'women'. Basically, users argued that power tried to control women through body politics. Also, Ayse Arman's article drew attention to this kind of power. 'Right' was mostly related to 'feminist' because of the 'abortion is a woman's right' appeal of feminist organisations, columnists and activists. *'rt @sfkfeminist: we organize as "abortion is right platform" a press conference at 11 am in 15 January...'* 'Decision' and 'women' both shared the second place as concepts related to 'feminist'. 'Protest', 'roboski' and 'pregnancy' were also associated with feminist.

'Women' as a keyword was mostly associated with the 'body' concept due to the feminist critique of the government's abortion and contraception policies: *'rt @kadinhaklarimiz: abortion is a women's issue, women's rights issue; nobody including state, government, assembly, erdogan, could not decide, my body, my decision, only me could decide about it'.* 'Decision' is on the second place because of the slogan 'My body, My decision'. Again, Ayşe Arman's article concerning women increased the use of the slogan. 'Right' is another concept mostly associated with 'body' due to the use of the campaign name: Abortion Right campaign. The 'headscarf ban' was mentioned as a body policy of the former government. Therefore, the second party CHP, in opposition to AKP, became the target of this ban. Women's bodies were the political battleground of the abortion debates.

When we analysed the debate based on the 'body' keyword, Özdemir and Arman were the figures and CHP was the party that were mainly mentioned. Cuneyt Ozdemir, a journalist, criticised Ayse Arman's protest by 'exposing' her own body during the campaign. *'rt @cuneytozdemir: there is a serious abortion debate, as soon as, catching a chance to undress herself by saying "my body, my decision" What does it mean?'* Users also tried to emphasise the duplicity of CHP politics, the Kemalist party founded by Mustafa Kemal Atatürk, which supported the headscarf ban because this party was once again involved in the women's debate.

Also, women's organisations which shared and were mentioned in the abortion debate. *Kurtaj_haktır* was the account mostly shared, whereas *sfkfeminist* was the most retweeted account (Table 8.3).

According to the list announced on the campaign website, the abortion campaign has been supported by 372 women's organisations. When tweets with the keyword 'abortion' are focussed, then only ten Twitter accounts were detected between May to July 2012 and December 2012 to January 2013 which shared 101 tweets. These organisations were left-wing political organisations: AmargiDergi (11 tweets), CHPKadinKollari (four tweets), filmmor_ (17 tweets), HakliKadin (one tweet), HalkevciKadin (31 tweets), lambda_istanbul (LGBTI) (one tweet), pembehayat_lgbt (LGBTi) (three tweets), sfkfeminist (five tweets), ucansupurgekff (26 tweets), YeniDemokratKad (two tweets). Out of all the tweets, 33 were retweeted tweets. Twitter use was limited due to women's Twitter account number which shared their tweet with the keyword 'abortion'. On the other hand, the number of tweets of women's organisations constitute 1% (799 tweets) compared to the overall tweets (60,917 tweets). In fact, the campaign signers with high followers had low contributions on Twitter. lambda_istanbul (13,972 followers) shared only one tweet, ucansupurgekff (12,924 followers) shared 26 tweets, sfkfeminist (12,571 followers) shared five tweets with the keyword 'abortion' during the debate. The accounts with a relatively high number of followers have unexpectedly less influence on the abortion debate appearing on Twitter.

This study could dismiss the campaign messages without abortion keywords. Judging by the scarcity of Twitter accounts of women's

Table 8.3 Women's Organisations Twitter Performance

Women Organisation	Message	Followers	Retweet Number
kurtaj_haktir	652	150	–
benim kararım	1	401	–
Kararkadinlarin	6	1.291	15
Kadinhaklarimiz	74	3.005	68
Kadinkolektifi	11	5.609	10
Filmmor	9	7.619	10
Sfkfeminist	38	11.618	94

organisations, the abortion debate is sustained mostly outside of women's organisations and particularly by individuals. Owing to demographic, sociological and economic reasons which create the digital gap – could be a possible subject of another research – organised women's voices are barely represented in the Twittersphere.

The Critical Role of Twitter

Statements of politicians sourced by mainstream media mostly shape the debate surrounding the abortion law on Twitter. This debate creates awareness among women that they can access the public sphere via Twitter in order to voice their opinions. Hence, people use Twitter effectively as a reaction to the body politics which victimised them. Moreover, they can respond instantly to government's arguments through this alternative space, organise campaigns and mobilise demonstrations. While Twitter is not used frequently as a political forum, it is important for making women's ideas, approaches and arguments visible, which historically have been silenced offline in the restricted sphere available to women. The debate on Twitter also played a critical role for the emergence and dissemination of the campaign. In Turkey, a patriarchal system has been encouraged in which women's abilities and opportunities for representation have been restricted by the dominant male discourse on women's issues. Women's feelings and expectations are mostly ignored and some duties (being a mother, being a wife) are exalted by the status quo. According to data of the Turkish Statistical Institute from 2012, the percentage of female politicians in the Grand National Assembly of Turkey was 4.5% in 1935; the percentage had increased to 14.4% in 2012, when only one female minister was in parliament (TÜİK 2013). On the other hand, according to Ministry of Justice data, the number of crimes against women increased by 1,400% from 2002 to 2009 (Bianet 2011). In this political and social climate, women should find other channels in order to proclaim their rights. Despite the large female population (37,671,216 in 2012), the number of women users on Twitter is only 5 million. Although Twitter use/usage has increased by 33% since 2012, the digital gap is still present. Campaign supporters on Twitter examined the issue in the context of women's health, individual preferences and rights. Mostly, they reacted to speeches made by the Prime Minister, the Minister of Health and the Minister of Religious Affairs. Ayse Arman and Cuneyt Özdemir are the persons most spoken of during the debate. Their shared tweets accounted for 40% of the news in the mainstream media. Those who oppose the abortion law criticise government intervention concerning their bodies as well as claims in the shared text on how hard it is for women to decide for an abortion. Both the supporters and opponents of the abortion law share the view that abortion should not be used as a birth control method. On the other hand, claims that the government was trying to manipulate the political agenda were frequently stated on Twitter. Noteworthy accusations stated that the abortion debate was a means of distraction from other important issues, such as the Uludere case (a military airstrike that killed 34 civilians in December 2011, also known as the Uludere massacre), the Syrian War, workers' strikes, the construction of the third bridge in Istanbul, and urban renewal laws. Despite the limited access of women's organisations on Twitter, the discussion of women's issues in this medium is significant for promoting citizen awareness and the mediation of women's rights in the public agenda. According to their Twitter performance, women's organisations need to improve their online activism activities by producing their own content.

Acknowledgement

The research was financially supported by the Scientific Research Projects (BAP) of Kadir Has University.

Note

1 Source: www.tjod.org/turk-jinekoloji-ve-obstetrik-dernegi-tjod-kurtaj-raporu/ (Accessed August 1, 2017).

References

Armstrong, A. (2003). Michel Foucault: Feminism. *Internet Encyclopedia of Philosophy (IEP)*. Accessed August 1, 2017. www.iep.utm.edu/foucfem/.
Benkler, Y. (2006). *The wealth of networks*. New Haven, CT: Yale University Press.
Bessant, J. (2014). The political in the age of the digital: Proposition for empirical investigation. *Politics, 34*(1), 33–44.
Bianet (2011). Kadın Cinayetleri 14 Kat Arttı. Accessed August 1, 2017. http://bianet.org/bianet/kadin/132742-kadin-cinayetleri-14-kat-artti
Brown, W. (1995). States of Injury: power and freedom in late modernity, Princeton, N.J.: Princeton University Press.
Bruns, A., and Burgess, J. (2011). #Ausvotes: How twitter covered the 2010 Australian federal election. *Communication, Politics & Culture, 44*(2), 37–56.
Butler, J. (1990). *Gender trouble and the subversion of identity*. London, UK & New York, NY: Routledge.
Calhoun, C. (2011). Civil society and the public sphere. In M. Edwards (ed.), *The Oxford handbook of civil society* (311–323). New York, NY: Oxford University Press.
Castells, M. (2005). *Ağ Toplumun Yükselişi*. İstanbul, Turkey: Bilgi Üniversitesi Yayınları.
Castells, M. (2012). *Redes de Indignacion y esperanza*. Madrid, Spain: Alianza Editorial.
Christensen, H. S. (2011). Political activities on the internet: 'Slacktivism' or political participation by other means? *First Monday, 16*(2).
Christoforou, S. (2014). Social media and political communication. Hate speech in the age of Twitter. Unpublished Master Thesis, Erasmus University

of Rotterdam. Accessed August 1, 2017. https://thesis.eur.nl/pub/17740/ Christoforou.pdf.

Dahlberg, L. (2001). Computer-mediated communication and the public sphere : A critical analysis. *Journal of Computer-Mediated Communication,* 7(10), 1–30.

Dahlberg, L. (2007). The internet and discursive exclusion: From deliberative to agonistic public sphere theory. In L. Dahlgren, and E. Siapera (eds.), *Radical democracy and the internet* (128–147). London, UK: Palgrave MacMillan.

Dahlgren, P. (2000). The internet and the democratization of civic culture. *Political Communication,* 17(4), 335–40.

Dahlgren, P. (2001). The public sphere and the net: Structure, space and communication. In W. L. Bennett, and R. E. Entman (eds.), *Mediated politics: Communication in the future democracy* (33–55). Cambridge, UK: Cambridge University Press.

Dahlgren, P. (2005). The internet, public spheres and political communication: Dispersion and deliberation. *Political Communication* 22 (2), 147–62.

Downey, J., and Fenton N. (2003). New media, counter publicity and the public sphere. *New Media & Society,* 5(2), 185–202.

Fenton, N., and Downey, J. (2003). Counter public spheres and global modernity. *Javnost–The Public,* 10(1), 15–32.

Fraser, N. (1989). Unruly practices: Power, discourse, and gender in contemporary social theory. *Minneapolis, MI: University of Minnesota Press*

Fraser, N. (1990). Rethinking the public sphere. *Social Text, 25/26,* 56–80.

Fuchs, C. (2014). *Social media. A critical introduction.* London, UK: Sage.

Gerbaudo, P. (2012). Twitler ve Sokaklar, Sosyal Medya ve Günümüzün Eylemciliği. (trans.) Osman Akınhay. İstanbul, Agora.

Gharib, A. (2012). *My body, my decision.* Bianet. Accessed August 1, 2017. http://bianet.org/english/english/138850-my-body-my-decision.

Goulding, A., and Spacey, R. (2003). Women and the information society: Barriers and participation. *IFLA Journal,* 29(1), 33–40.

Habermas, H. (2009). Kamusallığın Yapısal Dönüşümü. (trans.) Tanıl Bora. İstanbul, İletişim.

Hawthorne, S., and Klein, R. (1991). Cyberfeminism: An Introduction. In S. Hawthorne and R. Klein (eds.), CyberFeminism: Connectivity, critique and creativity (1–16). Melbourne: Spinifex.

Himelboim, I., McCreery, S., and Smith, M. (2013). Birds of a feather tweet together: Integrating network and content analyses to examine cross-ideology exposure on twitter. *Journal of Computer-Mediated Communication, 18*(2), 40–60.

Hindman, M. (2009). *The myth of digital democracy.* Princeton, NJ: Princeton University Press.

Howard, P. (2010) *The digital origins of dictatorship and democracy.* Oxford, UK: Oxford University Press.

Kalathil, S., and C. Boas, T. (2003). *Open networks closed regimes.* Washington, DC: Carnegie Endowment For International Peace.

Karaömerlioğlu, M. A. (2016). *Türkiye'de kürtajın kısa tarihi.* Bianet. Accessed August 1, 2017. http://bianet.org/bianet/bianet/139903-turkiye-de-kurtajin-kisa-tarihi.

Maireder, A., and Ausserhofer, J. (2016). Twitter'da Siyasal Söylemler: Ağlaştırma Konuları, Nesneleri ve İnsanları. In K. Weller et al. (eds.), *Twitter ve Toplum* (403–419). İstanbul, Turkey: Kafka.

Mavzer, B. (2013). *Turkish women speak up: My body, my decision.* Accessed August 1, 2017. http://globalvoicesonline.org/2013/02/27/turkish-women-speak-up-my-body-my-decision/.

Morozov, E. (2011). *The net dilusion. The dark side of internet freedom.* Accessed August 1, 2017. https://tropicaline.files.wordpress.com/2011/04/netdelusion.pdf.

Negt, O. and Kluge, A. (1993). *Public sphere and experience: Toward an snalysis of the bourgeois and proletarian public sphere.* (trans.) Peter Labanyi et al. Minneapolis: University of Minnesota Press.

Norris, P. (2001). *Digital divide: Civic engagement, information poverty and the internet worldwide.* Cambridge, UK: Cambridge University Press.

Papacharissi, Z. (2010). *A private sphere: Democracy in a digital age.* Cambridge, UK: Polity Press.

Poster, M. (1995). *CyberDemocracy: Internet and the public sphere.* Accessed August 1, 2017. www.hnet.uci.edu/mposter/writings/democ.html.

Rheingold, H. (2000). *Virtual community: Homesteading in the electronic frontier.* Cambridge, MA: MIT Press.

Salter, M. (2013). Justice and revenge in online counter-publics: Emerging responses to sexual violence in the age of social media. *Crime, Media, Culture, 9*(3), 225–242.

Schmidt, J.-H. (2014): Twitter and the rise of personal publics. In K. Weller, A. Bruns, J. Burgess, M. Mahrt, and C. Puschmann (eds.), *Twitter and society* (3–14). New York, NY: Peter Lang.

Schuster, J. (2013). Invisible feminists? Social media and young women's political participation. *Political Science, 65*(8), 24–31.

Segerberg, A., and Bennett, W. L. (2011). Social media and the organization of collective action: Using twitter to explore the ecologies of two climate change protests. *The Communication Review, 14*(3), 197–215.

Seibert, T. (2012). Anger from women's groups over Turkish abortion-law plan. *The National.* www.thenational.ae/news/world/europe/anger-from-womens-groups-over-turkish-abortion-law-plan.

Sharma, S. (2011). The biopolitical economy of time. *Journal of Communication Inquiry, 35*(4), 439–444.

Shirky, C. (2008). *Here comes everbody: The power of organizing without organizations.* London, UK: Penguin Press.

Sutton, J., and Pollock, S. (2000). Online activism for women's rights. *Cyberpsychology & Behaviour, 3*(5), 699–706.

Şener, G., Zengin S., Özkömürcü, H., and Yıldırım, B. (2013). TBMM'deki Milletvekillerinin Twitter Kullanımı Üzerine Bir Analiz (An analysis on Twitter usage of MPs in Turkish Parliament). *Uluslararası Medya Çalışmaları Sempozyumu,* Akdeniz Üniversitesi.

Turkle, S. (1997). *Life on the screen: Identity in the age of the internet.* New York, NY: Simon and Schuster.

TÜİK. (2013). İstatistiklerle Kadın, 2012. Sayı: 13458, Accessed August 1, 2017. http://www.tuik.gov.tr/PreHaberBultenleri.do?id=13458

UN Report. (2014). *Abortion policies and reproductive health around the world.* New York, NY: United Nations Publication.

Van Zoonen, L. (2002). Gendering the internet: Claims, controversies and cultures. *European Journal of Communication, 17*(1), 5–23.

Warner, M. (2002). Publics and counterpublics. *Public Culture, 14*(1), 49–90.

Webrazzi. (2013). Türkiye'deki Twitter kullanıcılarının sayısı 9.6 milyona ulaştı [infografik]. Accessed August 1, 2017. http://webrazzi.com/2013/02/12/twitter-turkiye-istatistikleri-2013/.

Wimmer, J. (2015). Counter public. In G. Mazzoleni (ed.), *The internet encyclopedia for political communication.* New York et al.: Wiley. doi:10.1002/9781118541555.wbiepc110.

Yardi, S. and Boyd, D. (2010). Dynamic debates: An analysis of group polarization over time on twitter. *Bulletin of Science Technology Society, 30*(5), 316–327.

9 Repeat, Remediate, Resist? Digital Meme Activism in the Context of the Refugee Crisis

Elena Pilipets and Rainer Winter

Introduction: Mediation of Political Activism in the Context of the Refugee Crisis

Since 2015, more than a million people, mostly from the Middle East, crossed into Europe, fleeing war, persecution and poverty in their home countries and sparking a global media discussion on the migrant and refugee crisis. The circulation of countless images of chaos at train stations and border crossings as well as journalistic reports and social media commentary on the overcrowded refugee camps and deaths in the Mediterranean have been fostering this discussion in contradictory ways, creating a division in the public imaginary (Appadurai 1996) over how to deal with the situation. Particularly the Syrian refugee crisis caused by the civil war and the growth of the militant group Islamic State (IS) claiming responsibility for recent terrorist attacks in France, Belgium, Turkey and the United States has become a central media issue and one of the most contentious points of the debate on the EU migration politics. Accompanied by the sharpening of the logic of inclusion and exclusion, the subsequent ambiguity of responses circulating across national borders and various media channels has created a highly contested environment of participation – a 'space of controversy' (Marres 2012) the enactment of which goes far beyond the question of what media represent.

On September 2, 2015, shortly before a series of IS coordinated mass shootings and suicide bombings occurred in Paris, an image of the dead body of Alan (Aylan) Kurdi appeared in social media, triggering a wave of intense personal, political, academic and artistic engagement with the controversy of the crisis. Alan (Aylan) Kurdi, a three-year-old Syrian boy, his mother, brother and other passengers in the inflatable boat that capsized in the Mediterranean Sea drowned while trying to reach the Greek Island of Kos. Turkish journalist Nilüfer Demir took a series of photographs of the bodies that were found washed up on the beach at Bodrum, of which one instantly went viral. The paradox of this particular photographic image is that, apart from the tragedy it *actually represents*, the impact of the ways in which it *became representative* of the entire crisis derives from *what it did* by means of the everyday media practices it set into motion.[1] The new 'relations of relevance' (Marres 2012, 145) it has given rise to in the course of its transnational and transmedia unfolding, for instance, by transforming the dominant narrative in social media discussions from that on migrants to that on refugees (D'Orazio 2015), continue to intervene in the world's (re)actions, revealing the controversy of political participation as dispersed among a variety of social, institutional, cultural and technical actors.

In the conclusion to the *Iconic Image on Social Media: A Rapid Research Response to the Death of Aylan Kurdi** performed by the researches of Visual Social Media Lab (2015), Olga Goriunova and Farida Vis address the changed conditions of how such images spread and what political and cultural forces they acquire with regard to new forms of viral visuality and its analytical challenges:

> Our kind of writing therefore is both intense and porous. [...] On the one hand, we, the authors, hope that we can do something, with words, and on the other hand, we feel quickly overpowered, with flows of events and political forces attempting to wrench what has been our focus out of sight. This is the nature of the rapid response: two months after the spread of the images of the body of Aylan on the Turkish beach shocked the world – leading to the large-scale, even though momentary, mobilization of publics to welcome and help those that were now addressed as refugees instead of migrants – new stories began to arise in the aftermath of the Paris terrorist attacks. [...] the tragic images of Aylan Kurdi were and continue to be used by different actors to achieve different ends. What we learned is that as forcefully shocking as they are in themselves, the images were efficient because they fit the visual canon we're trained in and move efficiently between contexts.
>
> (Goriunova and Vis 2015, 71)

Collective dynamics behind the capacity of viral media images to transform in their movement from context to context inform an important dimension of today's media and cultural activism the authors of the research report address under conditions of the 'visual-political and socio-affective regimes of today' (Goriunova 2015, 5). Drawing on the findings of the report, we will continue to explore the intensified ambiguity of political participation that has evolved with the widespread use of mobile visual and social media by looking at currently proliferating 'refugee memes'. Even though mostly associated with more ordinary, practices of slactivism or networking 'without a cause' (Joyce 2010; Gournelos and Gunkel 2011; Lovink 2012; Telofski 2012), participatory activities behind the circulation, replication and mutation of the memes become crucial when it comes to the ways in which we engage with conflictual phenomena. This is reflected by the resonating visions of migration the memes revive and foster in the context of social media debates on the refugee crisis, often in terms of simple binary opposi- tions, often as a variety of 'preposterous, uncultured, weird, humorous and "silly" expressions' (Goriunova 2014, 55). Precisely because of their persistent presence in our everyday media practice, the ambiguous ways in which the memes employ popular culture for public commentary (Milner 2013) acquire their ability to provoke change and need to be ad- dressed within a wider web of social, political and cultural connections.

In what follows, we suggest to discuss the affective temporality of their impact (1), their spatially distributed transcontextuality (2) and their complexly organised human-nonhuman agency (3) through a multiperspective, interdisciplinary approach of mediation.[2] Developed in the context of contemporary media theory and critical media and cultural studies, this approach opens up useful perspectives on follow- ing both the material and semiotic eventfulness of social life within an ongoing process of difference production, which is restricted nei- ther to the singular control of the human nor to the linear effects tech- nology has on society (Bolter and Grusin 1999; Lash and Lury 2007; Loon 2008; Parikka and Sampson 2009; Grossberg 2010; Grusin 2010; Kember and Zylinska 2012). Instead, it is orientated towards 'topological' questions to explore "how relations of continuity and dis- continuity are being made and unmade by describing the emergence of new kinds of connectivity" (Lury et al. 2012, 6). Using a combination of analytical perspectives from actor-network-theory (Latour 2005), Deleuze and Guattari's theory of relational becoming (1987, 1980) and anthropology of moving objects (Appadurai 1986), it emphasises the al- ways already relational, 'co-constitutive' (Kember and Zylinska 2012, 155) and heterogeneous aspect of agency, focusing on the contextually mutating forces behind the everyday politics of our lived experiences with and through media.

Repeat: Why Memes? Affect and Temporality of Meme Activism

Coincident with the viral mobilisation of the image of Alan (Aylan) Kurdi in September 2015, a variety of resonating narratives and images of ref- ugees emerged on social media, indirectly undermining or reinforcing the impact of the image in different contexts. On sites like 4chan, red- dit, Tumblr, Twitter or Facebook, some of them have found expression in populist memes circulated by far-right groups across Europe, United States and Canada. Suggesting that refugees either are 'invading' the receiving countries for terrorism or that they are undeserving because they themselves caused the conflict that they are fleeing (Thelwall 2015). Most of these memes are centred around nationalist hate, anti-Islamic propaganda and fear mongering which, in turn, attracts criticism from refugee supporters, mobilising a series of oppositional reactions within an ongoing feedback loop.

The recurrent temporality and 'ubiquity of the visual' (Highfeld and Leaver 2016, 49) within contemporary social media practices shape the dynamics of viral meme activism as part of what Richard Grusin (2010) describes as 'the affective life of our media everyday' in the climate of post-9/11 global (media) terror. The notion of effect he draws upon in the context of 'non-representational turn' (Thrift 2008) stands for 'packets of sensations and relations [...] that go beyond those who live through them (they become other)' (Deleuze 1995, 137). From this perspective, affects are not reducible to the emotional perceptions of an individual subject but circulate and can be 'attached to things, people, ideas, sensations, relations, activities, ambitions, institutions, and any other number of other things, including other affects' (Sedgwick 2003, 19). Understood in Spinozan-Deleuzian sense as 'the property of the active outcome of an encounter' (Thrift 2008, 178), the capacity of affect to circulate across contemporary media environments structures 'encounters as series of modifications' (ibid., 179) arising from the relations between human and nonhuman practices 'which may be more or less adequate and more or less empowering' (ibid.).

In this chapter, we will explore the increasing political ambiguity of viral meme activism through the capacity of digital memes to mobilise affect. Digital memes are serialised material-semiotic text-image re-enactments that move and change within the dynamics of mediation and connectivity, spreading beyond the boundaries of their original content, contexts and media through practices of everyday use and affective investment.[3] Following one of the most frequently used definitions by Limor Shifman (2013, 7–8), they come to work as 'a group of digital items that: (a) share common characteristics of content, form, and/or stance; (b) are created with awareness of each other; and (c) are circulated, imitated, and transformed via internet by multiple users'. The viral flows of engagement behind their 'always-active' character, as Ryan M. Milner suggests drawing on Liesbet van Zoonen (2005), are in their very form populist to the same extent as they are polyvocal, allow left-wing as well as right-wing sentiments, balance the familiar and the foreign, and therefore simultaneously enrich and complicate the notion of participation (Milner 2013, 2359–2362). A meme, therefore, as emphasised by Olga Goriunova, is not only content, but a collective behaviour, 'or rather systems of human-technical performances' that emerge from 'multiple sites, agents and ecologies which dynamically interlock to form networks that propel its coming into being' (Goriunova 2014, 56). Together, these 'techno-aesthetic methods of becoming [...], however stereotypical and imitative it might be' (Goriunova 2014, 57), prepare the way for mediation of controversy, opening repeated practices of meme activism to all kinds of variation and internet anomaly (Parikka and Sampson 2009; Sampson 2012) that can be used to anti-democratic ends as well as to provoke temporal subversions.

Due to the dynamics of repeated variation that shape both their content and the ways they move from context to context within everyday practices of media use, the memes transform and are transformed in a 'complex and overlapping network of heterogeneous feedback loops' (Grusin 2010, 97). Based on practices of 'coupling, doubling, replication, imitation and more or less independent distribution' (Maeder and Wentz 2014, 130), they increase their affective value as they are repeated. In doing so, the memes develop a specific serialised temporality that intensifies their capacity to affect further adaptations in the future by reworking visual and textual variations created in the past through practices of appropriation in the present. In this way, the 'prospective' (Shifman 2014) affectivity of engagement behind the mundane practices of meme activism works to make up what Grusin addresses as 'mediaphilia of anticipation' or 'premediation' (2010). By that, he means an affective and performative state of relations that marks our interactions with visual social media in a society of securitisation and control.

Dependent upon constant iteration and seriation, mediation of anticipation produces a 'temporality which is always divided, oriented towards both the immediate moment and the very near future' (Grusin 2010, 129). Inscribed in contagious virality of the memes, this anticipatory temporality "sometimes creates a heightened sense of alertness, while at other times [...] it generates a muted or low-level affect of waiting or passing time" (ibid.). Popular meme generators and databases materialise this experience by providing user-friendly and readily available platforms in which image macros 'awaiting witty captioning or visual manipulation are presented alongside banks of "exemplary" existing meme versions' (Shifman 2014, 354). Thus, for example, the popular 'imminent Ned' meme that is commonly used to warn of the impending arrival of 'winter' or other highly anticipated events creates its refugee variations with the German Chancellor Angela Merkel in the leading role by modifying Ned Stark's 'Brace yourself, [...] is coming'-template from the HBO TV-series *Game of Thrones*. [4] Yet, while maintaining this playful form of securitisation through reproduction of familiar popular culture imagery, the viral dynamics of 'anticipation and connection' (Grusin 2010, 128) that set the products and practices of meme activism into motion simultaneously partake in the development of a wider affective state. Within the 'premediated everyday' (ibid.) of a global media environment defined by 'too much connectivity' (van Dijk 2006), it fosters relations in which the separation between fact and fiction, the everyday and the anomalous event is increasingly difficult to reconcile (Parikka and Sampson 2009).

By showing how, in response to the ongoing war on terror since the shock of 9/11, socially networked global media circulate collective affects of anticipation, while also perpetuating low levels of apprehension or fear, Grusin outlines the main paradox of premediation: 'What premediation strives for is not to prevent future catastrophes but to prevent those catastrophes from having been unanticipated to protect us from being caught unawares and shocked' (2010, 176) so that we will be able to deal with the uncertainties of the future.

Referring to Jasbir Puar's work on terrorist assemblages (2007), he challenges the assumption of the signifying forces (positive versus negative images) of media representation by outlining the affective modalities of repetition, movement and transformation as part of the workings of premediation 'to catch a small hold of many futures, to invite futurity even as it refuses to script it' (Puar 2007, xix; Grusin 2010, 176). In calling attention to the forces of affectivity within the present political order of control and securitisation, he emphasises that 'if premediation is to have political agency it will be not chiefly a question of how premediation represents politics or is represented politically' but a question of 'political uses that humans and nonhumans, individually and collectively, make of it' (Grusin 2010, 141). It is from this perspective that we approach meme activism in the context of the refugee crisis, arguing that the rapid proliferation of refugee memes informs multiple articulations of its controversy, participating in 'a kind of temporality of premeditation in which the future impinges on the present' (ibid., 18) through remediation of prior media and cultural forms.

Remediate: Context, Movement, Transformation

Relations of affectivity behind viral spread of the internet memes are central to the controversial ways in which the images of refugees have been mobilised in response to political interests across various media, national borders and cultural practices. Situated in everyday interactions with networked social environments, the capacity of the memes to travel and change is determined not only by the specificity of each context they pass through but by the various articulatory forces and affects they accumulate in the course of their movement. The in-between dynamics of mediation that foster this movement through both narrative and navigational practices of everyday media use (Lash and Lury 2007; Maeder and Wentz 2014) are particularly interesting in their collective tendency to produce difference through what Bruno Latour (2005) calls 'translation' of material and semiotic relations from 'stage to stage, context to context' (Lash and Lury 2007, 16). Describing the premediation of affective potentialities of visual social media from this perspective, Richard Grusin emphasises the simultaneous forces of redistributed creation or 'remediation' of media images that come to work 'not just by reproducing meaning' (2010, 6) but by actively transforming relations between human, social and technical practices. To ensure the work of *pre*mediation, the logic of *re*mediation seeks both 'to erase mediation and to proliferate it in the practice of reforming or refashioning prior media forms' (Grusin 2010, 58). In doing so, it reworks multiple elements of a hybrid human-media assemblage 'in the service of establishing a territory' (Deleuze and Guattari 1987 [1980], 376) in which they 'coalesce and then regroup in changing but relatively stable formations' (Grusin 2010, 170).

Within this two-fold dynamic of assembling and reassembling the everyday eventfulness of media culture, the memes, along with other media objects circulating on the web, can be seen as transforming within and between a variety of situational relations – public and private, online and offline, fictional and non-fictional, local and global, semiotic and material, human and nonhuman. Following Jane Bennett's definition of an assemblage, such relations have an 'uneven topography' creating a 'living, throbbing grouping whose coherence coexists with energies and countercultures that exceed and confound it' (2005, 445). Shaping and channelling the contributions of heterogeneous actors while they are simultaneously being made, unmade and remade in their collective activities, practices of meme activism deploy the polysemic 'intertextuality' (Fiske 1987) of popular culture across multiple contexts of lived experience and media use (Winter 2007, 2010). Accordingly, their intrinsic 'polyvocality' (Milner 2013) becomes part of what cultural studies analyse in terms of articulation (Williams 1974; Hall 1981; Grossberg 1997) to emphasise that the question of relevance of cultural and media practice is more about the processes of meaning *making* than about the meaning itself.[5] Due to their operational processuality (Lash and Lury 2007; Shifman 2014), in which the overlapping relations between content and contexts constantly create new variations, the memes help to understand the contested political relevance of today's media assemblages as both the product of and as something that contributes to the process of articulation of its controversy.

To grasp the dynamic transcontextuality behind the circulation of images attached to social media activism in the context of the refugee crisis, we focused on the affective resonances between #refugeeswelcome and #refugeesnotwelcome movements provoked by the spread of refugee memes on Facebook and Twitter in September 2015. Arguing that the contradictory dynamics that fostered the spread of the memes were informed by multiple contextual articulations, we applied the methodological approach of 'following the object' (Appadurai 1986; Latour 2005; Lash and Lury 2007) that aims to reassemble the collective workings of mediation behind the ways the memes move and 'become reflexive in their self-modification over a range of territories, a range of environments' (Lash and Lury 2007, 5). By querying, collecting and comparing visual and textual data material through Twitter Search and Google Image Scraper (Digital Methods Initiative 2016) using the keywords *refugees welcome, refugee crisis, refugees not welcome, refugee memes* and *refugees* in the period from 1 to 30 September and by using the interactive network graphs created with the help of OSoME (Observatory on Social Media 2016) to visualise the contradictory co-occurrence of the hashtags #refugeeswelcome and #refugeesnotwelcome in the same period of time, we explored the appearance of the memes on different media platforms and the affects they triggered in the course of their circulation.

On September 3, 2015, one day after the image of Alan (Aylan) Kurdi went viral and two months before the terrorist attacks occurred in Paris, a side-by-side image allegedly showing an IS fighter as a Syrian refugee was posted on Facebook by Peter Lee Goodchild – a British social media blogger who, according to his current self-description on Twitter, identifies himself as an 'anti EU/anti Islam/political rebel'.[6] On the left side of the image a bearded man wearing camouflage and military gear holds a weapon in his hand. On the right side, a similar-looking man is shown 'at the Macedonian border' wearing sunglasses, a backpack and a T-shirt saying, 'Thank you'. The accompanying message that has received more than 70,000 shares, 7,000 likes and 2,500 comments within a short period of time completes the post in a sarcastic manner: 'Remember this guy? Posing in ISIS photos last year – now he's a "refugee" Are we suckers or what!' (Bartlett 2015).

Interestingly enough, though the earlier versions of the very same image already were addressed as deliberately misleading in other national contexts, its viral image macro-variations informing about the 'terrorist' past and the 'refugee' present of the man shown in the picture in different languages continued to circulate on Twitter, creating anti-Islamist hashtags such as #jihadfugees.[7] In the course of its circulation the geographical belongings of the image were changing as well. Re-shared by one of the German PEGIDA-leaders on August 30 with the link to an article on welt.de titled 'The Next Big Battlefield is Europe' (Hackensberger 2015), one of its variations introduced the very same 'ISIS fighter posing as refugee in Germany' even before it gained popularity in British anti-Islamist circles. On September 7, the image was prominently debunked in a BBC story that focuses on Goodchild apologizing for misrepresentation of the man shown in the photograph (Wendling 2015): Laith Al Saleh, a former Free Syrian Army rebel commander who claimed to fight against both IS as well as Syrian government troops in an interview with the Associated Press, was already profiled by the news agency on August 17 after he had arrived on the Greek island of Kos where the 'refugee part' of the photo-montage used on Facebook and Twitter was taken (Paphitis and Bennett 2015).

The photo that was published in the Atlantic report on the current situation of Syrian refugees the same day (Taylor 2015) was the one to become a viral image that had its first prominent appearance on Croatian Facebook on August 22.[8] Shared in a patriotic group Priznajem! Hrvat Sam from where it spread to the accounts of far-right German PEGIDA movements to transform into a photo-based meme superimposed with text in different languages, it introduces Laith Al Saleh on the 'Macedonian border' as one of the 'evil men invading Europe' with 2,800 shares and 2,700 likes appearing to be one of the first steps in the ongoing terrorist-refugee-before-after-feedback-loop.[9] Later variations of the image, no matter how often it was debunked in various national contexts, continued to be posted by right-wing politicians on Twitter and Facebook just to be retracted afterwards with statements that emphasised the need for 'detailed refugee screening'.[10] In addition, on September 9, a series of similar 'before-after' Facebook images presenting Laith Al Saleh and other men as 'refugees in Europe' appeared in a reportage of the Moscow-based international news channel RT as part of the Hungary's public broadcasting channel M1 story on 'at least two terrorists that were uncovered by Hungarian special forces via photographs on social media'. Though the RT reportage mentions that, with the exception of Laith al Saleh, the identities of other men in the images have not been clarified, it also emphasises that 'either way there are almost certainly individuals, who have belonged to terrorist groups in the past'.[11]

As we can see in relation to the ways its 'truthfulness' or 'untruthfulness' was constructed and deconstructed in different contexts, the viral image was working to present an impending catastrophe of 'terrorist invasion' as pre-mediated and distributed across various media platforms and national contexts. Moreover, as outlined below, it was not the image itself but the double presenting of 'the past' and 'the present' typical for photo-based meme genres (Shifman 2014) that was about to become the main focus of attention and the basis for further memetic appropriations and problematisations. The non-directionality of response and the immediate spreadability of socially and institutionally fostered rumours surrounding it in the course of its circulation transformed the image into an important visual participant within a sharply divided social media debate. Connected to the fact that Laith Al Saleh used to fight against IS with Free Syrian Army, it was centred on the possibility of 'terrorists' that were also addressed as 'militants' or 'males of fighting age' coming into Europe as part of the refugee flow.[12] Mobilizing affective reactions for individual expressions of threat, disgust, anxiety and hate or generalised political claims about whether national borders should be defended or opened and by or for whom: this debate was influenced by two main competing political visions on migration. In order to specify the complex relations of mediation between the two, we focused on memetic images that were attached to the proliferation of #refugeeswelcome and #refugeesnotwelcome hashtags on Twitter in September 2015. There, the controversy of the division in pro- and contra-refugee atmosphere found expression in a surprisingly frequent co-occurrence of the hashtags #refugeesnotwelcome and #refugeeswelcome that, accompanied by #stoptheinvasion, #saveeurope, #securetheborders, #hateoftheyear, #whitegenocide or #iamnorefugee, which were used in the same tweets to maintain the collective affects of confusion and anxiety. Connecting individual users with organised anti-refugee movements, news sources and institutional actors either by retweeting particular pieces of (mis-)information or by co-mentioning influential political figures in offensive contexts, the September 2015 #refugeesnotwelcome network employed memes to create negative, disturbing and cynical associations with its significantly more powerful #refugeeswelcome opponent.[13]

Along with the images of Laith Al Saleh and other men 'posing as refugees in Europe', the most frequently used meme in this overlapping media assemblage was the 'terrorist'-adaptation of the iconic immigration road and 'refugees welcome' sign showing the silhouette of a running family equipped with weapons and proclaiming, 'terrorists welcome'. Accompanied by its 'islamists not welcome'- and 'refugees not welcome'-variations, another frequently occurring theme was the one pointing out that most of the refugees are either 'young military-aged men' and 'invaders' or just 'cowards' leaving their women and children behind in the war zones to deal 'with whatever they are running from'. The third series of memetic response that, just as the image of Laith Al Saleh, was circulated by the anti-refugee movements under both pro- and anti-refugee hashtags are centred around another 'pose'. Showing in a self-contradicting way not only male but also female refugees making selfies with their smartphones when they reach land, it makes use of an even more cynical form of critique, implying that these are rich tourists rather than real victims of tragedy. Mutually reinforcing each other's impact, all these images worked in similar ways to maintain and establish an ongoing affective feedback loop in which the populist nature of controversy could be intensified by provoking further reactions. A prominent part of this feedback loop is an often-cited Vice Magazine article by Philip Kleinfeld titled 'Calling Bullshit on the Anti-Refugee Memes Flooding the Internet' that was published on September 10, 2015. It analyses a series of obviously faked photo-based memes from a number of far-right British Facebook pages such as EDL (English Defence League), Britain First or PEGIDA UK, addressing those responsible as 'racist jerks cranking up the meme generators', which, in turn, continues to provoke not only enthusiasm on the side of the refugee supporters but also further racist attacks directed against refugees and the author of the article himself.[14]

At the same time, the much more densely connected #refugeeswelcome network, which in the first half of September was dominated by photo-documentations of protest events and both friendly and unfriendly variations of the Alan (Aylan) Kurdi image (Vis and Goriunova 2015), continued to circulate the same memetic material. Yet, in addition to the memes described above, it also provided their counter-variations that both reflected on and worked against the #refugeesnotwelcome-program, remediating the 'now and then' logic of the anti-refugee memes by means of bricolage, satire and multiple pop culture references. One of the most prominent examples that was working to reverse the affect of connectivity behind the relational sprawl of the memes for purposes of subversion was designed as a look-alike of the 'terrorist posing as refugee' theme. Equipped with the logos of the two most influential British far-right movements, Britain First and the English Defence League, that both promote Islamophobic views it declares:

> This Muslim convert ISIS soldier is pictured here on a boat crossing from Syria to Greece on 23/08/15. The second picture is the same Muslim-convert ISIS soldier pictured in a block of high rise flats in Balsall Heath, Birmingham on 13/09/15. They're here. Don't say we didn't warn you. Please share to help stop this happening!

The 'before' image from the 2005 comedy *Are We There Yet* featuring US rapper and actor Ice Cube, sitting in a kayak with a life jacket under the caption 'fleeing Syria' along with the 'now' image captioned 'ready for war' that shows him with a gun in his early days with the hip hop crew N.W.A. complete the meme.

The resulting 'ISIS' Cube meme that started to circulate on Facebook after it was posted by Micky Williams on September 15 'to basically mock people who consistently share anti-refugee propaganda' (Hopkins 2015) is particularly telling of what misunderstanding political participation might result i as it was not only shared by those who understood the joke but also by those who misunderstood it by taking it seriously. On Twitter, the meme was reposted the same day as a screenshot of a UKIP Facebook account where it was introduced with the comment: 'this is a refugee who is living in the UK now!!!!' under #refugeesnotwelcome.[15] Retweeted 4.296 times with 2.373 likes, it started a lively discussion among refugee supporters creating ironic hashtags such as #brainsnotwelcome, #whensatirebackfires, #StraightOuttaSyria or #RefugeezWithAttitude. Further blurring the line between reality and fiction, even more 'terrorist-refugee' variations starring Dwayne Johnson 'entering UK on a Jet Ski', Sylvester Stallone 'posing for ISIS', Arnold Schwarzenegger 'now seeking asylum', Kenneth Williams 'planning Halal and Sharia attacks' and an 'ISIS lion' who 'came from Africa for a better life in London Zoo' were psoted as satirical responses after the meme was shared on the activist far-right Facebook parody page *Britain Furst* on September 16.[16] The page that works mainly by distributing memes using remix and irony for critique remediates the ambiguous workings of the 'logic of lulz' (Coleman

2011; Milner 2013) – or 'lols', an abbreviation for 'laughing out loud' – typical for subcultural image boards such as 4chan and reddit. This logic resonates with the politics of provocation or 'dètournement' popularised by Guy Debord and the Situationist International and used by culture jammers and online activists to grab attention to the constructedness or absurdity of dominant political attitudes (Lasn 1999; Kahn and Kellner 2005) through 'mocking the process of stereotyping by taking it to its extreme' (Shifman 2014, 350). Effective in its capacity to provoke affective response but not unproblematic in its openness to further 'hyper-humorous, hyper-ironic, hyper-distanced' (Milner 2013) adaptations, it works by 'rerouting spectacular images, environments, ambiences and events to reverse or subvert their meaning, thus reclaiming them' (Lasn 1999, 103).

Accordingly, the affect of 'networked laughter' (Rentschler and Thrift 2015) accompanying the counter-variations of anti-refugee memes in their movement across a variety of media platforms and national contexts worked in a double sense of reinforcing and complicating the technological, social and cultural conditions of participatory critique. Directed against racism, connected through the use of specific hashtags and intensified by countless lols, it opened the binary logic of inclusion and exclusion to alternative possibilities of how people feel about the dominant affective state of fear and anticipation that Grusin (2010) describes under conditions of post 9/11 premediation of the ongoing war on terror. Yet, at the same time, the practices of the very same network 'tied to finding shared humor and enjoyment through co-participation in the joke' (Rentschler and Thrift 2015, 10) necessarily continued the work of *re*mediation (Bolter and Grusin 1999) essential for the state of *pre*mediation (Grusin 2010) to be maintained. Mobilizing 'affective feedback loops in conjunction with our everyday media forms and practices' (ibid., 97) by making them fun and easily available to further articulations of protest and critique, the logic of lulz that was implied by the activist practices to subvert the sprawl of anti-refugee memes was constantly engaged in questioning its own political potential as part of a larger media assemblage. While it was helping to cope with the omnipresent media accounts of the threats posed by global terrorism through ironical dètournement of prior forms of its ongoing mediation, in the very act of multiplying its alternative visions it was not only fostering the affectivity of anticipation but also working to erase all evidence of how the dominant logic of securitisation and control operates within the controversy of the refugee crisis.

Resist? Digital Meme Activism and the Question of Political Agency

Based on the analysis of affective relations between cultural, social and technological practices through which viral image memes have been mobilised in response to various political interests in the context of refugee crisis, this chapter has explored the intensified ambiguity of political participation from the perspective of mediation. Rather than concentrate on exposing the evidence of power in structures of symbolic representation, mediation of affect has been discussed in its capacity to bring into focus the question of agency as distributed across an emergent environment of 'technological forms of life' (Lash 2002) that shapes our ordinary activities with digital technologies. Investigating material and semiotic contributions of both human and nonhuman actors within and between a variety of social and cultural contexts (Winter 2010, 19–22), we approached this environment as an assemblage 'that is not governed by a central power' (Bennett 2005, 445) but articulated through relatively stable temporal and spatial connections of heterogeneous elements. In the process of their circulation and exchange, these elements 'tend to fluctuate or perhaps overlap at various nodes or crossings' (Grusin 2010, 170), creating contagious viral visual media experiences.

In order to describe their constitutive transcontextuality, we drew on the notion of articulation developed within the frameworks of media and cultural studies (Williams 1974; Hall 1981; Grossberg 1997) and actor-network theory (Latour 2005; Marres 2012). From this hyprid perspective, both technological and cultural practices are understood in terms of 'contingent connections between heterogeneous elements [...] that need to be addressed in their dynamic contextual relations' (Winter 2010, 20). Focusing on the dynamics of repeated variation of the refugee memes in their circulation across different platforms in September 2015, we especially emphasised the necessity of exploring the co-emergence of their affective and performative forces.

In particular, we were trying to understand how the memes assemble and re-assemble themselves in the dual sense of being worked on (through repeated practices of attachment and detachment, use and differentiation) and actively working (as heterogeneous modes of viral contagion and redistributed creation). By following their relational movements as part of repetition of the 'affective life of our media everyday' (Grusin 2010, 118), we concentrated on the capacity of the memes to intervene in continuities and discontinuities of mediated experiences that constitute the post 9/11 state of relations in the context of current Syrian refugee crisis. In doing so, we could show how this state operates through ongoing remediation of relations of anticipation and connectivity in a society of securitisation, the main purpose of which, as Grusin suggests, is 'to make sure that no matter what tomorrow might bring, it will always feel as if it had already been premediated' (2010, 47).

As we have discussed earlier, the complex collective agency of activist practices behind the circulation of refugee memes was simultaneously reinforcing and undermining the affective forces of premediation. The remediation of their controversial material-semiotic outcome used by different actors to promote their own interests continues to unfold in multiple contexts of media use that have diverging spatial and temporal dynamics but can be approached only 'in resonance' with each other – in their collective capacity to 'recapitulate the same event in different ways' (Massumi 2002, 33). The main feature of meme activism can thus be seen through its repetitive eventfulness that continuously produces new affective relations, though the new constantly performs in the context of the familiar, creating what Inka Salovaara in her analysis of #JeSuisCharlie activism (2015) addresses as an assemblage that connects territory, historical moment as well as human and nonhuman actors. Under these conditions, the constitutive paradox of 'networked resistance' (Winter 2010), of which meme activism is an important and active part, is that its political potential can be nothing that is already known, decided upon a priori or premediated (Hall et al. 2010). Considering that it is derived not only from our everyday activities *with* media but also distributed *across* globally networked technologies that increasingly 'encourage mobility and the proliferation of transactions of transportation, communication and mediation' (Grusin 2010, 123), its participatory qualities are radically contingent. Accordingly, the situational breakthroughs of what Richard Kahn and Douglas Kellner call 'global/local technopolitics' (2005) can be empowering and democratic in some contexts, while in others they might continue to contribute to the workings of securitisation and control.

An essential part of this paradox, as Stefka Hristova similarly observes in her analysis of the Occupy activism (2014), is the inherent tendency of the memes to rework controversial political issues into cultural polysemy. Making use of Bernard Harcourt's Foucault-inspired distinction between civil and political disobedience (2012), she shows how practices of meme activism can take up the position of neutralising their own political potential. On the one hand, the performative and affective dynamics of repeated variation that are fundamental to the spread of digital memes foster the emergence of 'viral political dissent' (Hristova 2014, 273), emphasising the role that civil disobedience plays in the shaping of politics as everyday media practice. On the other hand, by using popular strategies of parody, satire and irony to demonstrate the injustice of the system, the memes neutralise their capacity to "resist() to the very ways in which we are governed" (Harcourt 2011, s.p.). Due to the repetitive dynamics of the everyday invested into their circulation from context to context, the memes provoke disruptions to the same extent as they provide a 'safe space in which […] images of repression are rendered mundane and even humorous, assuring the central and the commonsense primary purpose of the state to defend itself against internal and external threats' (Hristova 2014, 273).

The fact that both pro- and anti-refugee memes continue to be circulated in social media debates on the possibility of terrorists entering Europe highlights the ambigous ways in which the anticipatory affectivity of today's networked media practices is coupled with the framework of securitisation. It's 'contagious relationality' (Sampson 2012, 12) unfolds both pre- and re-mediated aspects of participation as a 'double movement of containment and resistance' (Hall 1981, 228). Unlike opposition, this relational movement also involves hybridisations as well as the questioning of boundaries that underlie the logic of 'preemptive modulation of action potential' (Massumi 2015, 86) in both temporal and spatial terms. Drawing together affect, meaning and practice, it is embedded in an ongoing transition from where tensions in current participatory politics emerge. As Lawrence Grossberg has noted, regarding its dynamic conditions: 'What was resistant can be contained, perhaps later to escape and become resistant again [...] what resists over here, is contained over there'. (2010, 209)

Notes

1 The workings behind the paradox agency of the image also affected the use of the boy's name. While Alan was the actual name of the boy, the name Aylan emerged in attachment to the image and collective practices behind its global circulation. According to Goriunova and Vis, the problem is

> that the images spread as the ones depicting Aylan [...]. The events of transformation triggered by the images are related to the wrong spelling of the child's name both in human and in technical memory, much of which is now hard to change.
>
> (2015, 71)

2 The authors refer to the concept of mediation that has been developed either outside of or as an alternative to the framework of the concept of mediatisation (e.g. Krotz 2007; Hepp et al. 2015; for the discussion of both concepts in relation to each other see Couldry 2008; Livingstone 2009; Hartmann 2010). Unlike the concept of mediatisation that tends to describe the workings of media as a metaprocess – 'a single "media logic" that is simultaneously transforming the whole of social space at once' (Couldry 2008, 375) – the concept of mediation encourages us to look at the nonlinearity, discontinuity and asymmetry of this process in terms of multiple entangled processes of differentiation (Kember and Zylinska 2012, 155, see Chapter 2). Focusing on specific questions about the transformation of practices in and between specific contexts through investment of both human and nonhuman agency, it describes 'the complex foldings of technological components with other aspects of social and cultural reality' (Parikka and Sampson 2009, 5).

3 Most definitions of digital memes are derived from Richard Dawkins' (1976) and Susan Blackmore's (2000) memetics, where the meme is discussed as a unit of cultural information that is able to spread analogous to the genetic principles of fidelity, fecundity and longevity. In this chapter we draw on Tony Sampson's critique of the deterministic neo-Darwinian logic that is attached to this tradition (2012, 61–97), suggesting instead to explore the affective and performative conditions of social relationality behind the viral workings of the memes.

4 Sources: http://knowyourmeme.com, http://memegenerator.net, http://
lolworthy.com and http://9gag.com. (all accessed August 1, 2017).
5 According to Lawrence Grossberg, 'articulation is [...] the methodological
face of a radically contextualist theory. It describes a nonlinear expansive
practice of drawing lines, of mapping connections' (1997, 260).
6 See https://twitter.com/peterpanohno (accessed August 1, 2017). Though
the original post is no longer available on Facebook, it continues to circulate
across different official and unofficial news websites. In an interview with
BBC News Goodchild apologised 'for getting the facts wrong' after he was
blocked out of his Facebook account.
7 The German story on debunking PEGIDA (Patriotische Europäer gegen
die Islamisierung des Abendlandes) variations of the image that were re-
shared from one of the Croatian patriotic Facebook pages on August 30,
2015 was published in a Facebook screen-shot album titled 'Fälschungen'
(Fakes) by a German anti-PEGIDA group and is accessible under www.
facebook.com/Zugespielt/photos/a.1603991229852725.1073741838.
1575736682678180/1603991393186042/?type=1&theater (01.07.2017). One
of the examples of the right-wing Twitter-mobilisation of the image in the
German context shared under #jihadfugees and #fluechtlinge on September
2, 2015 is accessible under https://twitter.com/hashtag/Jihadfugees?src=hash
(accessed August 1, 2017).
8 The post from the Croatian patriotic group Priznaem! Hrvat Sam
from August 22 that was reshared by Pegidanorth the same day is
available under www.facebook.com/priznajem.HRVATsam/photo
s/a.138572839557155.35858.138368646244241/871156096298822/?-
type=1&theater (01.07.2017).
9 Before the image appeared on Facebook, it already started to circulate
on Twitter. According to Twitter image search, the first Tweet featuring
the image of 'the militant commander' Laith al Saleh '/On the way to the
Nederland/' appeared on August 17, 2015 without any reference to IS from
where it was reshared twice https://twitter.com/search?f=images&verti-
cal=default&q=Laith%20Al%20Saleh%20&src=typd (accessed August 1,
2017). The image gained more popularity on Tweeter after it was debunked
in the BBC story described above.
10 A Canadian example of such postings comes from the conservative candidate Peter Kent who retweeted the image commenting on September 8, 2015:
'These then and now pix chilling reminders why prudent/detailed refugee
screening essential.' The Twitter debate around this can be accessed under:
https://twitter.com/KentThornhillMP/status/641287892443209728 (accessed
August 1, 2017). In Austria it was the FPÖ chef Heinz Strache on September
9 with a similar comment that can be accessed under: https://twitter.com/
fpoeticker/status/641556952024260608 (accessed August 1, 2017). Afterwards, both politicians were sharply criticised for the use of unreliable sources.
11 More on the RT-report under: https://www.rt.com/news/314788-hungary-
migrants-isis-terrorists/ (accessed August 1, 2017).
12 Examples of such debates from different national and political perspectives
(Germany, Syria, UK, US) can be accessed under www.buzzfeed.com/alan-
white/a-viral-facebook-post-claims-a-refugee-was-a-member-of-isis?utm_
term=.ps3AWmAma#.hc2n6ZnZ2 (accessed August 1, 2017) or https://
medienredaktion.wordpress.com/2015/09/30/ bilder-von-als-fluechtling-
getarnte-terroristen-brd-beluegt-das-gesamte-volk/ (accessed August 1, 2017).
13 Two Twitter co-occurrence networks were created with the help of the
Social Media Observatory Interactive Network Graph developed at the
Indiana University and available online under http://truthy.indiana.edu

(01.07.2017). Regarding the hashtag #refugeesnotwelcome in September 2015 most of the tweets were tagged in connection to #refugeeswelcome followed by #refugees, #refugeecrisis, #fluechtlinge, #isis, #schauhin and the official hashtag of the British far-right populist anti-EU organisation #ukip. The co-occurence network of the significantly more powerful #refugeeswelcome hashtag in the same period of time indicates a strong impact of the Alan (Aylan) Kurdi image and the most frequent co-occurence of the hashtags #refugees, #syria and #refugeecrisis.

14 See www.dailystormer.com/vice-kike-philip-kleinfeld-calls-bullshit-on-polmigrant-video/ and discussions on Vice homepage www.vice.com/read/kleinfeld-refugee-memes-debunking-846 (01.07.2017).

15 An example of Twitter commentary on the use and misuse of the satirical Ice or 'ISIS Cube' meme is available under https://twitter.com/junayed_/status/643911141383651328 (accessed August 1, 2017).

16 The memes along with the discussion can be accessed under www.facebook.com/BritiainFurst/photos/a.722782891130445.1073741828.7 22772297798171/985594068182658/?type=3&theater (accessed August 1, 2017).

References

Appadurai, A. (1986). *The social life of things. Commodities in cultural perspective.* Cambridge, UK: Cambridge University Press.

Appadurai, A. (1996). *Modernity at large. Cultural dimensions of globalization.* Minneapolis and London, UK: University of Minnesota Press.

Bartlett, E. (2015). 'No, this refugee is not a terrorist for Isis.' In *Independent*, 10 September. Accessed August 1, 2017. http://indy100.independent.co.uk/article/no-this-refugee-is-not-a-terrorist-for-isis--ZkHvS_d6Hl.

Bennett, J. (2005). The agency of assemblages and the North American blackout. *Public Culture, 17*(3), 445–465.

Blackmore, S. (2000). *The meme machine.* Oxford, UK: Oxford University Press.

Bolter, J. D., and Grusin, R. (1999). *Remediation. Understanding new media.* Cambridge, MA: MIT Press.

Coleman, G. (2011). Anonymous: From the Lulz to collective action. In *The New Everyday. A Media Commons Project*, 6 April. Accessed August 1, 2017. http://mediacommons.futureofthebook.org/tne/pieces/anonymous-lulz-collective-action.

Couldry, N. (2008). Mediatization or mediation? Alternative understandings of the emergent space of digital storytelling. *New Media & Society, 10*(3), 373–391.

Dawkins, R. (1976). *The selfish gene.* Oxford, UK: Oxford University Press.

Deleuze, G. (1995). *Negotiations, 1972–1990.* New York, NY: Columbia University Press.

Deleuze, G., and Guattari, F. (1987) [1980]. *A thousand plateaus. Capitalism and schizophrenia,* translated by B. Massumi, Minneapolis and London, UK: University of Minnesota Press.

Digital Methods Initiative (2016). Google Image Scraper. Accessed August 1, 2017. https://tools.digitalmethods.net/beta/googleImages/.

Dijk, J. (2006). *The network society.* London, UK: Sage.

D'Orazio, F. (2015). Journey of an image: From a beach in Bodrum to twenty million screens across the world. In F. Vis, and O. Goriunova (eds.), *The iconic image on social media: A rapid research response to the death of Aylan Kurdi* (11–19). Visual Social Media Lab. Accessed August 1, 2017. http://visualsocialmedialab.org/projects/the-iconic-image-on-social-media.

Fiske, J. (1987). *Television culture.* (Second edition). New York, NY: Routledge.

Goriunova, O. (2014). The force of digital aesthetics. On memes, hacking, and individuation. *The Nordic Journal of Aesthetics, 47,* 54–75.

Goriunova, O. (2015). Introduction. In F. Vis, and O. Goriunova (eds.), *The iconic image on social media: A rapid research response to the death of Aylan Kurdi* (5–10). Visual Social Media Lab. Accessed August 1, 2017. http://visualsocialmedialab.org/projects/the-iconic-image-on-social-media.

Goriunova, O., and Vis, F. (2015). Conclusion. In F. Vis, and O. Goriunova (eds.), *The iconic image on social media: A rapid research response to the death of Aylan Kurdi* (71–72). Visual Social Media Lab. Accessed August 1, 2017. http://visualsocialmedialab.org/projects/the-iconic-image-on-social-media.

Gournelos, T., and Gunkel, D. J. (2011). *Transgression 2.0. Media, culture, and the politics of a digital age.* London, UK: The Continuum International Publishing Group.

Grossberg, L. (1997). *Dancing in spite of myself: Essays on popular culture.* Durham, NC: Duke University Press.

Grossberg, L. (2010). *Cultural studies in the future tense.* Durham, NC and London, UK: Duke University Press.

Grusin, R. (2010). *Premediation. Affect and mediality after 9/11.* Chippenham and Eastbourne, UK: Palgrave Macmillan.

Hackensberger, A. (2015). Das nächste große Schlachtfeld ist Europa. *Die Welt,* 29 June. Accessed August 1, 2017. www.welt.de/politik/ausland/article143186475/Das-naechste-grosse-Schlachtfeld-ist-Europa.html.

Hall, S. (1981). Notes on deconstructing "the Popular". In R. Samuel (ed.), *People's history and socialist theory* (227–240). Boston, MA: Routledge and Kegan Paul.

Hall, G., Birchall, C., and Woodbridge, P. (2010). Deleuze's postscript on the societies of control. *Culture Machine, 11.*

Harcourt, B. E. (2011). Occupy Wall Street's 'political disobedience. Accessed August 1, 2017. https://opinionator.blogs.nytimes.com/2011/10/13/occupy-wall-streets-political-disobedience/

Hartmann, M. (2010). Mediatisierung als Mediation: Vom Normativen und Diskursiven. In M. Hartmann, and A. Hepp (eds.), *Die Mediatisierung der Alltagswelt* (35–47). Wiesbaden, Germany: VS.

Hepp, A., Hjarvard S., and Lundby, K. (2015). Mediatization: Theorizing the interplay between media, culture and society. *Media, Culture & Society, 37,* 314–324.

Highfeld, T., and Leaver, T. (2016). Instagrammatics and digital methods: Studying visual social media, from selfies and GIFs to memes and emoji. *Communication Research and Practice, 2*(1), 47–62.

Hopkins, S. (2015). Rapper Ice Cube mistaken as "ISIS convert living in birmingham" in latest meme fooling far-right supporters. *The Huffington Post,* 17 September. Accessed August 1, 2017. www.huffingtonpost.co.uk/2015/09/17/rapper-ice-cube-mistaken-for-isis-fighter_n_8150916.html.

Hristova, S. (2014). Visual memes as neutralizers of political dissent. *TripleC*, 12(1), 265–276.

Joyce, M. (2010). *Digital activism decoded. The new mechanics of change*. New York, NY and Amsterdam, the Netherlands: International Debate Education Association.

Kahn, R., and Kellner, D. (2005). Oppositional politics and the internet: A critical/reconstructive approach. *Cultural Politics*, 1(1), 75–100.

Kember, S., and Zylinska, J. (2012). *Life after new media. Mediation as a vital process*. Cambridge, MA: The Mit Press.

Kleinfeld, P. (2015). Calling bullshit on the anti-refugee memes flooding the internet. *Vice*, 10 September. Accessed August 1, 2017. www.vice.com/read/kleinfeld-refugee-memes-debunking-846.

Krotz, F. (2007). *Mediatisierung: Fallstudien zum Wandel von Kommunikation*. Wiesbaden, Germany: VS.

Latour, B. (2005). *Reassembling the social: An introduction to actor-network-theory*. Oxford, UK: Oxford University Press.

Lash, S. (2002). *Critique of information*. London, UK: Sage.

Lash, S., and Lury, C. (2007). *Global culture industry*. Cambridge, UK: Polity Press.

Lasn, K. (1999). *Culture jam: The uncooling of America*. New York, NY: William Morrow & Company.

Livingstone, S. (2009). On the mediation of everything. ICA Presidential Address 2008. *Journal of Communication*, 59(1), 1–18.

Loon, J. van. (2008). *Media technology. Critical perspectives*. Maidenhead, UK: Mc-Graw-Hill/Open University Press.

Lovink, G. (2012). *Networks without a cause. A critique of social media*. Bodmin and Cornwall, UK: Polity Press.

Lury, C, Parisi L., and Terranova, T. (2012). Introduction: The becoming topological of culture. *Theory, Culture & Society*, 29(4/5), 3–35.

Maeder, D., and Wentz, D. (2014). Digital seriality as structure and process. *Eludamos. Journal for Computer Game Culture*, 8(1). Accessed August 1, 2017. www.eludamos.org/index.php/eludamos/article/view/vol8no1-9/8-1-9-pdf.

Marres, N. (2012). *Material participation. Technology, the environment and everyday publics*. Chippenham and Eastbourne, UK: Palgrave Macmillan.

Massumi, B. (2002). *Parables for the virtual movement, affect, sensation*. Durham, NC and London, UK: Duke University Press.

Massumi, B. (2015). *Ontopower: War, powers, and the state of perception*. Durham, NC and London, UK: Duke University Press.

Milner, R. M. (2013). Pop polyvocality: Internet memes, public participation, and the Occupy Wall Street movement. *International Journal of Communication*, 7, 2357–2390. Accessed April 9, 2016. http://ijoc.org/index.php/ijoc/article/view/1949.

Observatory on Social Media (2016). Networks. Accessed August 1, 2017. http://truthy.indiana.edu/tools/networks/.

Paphitis, N., and Bennett, D. (2015). Syrian rebel leader seeks Europe fleeing gov't and jihadis. *Associated Press*, 17. Accessed August 1, 2017. http://bigstory.ap.org/article/d57a8149607b494ea7d6a317a50980b4/syrian-rebel-leader-seeks-europe-fleeing-govt-and-jihadis.

Parikka, J., and Sampson, T. D. (2009). *The spam book: On viruses, porn, and other anomalies from the dark aide of digital culture.* Cresskill, NJ: Hampton Press.

Puar, J. K. (2007). *Terrorist assemblages. Homonationalism in queer times.* Durham, NC and London, UK: Duke University Press.

Rentschler, C. A., and Thrift, S. A. (2015). Doing feminism in the network: Networked laughter and the "binders full of women" meme. *Feminist Theory,* 16(3), 329–359.

Salovaara, I. (2015). #JeSuisCharlie: Networks, affects and distributed agency of media assemblage. *Conjunctions: Transdisciplinary Journal of Cultural Participation,* 2(1), 103–115.

Sampson, T. D. (2012). *Virality. Contagion theory in the age of networks.* Minneapolis: University of Minnesota Press.

Sedgwick, E. K. (2003). *Touching feeling: Affect, pedagogy, performativity.* Durham, NC: Duke University Press.

Shifman, L. (2013). *Memes in digital culture.* Cambridge, MA and London, UK: The MIT Press.

Shifman, L. (2014). The cultural logic of photo-based meme genres. *Journal of Visual Culture,* 13(3), 340–358.

Taylor, A. (2015). Escaping from war-torn Syria to Western Europe. *The Atlantic,* 17 August. Accessed August 1, 2017. www.theatlantic.com/photo/2015/08/escaping-from-war-torn-syria-to-western-europe/401510/.

Telofski, R. (2012). *Living on a meme. How anti-corporate activists bend the truth, and you, to get what they want.* Bloomington, IN: iUniverse.

Thelwall, M. (2015). Undermining Aylan: Less than symphathetic international responses. In F. Vis, and O. Goriunova (eds.), *The iconic image on social media: A rapid research response to the death of Aylan Kurdi** (31–37). Visual Social Media Lab. Accessed August 1, 2017. http://visualsocialmedialab.org/projects/the-iconic-image-on-social-media.

Thrift, N. (2008). *Non-representational theory. Space/politics/affect.* London, UK and New York, NY: Routledge.

Wendling, M. (2015). Laith Al Saleh: This viral photo falsely claims to show an IS fighter posing as a refugee. *BBC Trending.* Accessed August 1, 2017. www.bbc.com/news/blogs-trending-34176631.

Williams, R. (1974). *Television, technology and cultural form.* London, UK: Routledge.

Winter, R. (2007). Perspektiven der Cyber-Society. Plädoyer für eine kritische und kontextuelle Analyse digitaler Praktiken. In J. Fromme, and B. Schäffer (eds.), *Medien-Macht-Gesellschaft* (29–44). Wiesbaden, Germany: VS.

Winter, R. (2010). *Widerstand im Netz. Zur Herausbildung einer transnationalen Öffentlichkeit durch netzbasierte Kommunikation.* Bielefeld, Germany: transcript.

Zoonen, L. van (2005). *Entertaining the citizen: When politics and popular culture converge.* Lanham, MD: Rowman and Littlefield.

Part III

(Re-)Framing Participation and Citizenship

10 Towards a Framework for Studying Political Participation in Social Media

Julie Uldam and Anne Kaun

Social media have been praised regarding their potential for facilitating political participation. Before we can begin to assess this potential, we first need to address fundamental questions about what political participation entails. In this chapter, we address some of these questions and suggest the contours of an analytical framework for studying political participation in social media.

One of the most difficult problems facing democracy in the Western hemisphere is the decline in citizens' participation in parliamentarian politics (Dahlgren 2009). In contrast, suggestions for social and political change often originate from civic initiatives. At the same time, corporations play an increasingly central role in the political arena (Matten and Crane 2005). Therefore, we need to look beyond parliamentarian politics and the rights and obligations of liberal citizenship such as voting. Social media have been vested with hopes that they can help reinvigorate political participation by providing new possibilities for bottom-up, self-organizing participation such as direct democracy and for bypassing mass media gatekeepers and taking action to hold governments and corporations to account (e.g. Van Laer and Van Aelst 2010; Castells 2013). At the same time, sceptics have pointed to challenges social media pose to extra-parliamentarian political participation. These accounts have highlighted the dominance of commercial interests, individualisation, non-committal participation – or 'clicktivism'– and security and censorship (e.g. Gladwell 2010; Juris 2012; Dahlgren 2013; Dahlberg 2015).

Rather than taking any of these perspectives for granted, this chapter explores key aspects of political participation, including extra-parliamentarian engagement, in social media. We do so by first outlining examples of political participation that criticise government and business practices, considering their modes in terms of a formal-informal distinction and their agenda in terms of a reformist-systemic distinction. On the basis of this, we suggest a framework for studying political participation in (social) media that considers the issues of power relations, affordances, practices/literacy and discourses that condition political participation in social media.

Expanding the Political: Alternative Forms of Political Participation

Government practices at transnational, national and local levels have been criticised by civic actors. At a transnational level, counter-summits criticise international organisations such as WTO, IMF or UNFCCC for their exclusive processes and privileging of economic growth (Della Porta and Tarrow 2005; Uldam and Askanius 2011). Such alternative summits have typically been grounded in protest and antagonistic political participation (Uldam and Askanius 2011). Transnationally and nationally, citizens have protested governments' austerity policies, for example the Indignados and Occupy movements (Pianta and Gerbaudo 2015). Antagonistic political participation has also been directed at business, for example criticising companies' CSR policies and sponsorships as pretence of prioritising environmental and social issues (Uldam 2016). Expectations that businesses assume responsibility for the consequences of their actions beyond what is required legally have fundamentally altered the relationship between corporations and civic actors. While business-centred political participation often involves civil society groups and activists targeting individual companies, this is done with a view towards systemic change rather than single-issue demands (Greenwood et al. 2002). Business-centred political participation is thus not removed from systemic critique and demands for change to the current political and economic organisation of society altogether (Starr 2000; Karagianni and Cornelissen 2006; Uldam 2013).

While protest – directed at international organisations, governments or business – is certainly a crucial part of political participation without which politics would be "replaced by a confrontation between non-negotiable moral values or essentialist forms of identifications" (Mouffe 1998: 13f.), extra-parliamentarian political participation also involves proposals for solutions and alternatives to contested issues (Calhoun 2014). One of the most recent examples is the transnational Occupy movement with its protest camps which served both to protest the influence of corporate power on parliamentarian politics (among other issues) as well as to enact a community-driven alternative to the current neoliberal organisation of society, for example with free libraries, free seminars and experiments in direct democracy. Another example is the community-driven Transition Towns network (initiated in the United Kingdom and now with projects mushrooming across Europe and in Australia, New Zealand and South Africa), which facilitates local, self-organised food and energy provision in a growing number of cities. Political participation is also expressed through creative, subversive tactics such as the actions by culture jammers like the Yes Men, who, for example, impersonating WTO officials, announced the refounding of the WTO campaign to ensure businesses help people rather than businesses (Cammaerts 2007; Boyd 2013). From this perspective, political participation is not necessarily in decline, but rather in flux. Consequently, questions about civic engagement should not just focus on declining participation in parliamentarian politics, but also on what alternative modes of participation are emerging and how they are facilitated and constrained by social media.

Key discussions on political participation argue for an understanding that captures the efforts of civil society actors to address issues of public concern beyond parliamentarian politics for which media are crucial (e.g. Bennett 2003, 2012; Fenton 2008; Dahlgren 2009; Carpentier 2012). In this way, we can distinguish between, on the one hand, parliamentarian political participation such as voting and, on the other hand, extra-parliamentarian political participation such as volunteer work, activism and involvement in community-driven initiatives (Ekman and Amnå 2012). Political participation is thus understood here as engagement with political and social issues, an engagement expressed in a variety of ways that do not always adhere to traditional perceptions of parliamentarian politics. This includes trade union strikes, NGO campaigning as well as participation 'outside official politics' such as collectively organised protest events, culture jamming, direct action and community-driven initiatives (Böhm et al. 2008). Such forms of political participation have also been described as subactivism (Bakardjieva 2009) and microactivism (Mascheroni 2013). When studying and assessing political participation, we therefore need to consider both parliamentarian as well as extra-parliamentarian political participation to understand their interrelations. For example, the decline in voting among young people in many countries should not unequivocally be taken as disinterest in politics altogether. Rather, an increase in young people's extra-parliamentarian political participation can be seen as disillusionment with parliamentarian politics and an assertion of political agency outside parliamentarian politics (Dahlgren and Olsson 2007; Bennett 2008).

The advent and increasing popularisation of social media has been noted as an important vehicle for political participation, in parliamentarian as well as extra-parliamentarian politics. In relation to extra-parliamentarian political participation, especially the Arab Spring uprisings and the Occupy and Indignados movements have been noted as celebratory examples (DeLuca et al. 2012). Here, the capacity of social media for facilitating mobilisation, organisation and visibility has been highlighted. These accounts often focus on technological affordances of social media such as instantaneous, dialogical communication that bypass traditional mass-media filters (DeLuca et al. 2012). While these affordances are important to the emancipatory potential of social media, they are merely one part of a much bigger picture. We need to look beyond affordances and also consider user practices and media power. When we do so, we can move beyond the celebratory and simplistic focus on technological affordances and better understand both the possibilities for and limits to political participation in social media. Paying attention to media practices like Gerbaudo's (2012) ethnographic study of the protests in Tahir Square (Egypt), Puerta del Sol square (Spain) and Zuccotti Park (United States) shows that the role of social media affordances in mobilising and organising the protests was relatively small compared to the significance of collective identity formation and the particularity of physical spaces. Similarly, Fenton and Barassi (2011) draw on ethnographic methods in their study on the Labour Movement in Britain, showing how people in the UK-based Cuba Solidarity Campaign preferred alternative media rather than mainstream social media because they found the latter to be underpinned by individualistic logics. Mattoni and Treré (2014) also focus on media practices rather than merely affordances, showing how the Italian student movement in 2008 only used social media for mobilising protesters and relied on email listservs to organise the protests because participants were worried about surveillance. Paying attention to media power, Youmans and York (2012) show how the policies and user agreements of commercial social media platforms inhibit some forms of political participation by preventing anonymity and prohibiting certain content, resulting, for example, in Facebook banning the page 'We Are All Khaled Said', which was used to mobilise protesters during the Egyptian uprising. Uldam (2016) has also addressed the influence of policies and user agreements of commercial social media platforms on political participation, showing how the blog hosting site Wordpress.com referred to their policy of no anonymity and removed a website that criticised the oil company BP following a request from the company. This emphasises the ways in which social media and their technological affordances are embedded in wider societal structures and practices.

An Analytics of Political Participation and (Social) Media

In order to better understand the possibilities and challenges that social media can offer political participation – including the nitty-gritty of everyday organising, struggles to mobilise for systemic change to which only a few pay attention, let alone engage with, and corporate and government impediments to visibility among wider publics – we need to look beyond affordances. Therefore, we suggest an analysis of political participation in social media that looks beyond affordances and pays attention to other key issues that condition political participation. Our aim is to avoid techno-determinism and media-centric focal points. More specifically, the approach we suggest considers the context of political participation in social media, paying particular attention to (1) affordances, (2) power relations, (3) practices and (4) discourses. In doing so, we draw on Couldry's (2012) model of a socially oriented media theory that considers media in the context of other social institutions that shape our sense of reality and questions media's overemphasised role for constructing social reality. Like Couldry's model, the analytics of social media that we suggest could potentially be applicable to an analysis of political participation beyond social media, since it is non-media centric. However, our focus is on political participation and social media. In this way, the four dimensions are adapted so as to consider social media specifically. In outlining his model, Couldry (2012, 6) proposes a pyramid with four apexes that each represents a focal point in media research:

We can turn the pyramid four ways up, with the type of research we want to prioritize at the top, while others form the pyramid base. No way of turning the pyramid is 'right', or 'better', since the apexes name different priorities for research: media *texts*; the *political economy* of media production, distribution and reception; the *technical properties* of each medium; and the *social uses* to which media technologies and media contents are put.

It is important to note that paying equal attention to all four dimensions is often not feasible. It is, nonetheless, important to consider their role, even if just one apex is in focus. We find this approach to studying media highly useful, because it acknowledges the interrelations between the four aspects of the role of the media while also allowing for pragmatic choices regarding delimitations. We therefore adopt this approach while fine-tuning it for studying political participation in social media. In the following, we outline each of the four dimensions and discuss their interrelated roles in conditioning political participation in social media.

Power Relations

While social media can potentially help civil society actors access and circulate information in unprecedented ways, these technologies are embedded in unequal power relations that privilege government and corporate elites (Dahlgren 2013). Social media platforms are characterised by increasing ownership concentration, with multinational media corporations such as Google and Facebook dominating the majority of social media platforms (van Dijck 2013; Dahlberg 2014). Particularly government policies and regulation as well as platforms' Terms of Service (ToS) are important in this respect. Recent examples of Facebook deleting left-wing political group pages show that the platform is all but neutral (Gillespie 2010). Rather, social media platforms' ToS play a key role in conditioning possibilities for political participation. This is propelled by the commercial logics that underpin popular social media platforms such as Facebook and YouTube (and the relegation of non-profit alternative media platforms such as IndyMedia to the margins of the internet) (Youmans and York 2012; Uldam 2014). The commercial logic of popular social media platforms means that companies such as Facebook must cater for broad segments of users and advertisers (Youmans and York 2012). This often entails ToS that impede anonymity and privileges copyright over subvertising, in some cases enabling corporations to censor antagonistic political participation (Youmans and York 2012; Uldam 2014). In addition to revenues from advertising, commercial social media have developed business models based on the collection of data that is reanalysed and sold to third parties (Andrejevic 2013). Access to the data gathered as well as tools for analysis is limited to the major commercial players, thus contributing another layer of unequal power relations (Dahlberg 2015). These interests and conditions of unequal power relations further spur asymmetrical visibilities because the specifics of their collection and price are not made transparent. This obscures exactly what is being observed, on what basis and logics, enabling governments and corporations to monitor citizens' activities without being seen themselves and instilling uncertainty in those being watched (Brighenti 2010). In this way, social media augment visibility asymmetries by rendering them less transparent and accountable (Brighenti 2010). To the extent that civic users are aware of these asymmetries of visibility, they risk impeding participation in radical politics by instilling self-censorship.

Technological Affordances

While we argue for the importance of looking beyond affordances, we also want to stress the importance of paying attention to affordances and their implications for political participation in social media. The notion of affordances is often used to refer to 'action possibilities' (Gibson 1979) provided by an object or technological infrastructure. Following this definition of affordances, media technologies in general and social media in particular are constructed following a certain set of ideas (Kaun and Stiernstedt 2014). For example, as a commercial platform, Facebook follows a business model that is largely based on dispossession of creative expressions in the form of data (Andrejevic 2013) and the near impossibility of organic reach (Collister 2015). Organic reach refers to the possibility of a post appearing in users' newsfeed without paying for it. However, as Facebook's business model relies on revenue from users (companies, NGOs, politicians, artists) paying to reach their constituencies and stakeholders, significant organic reach is almost unattainable. This business model is embodied in technological affordances, namely the algorithm that determines the visibility of posts and tweets in social media platforms impede organic reach so as to motivate users

to pay for boosted reach (Dahlberg 2014). Further, social media algorithms grant visibility to posts on the basis of interaction. For example,
our posts are most likely to be featured in the newsfeeds of those of our
Facebook friends with whom we frequently interact (whether via likes,
comments, posts, messenger, etc.). One of the consequences is that organisations and social actors with resources – either capital to pay for
reach or people with skills to circumvent the algorithm – are privileged
in struggles for visibility in Facebook. This illustrates the interplay between affordances (the algorithm), power relations (the business model)
and practices/social media literacy (skills). Another consequence is that a
lot of the information that we receive via social media platforms presents
merely one aspect of an issue, bits of information or factoids, connecting
likeminded users rather than challenging our presumptions or offering
new perspectives. This illustrates the interplay between affordances and
practices. This interplay is further illustrated by the transient features
of many social media platforms which facilitate the instant agency of
point-and-click activism, offering easy, non-committal modes of civic
participation (Fenton 2008). Consequently, citizens' engagement with
an issue may end after a single click of a mouse, as is often the case
when joining a Facebook group or signing an online petition (Fenton
and Barassi 2011).

Social Media Practices

The notion of media practices refers to what we do with media (Couldry
2004). What we do when we use media is not necessarily what we were
intended to do. Just think of text messaging (SMS), which was intended
as an emergency communication tool and not the popular everyday communication channel that it is today. Paying attention to media practices
is also important in relation to political participation. Couldry (2012)
develops the notion of media practices as an 'open set of practices relating to, or oriented around, media' (Couldry 2004, 117). He argues
that media practices are concerned with specific regularities in actions
relating to media and regularities of context and resources that enable
media-related actions. He details further that media practices are concerned with the need for coordination, interaction, community, trust
and freedom. In that sense, focusing on media practices provides a
fruitful link to questions of political participation, particularly in extra-
parliamentarian contexts, because it opens up for considering the ways
in which social media enable practices of political participation that do
not necessarily cohere with formal participation such as voting. For example, drawing on a study of video responses to the Dutch-produced
anti-Islam film *Fitna*, Van Zoonen et al. (2010) explore playful modes
of engaging with politics, arguing that we need to look beyond politically oriented platforms to find political participation in online media.

Similarly, the ways in which political participation is performed on social media platforms require us to look for forms of participation beyond formal modes. In exploring political participation in social media, prominent studies have proposed alternative notions of participation and citizenship such as 'silly citizenship' (Hartley 2010) 'unlocated citizenship' (Van Zoonen et al. 2010) and 'self actualizing–dutiful citizenship' (AC–DC) (Bennett et al. 2014, see also Dahlgren 2003; Couldry et al. 2007). Drawing on examples of spoof election campaign videos, Hartley traces the historical trajectory of conceptions of citizenship, arguing that young people's uses of irony and satire – the playful performance of self-organised and self-represented deliberation – to represent themselves in YouTube videos should also be taken as citizens' practices of political participation. Bennett et al. (2014) identify loosely networked activism that addresses issues that reflect personal values in social media that transcends institutional or communal affinities. In this way, they share the idea that social media enable participation with politics in ways that are self-actualizing rather than dutiful, in Bennett's terms, thus contributing to a vivid civic culture that is understood in much broader terms than suggested by Almond and Verba (1963) in their seminal study of civic culture and politics (Bennett et al. 2011, 2014). While social media thus provide new platforms for expressing and acting out various forms of political participation, they have also been shown to privilege formal (reformist and institutional) modes of political participation over informal (radical and anti-systemic) modes (Van Laer and Van Aelst 2010; Uldam 2013) and individual over collective participation (Fenton and Barassi 2011; Bennett and Segerberg 2013). For example, increasing surveillance from government and business has led many activists to avoid social media for uses that relate to organising, and even sometimes mobilising for, protests (Gerbaudo 2013; Uldam 2016). Activists with insight into online surveillance risks and possibilities for circumventing surveillance – i.e. a high degree of media literacy – instead use alternative social media platforms such as Crabgrass or RiseUp, or use social media platforms in alternative ways (Uldam 2013). While face-to-face meetings remain crucial in organising protests, this highlights the interplay between media practices, literacy and power relations.

Through social media, information flows have become more complex – changing from a privileged position of broadcast media and mainstream press towards networked digital media, as Lotan et al. (2011) argue. Investigating the news flows on Twitter during the Tunisian and Egyptian uprising, they find that news is increasingly co-constructed by bloggers, activists and journalists. These and similar findings from other studies point towards changing power relations in the media landscape that need to be taken into consideration when studying political participation in social media.

Discourses

Discourse itself signifies a certain part of social practice incorporating a particular perspective and interpretation of social reality. The particular discursive practice and the specific fields of action are dialectically interrelated. Hence, discourse can be understood as a complex set of simultaneous interrelated linguistic acts that take place within and across fields of social action (Kaun and Jurkane 2016). As discourses condition our understandings of the world, they also condition our possibilities to act in that world. In that sense, discourses have performative power to condition political participation and political identities. However, for our discourses to be given a kind of reality that they would not have otherwise, they need to be seen and heard by others in the space of appearance (Arendt 1958). As social media can potentially help social and political actors access the space of appearance, we also need to pay attention to the discourses and counter-discourses that the affordances, power relations and practices facilitate and constrain in social media. One of the key democratic potentialities of social media platforms relates to their capacity for circulating counter-discourses to wider publics (Dahlberg and Phelan 2013). It is not only the affordances, power relations and practices that condition possibilities for gaining visibility for discourses that are important, but also the discourses as such for which social and political actors struggle to gain visibility and support (Chouliaraki 2000). For example, competing discourses try to establish different causes, identify different villains and different solutions to the Euro crisis (Kyriakidou et al. in this volume). As a wide range of actors, including capitalists, anti-capitalists, social democrats and nationalists, struggle to promote their discourse on Europe, social media have become a key arena for these struggles. Other discursive struggles and representations include climate change (Uldam and Askanius 2011; Uldam 2016), corporate responsibility (Vestergaard 2014) and movements of the dispossessed (Kaun 2015).

Power relations, practices, affordances and discourse form the basis of our suggestion for an analysis of political participation in social media. As we have indicated in relation to the four dimensions, they each play a key role for possibilities of political participation. Therefore, studies focusing on any of the four dimensions are important. At the same time, we want to stress the significance of considering all four dimensions and their interrelations, even when highlighting on one of them. It is precisely the interplay between the four dimensions that allows us to understand the conditions of possibility behind questions such as: Who participates? Who listens? It allows us to better understand phenomena such as virality and spreadability, the interplay with the mainstream press and between online/offline dynamics.

Towards an Analytics of Political Participation in Social Media

In illustrating our suggestion for an approach to studying political participation in social media on the basis of the four dimensions outlined in this chapter, we find the following figure useful, because its circular connectors illustrate the continuous interrelations between all four dimensions (Figure 10.1).

Adopting a four-dimensional analysis of affordances, power relations, practices and discourses warrants questions about what kinds of methods are required. A wide range of methods can be employed to shed light on various aspects of the four dimensions. Our suggestion is to adopt mixed-method approaches that allow investigating the four dimensions in conversation with each other. For example, ethnographic approaches such as in-depth interviews, participant observation and nethnography can provide important insights into social media practices of political participation (Rokka and Moisander 2009; Gerbaudo 2013; McCurdy and Uldam 2014; Varnali and Gorgulu 2015), while document analysis of, for example ToS and government and agency reports along with user rights can provide important insights into the governance logics of social media (Fernback and Papacharissi 2007; Youmans and York

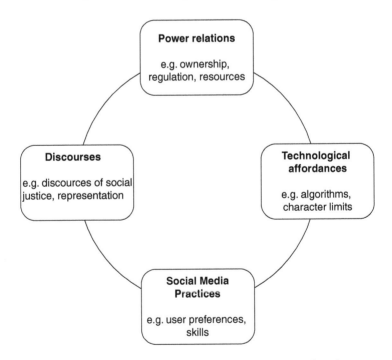

Figure 10.1 Four dimensions of political participation in social media.

2012; Fuchs 2014). Combining different methods allows capturing the complex interplay between power relations, practices, affordances and discourse while paying attention to the multi-dimensional character of each individual dimension. In this way, empirical research may focus on one dimension, but the other three dimensions provide the necessary context for making sense of the dimension in focus. While considering, for example, the affordances of Facebook to facilitate political mobilisations, one would need to keep in mind that affordances emerge in the complex multi-dimensional context of power relations, discourses and ways of using Facebook.

Implications and Avenues for Future Research: Assessing Political Participation in Social Media

In this chapter, we have proposed a four-dimensional model to assess political participation in social media. Current approaches have been criticised for focusing solely on one medium and neglecting the complex media ecology within in which political participation takes shape (Mattoni and Treré 2014). We argue that whether we study political participation in a single platform or medium, we need to pay attention to the interplay between the material and the discursive, the structural and the cultural. Thus, pushing beyond this one medium critique and media-determinism critiques, we take the multi-layeredness of social media dynamics as a starting point and propose power relations, technological affordances, discourses and practices as four dimensions to investigate when assessing possibilities for political participation in social media. This approach is based on a non-media-centric approach that acknowledges the importance of technological affordances, but considers them as embedded in and interconnected with power relations, practices and discourses (Couldry 2012). In that endeavour it is, hence, crucial to acknowledge the interconnectedness of all four dimensions. We suggest that to understand political participation in social media, future research should not only include multiple media platforms and practices in the analysis, but also pay attention to their embeddedness in wider societal conditions. Doing so will often entail mixed-method approaches, including ethnographic methods, multimodal analysis, network analysis, content analysis, policy analysis and discourse analysis.

References

Almond, G. A., and Verba, S. (1963). *The civic culture: Political attitudes and democracy in five nations*. London, UK: Sage.
Andrejevic, M. (2013). *Infoglut: How too much information is changing the way we think and know*. New York, NY; London, UK: Routledge.

Arendt, H. (1958). *The human condition*. Chicago, IL: University of Chicago Press.

Bakardjieva, M. (2009). Subactivism: Lifeworld and politics in the age of the Internet. *The Information Society, 25*(2), 91–104.

Bennett, W. (2003). Communicating global activism. *Information, Communication & Society, 6*(2), 143–168.

Bennett, W. L. (2008). *Civic life online: Learning how digital media can engage youth*. Cambridge, UK: MIT Press.

Bennett, W. L. (2012). The personalization of politics. Political identity, social media, and changing patterns of participation. *The Annals of the American Academy of Political and Social Science, 644*(1), 20–39.

Bennett, W. L., and Segerberg, A. (2013). *The logic of connective action: Digital media and the personalization of contentious politics*. Cambridge, UK: Cambridge University Press.

Bennett, W. L., Segerberg, A., and Walker, S. (2014). Organization in the crowd: Peer production in large-scale networked protests. *Information, Communication & Society, 17*(2), 232–260.

Bennett, W. L., Wells, C., and Freelon, D. (2011). Communicating civic engagement: Contrasting models of citizenship in the youth web sphere. *Journal of Communication, 61*(5), 835–856.

Böhm, S., Spicer, A., and Fleming, P. (2008). Infra-political dimensions of resistance to international business: A Neo-Gramscian approach. *Scandinavian Journal of Management, 24*(3), 169–182.

Boyd, A. (2013). Prefigurative intervention. In A. Boyd, and D. O. Mitchell (eds.), *Beautiful trouble: A toolbox for revolution* (82–85). New York, NY: OR Books.

Brighenti, A. M. (2010). *Visibility in social theory and social research*. London, UK: Palgrave MacMillan.

Cammaerts, B. (2007). Jamming the political: Beyond counter-hegemonic practices. *Continuum, 21*(1), 71–90.

Carpentier, N. (2012). Discursive structures in the network society. *Javnost – The Public, 19*(4), 25–40.

Castells, M. (2013). *Networks of outrage and hope: Social movements in the internet age*. Malden, MA: Polity Press.

Chouliaraki, L. (2000). Political discourse in the news: Democratizing responsibility or aestheticizing politics? Discourse and Society, *11*(3), 293–314.

Collister, S. (2015). Algorithmic public relations. In J. L'Etang, D. McKie, N. Snow, and J. Xifra (eds.), *The Routledge handbook of critical public relations* (360–370). London, NY: Routledge.

Couldry, N. (2004). Theorising media as practice. *Social Semiotics, 14*(2), 115–132.

Couldry, N. (2012). *Media, society, world. Social theory and digital media practice*. Cambridge, NY: Polity.

Couldry, N., Livingstone, S. M., and Markham, T. (2007). *Media consumption and public engagement: Beyond the presumption of attention*. Basingstoke, UK: Palgrave Macmillan.

Dahlberg, L. (2014). The Habermasian public sphere and exclusion: An engagement with poststructuralist-influenced critics. *Communication Theory, 24*(1), 21–41.

Dahlberg, L., and Phelan, S. (2013) (eds.), *Discourse theory and critical media politics*, New York, NY: Palgrave Macmillan.

Dahlgren, P. (2003). Reconfiguring civic culture in the new media milieu. In J. Corner (ed.), *Media and the restyling of politics* (151–170). London, UK: Sage.

Dahlgren, P. (2009). *Media and political engagement*. Cambridge, UK: Cambridge University Press.

Dahlgren, P. (2013). *The political web: Participation, media, and alternative democracy*. Basingstoke, UK: Palgrave Macmillan.

Dahlgren, P., and Olsson, T. (2007). From public sphere to civic culture: Young citizens' internet use. In R. Butsch (ed.), *Media and public spheres* (198–209). Basingstoke, UK: Palgrave Macmillan.

Della Porta, D., and Tarrow, S. (2005). Transnational processes and social activism: An introduction. In D. Della Porta, and S. Tarrow (eds.), *Transnational protest and global activism* (1–19). Lanham et al., MD: Bowman & Littlefield.

DeLuca, K., Lawson, S., and Sun, Y. (2012). Occupy Wall Street on the public screens of social media: The many framings of the birth of a protest movement. *Communication, Culture & Critique, 5*(4), 483–509.

Ekman, J., and Amnå, E. (2012). Political participation and civic engagement: Towards a new typology. *Human Affairs, 22*(3), 283–300.

Fenton, N. (2008). Mediating hope: New media, politics and resistance. *International Journal of Cultural Studies, 11*(2), 230–248.

Fenton, N., and Barassi, V. (2011). Alternative media and social networking sites: The politics of individuation and political participation. *The Communication Review, 14*(3), 179–196.

Fernback, J., and Papacharissi, Z. (2007). Online privacy as legal safeguard: The relationship among consumer, online portal, and privacy policies. *New Media & Society, 9*(5), 715–734.

Fuchs, C. (2014). *Digital labour and Karl Marx*. New York, NY: Routledge.

Gerbaudo, P. (2012). *Tweets and the streets: Social media and contemporary activism*. London: Pluto Press.

Gibson, J. J. (1979). *The ecological approach to visual perception*. Boston, MA: Houghton Mifflin Harcourt.

Gillespie, T. (2010). The politics of 'platforms'. *New Media & Society, 12*(3), 347–364.

Gladwell, M. (2010). Why the revolution will not be tweeted. *The New Yorker*.

Greenwood, R., Suddaby, R., and Hinings, C. R. (2002). Theorizing change: The role of professional associations in the transformation of institutionalized fields. *Academy of Management Journal, 45*(1), 58–80.

Hartley, J. (2010). Silly citizenship. *Critical Discourse Studies, 7*(4), 233–248.

Juris, J. S. (2012). Reflections on #Occupy everywhere: Social media, public space, and emerging logics of aggregation. *American Ethnologist, 39*(2), 259–279.

Karagianni, K. S., and Cornelissen, J. (2006). Anti-corporate movements and public relations. *Public Relations Review, 32*(2), 168–170.

Kaun, A. (2015). Regimes of time: Media practices of the dispossessed. *Time & Society, 24*(2), 221–243.

Kaun, A., and Jurkane Hobein, I. (2016). Occupy narratives in Sweden and Latvia: How mainstream media tell the story of a movement. *Interactions: Studies in Communication and Culture, 7*(1), 23–39.

Kaun, A., and Stiernstedt, F. (2014). Facebook time: Technological and institutional affordances for media memories. *New Media & Society*, 16(7), 1154–1168.

Lotan, G., Graeff, E., Ananny, M., Gaeffney, D., Pearce, I., and boyd, d. (2011). The revolutions were tweeted: Information flows during the 2011 Tunisian and Egyptian revolutions. *International Journal of Communication*, 5, 1375–1405.

Mansell, R. (2010). Commentary: Mediating the public sphere: Democratic deliberation, communication gaps, and the personalization of politics. *Annals of the International Communication Association*, 34(1), 259–274.

Mascheroni, G. (2013). Performing citizenship online: Identity, subactivism and participation. *Observatorio*, 7(3), 93–119.

Matten, D., and Crane, A. (2005). Corporate citizenship: Toward an extended theoretical conceptualization. *Academic of Management Review*, 30(1), 166–179.

Mattoni A., and Treré, E. (2014). Media practices, mediation processes, and mediatization in the study of social movements. *Communication Theory*, 24(3), 252–271.

McCurdy, P., and Uldam, J. (2014). Connecting participant observation positions: Toward a reflexive framework for studying social movements. *Field Methods*, 26(1), 40–55.

Mouffe, C. (1998). The radical centre. A politics without adversary. *Soundings*, 9, Summer: 11–23.

Pianta M., and Gerbaudo P. (2015). In search of European alternatives: Anti-austerity protests in Europe. In M. Kaldor and S. Selchow (eds.), *Subterranean Politics in Europe* (31–59). London: Palgrave Macmillan.

Rokka, J., and Moisander, J. (2009). Environmental dialogue in online communities: negotiating ecological citizenship among global travellers. *International Journal of Consumer Studies*, 33, 199–205.

Starr, A. (2000). *Naming the enemy: Anti-corporate movements confront globalization*. London, UK: Zed Books.

Uldam, J. (2013). Activism and the online mediation opportunity structure: Attempts to impact global climate change policies? *Policy & Internet*, 5(1), 56–75.

Uldam, J. (2014). The power of words and the words of the powerful. Management of visibility: Silencing critical voices in the online public sphere. Paper presented at The Academy of Management Annual Meeting 2014, Philadelphia, United States.

Uldam, J. (2016). Corporate management of visibility and the fantasy of the post-political: Social media and surveillance. *New Media & Society*, 18(2), 201–219.

Uldam, J., and Askanius, T. (2011): Mediation, antagonism and the formation of oppositional political identities: Conflictual activism and climate change protests. Paper presented at The 61st Annual International Communication Association Conference. Boston, United States.

Varnali, K., and Gorgulu, V. (2015). A social influence perspective on expressive political participation in Twitter: the case of #OccupyGezi. *Information, Communication & Society*, 18(1), 1–16.

Van Dijck, J. (2013). *The culture of connectivity: A critical history of social media*. Oxford, UK: Oxford University Press.

Van Laer, J., and Van Aelst, P. (2010). Internet and social movement action repertoires: Opportunities and limitations. *Information, Communication & Society, 13*(8), 1146–1171.

Van Zoonen, L., Vis, F., and Mihelj, S. (2010). Performing citizenship on You-Tube: Activism, satire and online debate around the anti-Islam video Fitna. *Critical Discourse Studies, 7*(4), 249–262.

Vestergaard, A. (2014). Mediatized humanitarianism: Trust and legitimacy in the age of suspicion. *Journal of Business Ethics, 120*(4), 509–525.

11 Protest or Collaboration? How Perceived Opportunities and Constraints Shape the Activities of Anti-Infrastructure Citizen Action Groups

Marco Bräuer and Jens Wolling

Participatory Demands and Citizen Action Groups

It is the normative pretension of democracies that citizens are the "sovereign". Nevertheless, the normatively desired extent and kind of citizens' *political participation* is disputed: Precisely how much and which kind of engagement is perceived as appropriate depends on the perspective of the theory of democracy consulted. The decision-making systems in most Western democracies are focused on general parliamentary and presidential elections. These democratic systems provide various statutory rights that enable citizens to engage in processes like voting or engagement in political parties. Political parties are traditionally regarded as those institutions that integrate and articulate the values, preferences and interests of the citizens. In practice however, the capacities of these intermediaries are limited: Considering the growing complexity of political decision-making, it is not surprising that in many instances representative and/or presidential democracies are not able to comprehensively integrate their citizenries' interests and demands by means of the designated means of collaboration (see Hilgartner and Bosk 1988). The emergence of *social movements* as collective actors who challenge established authorities (Snow et al. 2004, 14) can be seen as one reaction to a lack of actual integration of interests into political decision making by these established forms of participation. Facing these deficits, citizens look for alternative forms of sociopolitical organisation and approach other means of participation. Within the legal spectrum of alternative sociopolitical organisations, two major forms can be differentiated: social movements and citizen action groups. Frequently, citizen action groups function as germ cells for social movements. Whether a social movement actually emerges from the activities of citizen action groups depends on the topic. If the topic of a citizen action group is relevant for a broader public, it is likely that a social movement might develop.

For social movements and citizen action groups, *protest* is the central form of collective action as they usually perceive the institutionalised channels of political influence as closed, at least in the emergent phase of a respective movement. The environmental movement in Germany can be considered as an example of this development. It started with mobilisations of mass protests in front of nuclear power plants. These activities were the crucial and visible site of contention. At the same time, the movement gained access to the political decision-making system through the foundation and subsequent electoral success of the Green party.

Not only the objectives of social movements but also the occasions of their appearance differ. Tilly (1978) distinguishes between the *proactive* and *reactive* demands of movements. In the case of the environmental movement, reactive demands are characterised as reactions vis-à-vis the implementation of political decisions (e.g. opposition against the construction of dams in order to protect natural habitats), whereas proactive demands encompass an environmental policy that supports the transition of the energy system by fostering the use of renewable energies. Reactive claims can be observed almost everywhere in the world. Of course, not all of them are related to a broader social movement. Quite often, single local groups of citizens mobilise against the realisation of a specific project like for instance a high-speed railway system or an airport (mobility infrastructure), the construction of a wind farm, hydraulic fracturing or the construction of power lines (energy infrastructures).

Some observers classify this kind of activism as being merely "NIMBY" (not in my backyard). Research, however, has shown that the picture is more complex (Wolsink 2000). In some cases, the resistance against infrastructure projects may indeed equate solely to NIMBY opposition. But frequently it is motivated differently: Reactive protests demonstrate citizens' willingness and desire to be involved in political and administrative decisions. Taking into account the general value change in modern societies (Inglehart and Flanagan 1987), such resistance can be explained by the increasing importance of post-materialistic values: people are becoming more concerned with their environment and the protection of cultural landscapes and they subsequently have a stronger need for political participation.

Such participatory demands are a common European phenomenon that is illustrated by findings from a representative survey asking people for their desired involvement in the decision-making process regarding technology and science (an area that is strongly connected to the field of many infrastructure projects). Table 11.1 presents results from the EU-ROBAROMETER 79.2, conducted in spring 2013. Citizens were asked, 'What is the level of involvement citizens should have when it comes to decisions made about science and technology?' Participatory demands and activities are influenced by several factors like features of the political system, culture, history, the media system, economic development, etc. To get a first insight into the different participatory demands in Europe, we grouped the countries according to their geographical position.

As geography is closely linked to several of the aforementioned relevant factors, this approach takes such multifaceted influences into account. We grouped the countries in the following four geographical regions (North: Denmark, Finland and Sweden; West/Middle: Austria, Belgium, France, Great Britain, Ireland, Luxembourg and the Netherlands; South: Cyprus, Greece, Italy, Malta, Portugal and Spain; and East/South-East: Bulgaria, Croatia, Czech Republic, Estonia, Hungary, Latvia, Lithuania, Poland, Slovakia, Slovenia and Romania). In Table 11.1, two countries from each region are presented. The one with the highest percentage of people who believe that citizens don´t need to be involved (column 1) and the country with the highest percentage of people demanding that the public should at least be consulted before decisions are taken (sum of column 3–5). As the focus of this chapter is on the case of anti-infrastructure mobilisation in Germany, data from the eastern and western parts of Germany are also included separately. The comparison of east and west gives information on how far political socialisation in different regimes influences the kind and extent of participation desired.

The results reveal that almost in all countries, the majority wants to be at least consulted. Furthermore, between 13.4% (Great Britain) and 29.3% (Croatia) of the interviewees even demand an active role in the decision-making process (sum of column 4 and 5). These attitudes are a challenge for representative democratic systems and their respective governmental, administrative and parliamentary institutions. Clearly defined and practiced participatory options provided by political and administrative bodies are needed. If such options are missing, the probability of civic protests increases, especially when it comes to the implementation of political decisions regarding science and technology. This is because it is in this phase that the consequences of political decisions become visible and citizens begin to feel directly affected, e.g. by the installation of big wind farms or by power grid extensions.

Citizen action groups are the most widespread organisational form of project-related opposition (Marg et al. 2013; Kubicek 2014). Nevertheless, the existing research on citizen action groups is scarce. Accordingly, little systematic knowledge is available regarding their activities and convictions.

This chapter addresses these questions. At first, a conceptual framework is developed for the analysis of the actions applied by citizen action groups against infrastructure projects. These actions can in practice encompass various forms: from collecting signatures, through writing letters to MPs, up to the organisation of demonstrations and the creation of own forms of alternative media. Some of these activities are publicly visible protest mobilisations. However, it would be too limited to focus attention solely onto such phenomena. Also, more covert forms of political participation are part of their repertoires. Using the two dimensions, protest and collaboration, in this chapter we develop a conceptual map

Table 11.1 Civic Demand to Be Heard in Decision Making Processes Regarding Science and Technology

Country	Citizens Do Not Need to Be Involved or Informed	Citizens Should only Be Informed	Citizens Should Be Consulted and Their Opinion Should Be Considered	Citizens Should Participate and Have an Active Role	Citizens' Opinions Should Be Binding	Don't Know
Germany West (N=943)	3.6%	24.1%	49.2%	14.5%	3.3%	5.3%
Germany East (N=537)	3.4%	26.1%	48.6%	14.9%	4.3%	2.8%
Ireland (N=984)	10.6%	26.9%	33.3%	14.1%	2.8%	12.2%
Great Britain (N=999)	6.5%	23.1%	49.9%	10.8%	2.6%	7.0%
Italy (N=995)	7.9%	38.1%	34.6%	9.5%	4.1%	5.7%
Malta (N=498)	5,4%	13.1%	45.4%	13.9%	2.6%	19.7%
Finland (N=1.000)	4.0%	35.3%	40.8%	14.2	4.1%	1.6%
Denmark (N=1.000)	4.0%	19.2%	51.4%	18.2%	3.3%	3.9%
Slovenia (N=1.000)	10.6%	44.6%	24.7%	13.3%	2.6%	4.2%
Croatia (N=978)	7.3%	31.7%	28.0%	20.6%	8.7%	3.8%

Source: EUROBAROMETER 79.2, April–May 2013, own calculations.

of these options. This framework is aimed at helping to classify the adopted forms of collective action as the basis for comparative research.

Based on this classification of activities, differences in the repertoires can be identified not only between the groups but also between different phases in the policy-making cycle and between different countries. Thus, the second objective guiding this chapter is the identification of explanations for these differences. We suggest the concept of opportunity structures from social movement research as an appropriate approach. In order to empirically investigate these conceptual assumptions, we present results from a case study on protests against the installation of high-voltage power lines in the German electricity grid. The results reveal that varying contexts lead to specific forms of protest and collaboration that differ considerably even within one given region. It is important to keep these differences on the micro-level in mind when it comes to comparing different anti-infrastructure protests on the macro level, e.g. between different regions or actually between different countries.

Political Participation between Protest and Collaboration

From a functional perspective, political participation is defined as "any voluntary activity that citizens do in order to influence political decisions on every layer of the political system" (Kaase 1995, 521). A more concrete approach is presented by van Deth (2009, 146), who provides a list of 70 forms of participation. To systemize these forms of participation, the author suggests a differentiation that was developed by Teorell et al. (2007), who distinguished *channels of representation* from activities in *extra-representational channels*. Channels of representation encompass activities that directly address the political system, like for example voting or submitting a petition to parliament. Here, the political system offers the citizens participatory options. If they go beyond the mere act of voting, e.g. public consultations and round tables, these activities can be described as collaboration. Extra-representational channels are directed at mass media or at directly influencing the public opinion, for example demonstrations and boycotts (Teorell et al. 2007, 431). We would coin these activities as *channels of public awareness*. By employing such activities, people indirectly exert pressure on the political decision-making system. These are usually labelled "protest" due to their use of indirect and non-routinized channels to influence political decisions (Della Porta and Diani 2006, 165f.).

Another distinction focuses on the initiator of participation: On the one hand, it is the political parties and political institutions that initiate traditional forms of political collaboration. These can be considered as forms of *top down participation*. However, not only actors from the political realm offer these prospects of collaboration. Especially in the context of science and technology, also private enterprises and stakeholder groups recently started employing different forms of collaboration (e.g. round tables) mainly with the purpose of avoiding protests. In the past, these arenas were dominated almost exclusively by policy makers and expert networks. Nowadays, also normal citizens can become involved in these processes, forming the so-called sphere of "subpolitics" (Beck 1997). Such *bottom up activities* aimed at influencing the political process often take place outside institutionalised channels of representation and are employed to create public awareness. They frequently have the character of protest (e.g. manifestations or boycotts). But bottom up participation can also address the channels of representation, e.g. when citizen write a letter to their local member of parliament to influence the politicians´ decision-making. Such an activity can also be coined as collaboration. Furthermore, political participation activities are shaped by the policy-making cycle, as the *policy formation phase* provides different participatory options compared to the *implementation phase*.

All three distinctions (channels of representation vs. channels of public awareness; citizen-driven vs. elite-driven; policy formation vs. policy implementation) were combined into a matrix as presented in Figure 11.1. From the matrix, it becomes clear that protest and collaboration both constitute possible options in all phases and for all actors. Political or other elite actors offer channels of public awareness like round table processes and other forms of public deliberation. On some occasions, it might be also in the interest of powerful elites themselves to initiate protest events. The matrix provides just a rough overview of the distinctions necessary for a sound analysis. Protest and collaboration could be relevant in all phases and also for all actors. But which concrete options are finally chosen by which actor and in which phase remains an open question and must be the subject of research.

As pointed out above, citizen action groups are not limited to *protest* – neither in the policy formation phase nor in the implementation phase. They also have various options of *collaboration*. In this chapter, we will focus on the activities of citizen action groups with reactive demands in the implementation phase of infrastructure projects. In the case of these projects, the political system offers several opportunities of collaboration provided by official channels of representation like compulsory hearings where citizens have the right to make comments and enter objections. Besides that, also non-mandatory forms of top down collaboration are occasionally employed. However, the public perception of the collective action of citizen action groups is often primarily focused on protest. Moreover, researchers also often limit their studies to the visible forms of collective action and hence might omit to investigate the activities performed in formalised or informal channels of representation. Summarising these arguments, it becomes clear that forms of protest and forms of collaboration can and should be distinguished and that both must be included in the analysis of collective action.

	Policy formation		Political decision	Policy implementation	
	citizen-driven (bottom-up)	elite-driven (top-down)		citizen-driven (bottom-up)	elite-driven (top-down)
Channels of representation	collaboration	collaboration		collaboration	collaboration
Channels of public awareness	protest	both		protest	both

Figure 11.1 Collaboration and protest.

In the following sections, theoretical concepts will be proposed that might explain why citizen action groups engage in specific forms of collaboration and/or protest activities.

The Concept of Opportunity Structures

Opportunity structures are conceptualised as frame conditions that citizens must take into account if they want to successfully gain influence (Tilly and Tarrow 2007, 49). In Eisinger's seminal study, the author conceptualised the perception and evaluation of opportunity structures as a learning process: examples of success or failure make the structures of opportunities and constraints visible to the activists (Crossley 2002, 109). If previous protests are perceived as unsuccessful, it will be difficult to mobilise citizens for future collective action; whereas if claimants attain their goals, it will be easier to motivate them (Eisinger 1973, 27). It cannot be denied that objective opportunity structures do exist. However, individual and collective action depends on the sense-making processes of the citizens involved (Kriesi 2004, 68).

Political Opportunity Structures

The concept of *political opportunity structures* introduced by Eisinger (1973) states that the general openness of the political system is the essential variable to explain the collective action of protestors. Eisinger regarded protests, especially violent collective behaviour, as a consequence of closed political structures. Tarrow (1996) defined political opportunity structures as 'signals to social or political actors which either encourage or discourage them to use their internal resources to form social movements' (Tarrow 1996, 54). It is expected that responsive and inclusive political opportunity structures would assimilate potential protests (Kitschelt 1986, 62). Thus, one would assume that public deliberation of planning projects would minimise protests (Barnes et al. 2006). Another dimension of the concept is the level of centralisation of the state: Federal systems in general provide more opportunities for political participation than centralised ones (Kriesi 2004, 70). An additional aspect are the *prevailing strategies* for dealing with opponents: political representatives can react with exclusion (e.g. via confrontation, repression and polarisation) or with inclusion (e.g. cooperation and support) (Kriesi 2004, 71).

Assessing the concept of political opportunity structures, protest activities can be defined as the reaction of citizens who are confronted with closed political opportunity structures. From that, it can be concluded that the protest level should be higher in centralised states without official possibilities of collaboration and ruled by representatives that react with exclusion. The theory of political opportunity structures hence provides an explanatory framework that helps to understand when citizen action groups make use of participatory forms and when they mobilise for protest activities.

Media Opportunity Structures

The original approach of political opportunity structures, however, has not focused on the role of media and the public sphere. Crossley (2002) therefore suggested adding the concept of mass media opportunity structures in order to better understand the various opportunities and constraints that protest actors face (Crossley 2002, 123). Mass media either enable or constrain the visibility of protestors (Cammaerts 2012, 119). Taking the model of the public sphere as intermediate system into consideration (Gerhards and Neidhardt 1991), protests aim at creating awareness, public pressure and the mobilising of public opinion in order to force political authorities to negotiate with the protestors and their respective claims. Some authors even argued that protests without media coverage must be regarded as non-existent (Lipsky 1969). With the internet and social media, the elementary relevance of traditional mass media obviously diminished. Nevertheless, many political activities, even those organised in the internet or by social media, still aim at gaining attention from mass media.

Societal Opportunity Structures

But claimants do not only depend on the attention of mass media. They also need to mobilise direct public support. They must motivate people to join the action groups and to take part in protest and collaboration activities. As outlined above, protest is strongly related to the general societal value change. This is also true for many opponents of infrastructure projects, who are motivated because the projects challenge their values. If the regional population shares these values and the activists are able to demonstrate that the project is a threat to these values, the population might be mobilised. If their claims do not match the value system of the population or if they have only a low priority, the action groups will receive less support, not only from the mass media, but also from the population. We define this general readiness of the population to support citizen action groups as *societal opportunity structure*.

Empirical Analysis of Citizen Action Groups

The expounded framework of opportunity structures was applied to the investigation of protest and collaboration activities of citizen action groups in Germany that oppose the building of new high-voltage power lines. Several citizen action groups in many parts of the country have started to struggle against the construction of such new "energy highways", arguing that they are unneeded, represent a danger for the environment and public health, mutilate the landscape and serve primarily the interests of the deregulated energy industry rather than sustainability. This resistance was analysed in several qualitative case studies. The sample consists of eight action groups opposing different high voltage power line projects. Five groups from the eastern and three from the western part of Germany were selected. Each case study comprised semi-structured interviews with the core activists and analyses of documents produced by the action groups (leaflets, placards, web sites, etc.). In addition, group meetings and protest events were observed and field notes were taken. The analysed material encompasses 25 semi-structured interviews and one focus group. The case studies were conducted between 2012 and 2014. The diversity of the material allows for comparisons between the activists within the groups as well as between the activists of different groups, in order to understand the individual and collective perception and evaluation processes. The collected data were analysed with the method of qualitative content analysis. The coding scheme was developed in a combination of a concept-driven and data-driven strategy, i.e. the main categories were derived from the theoretical concepts introduced above (political opportunity structure, media opportunity structure and societal opportunity structure) and were supplemented by sub categories that were inductively built from the material to ensure the explorative character of qualitative research and allowing the detection of new and unexpected aspects.

Context of Case Study

Before the research findings are presented in detail, the general context of the infrastructure projects under investigation will be introduced. Renewable energy sources are widely acknowledged to contribute to a sustainable economy and to offset climate change. In Germany, a vast political majority demands that nuclear and fossil energy should be replaced with green energy (the so-called energy transition). The German energy industry and many political actors claim that in order to successfully implement this transformation process, an extension of the national power grid is needed for the transmission of (offshore) wind energy from the North Sea and the Baltic Sea to the urban and industrial centres in the South. Accordingly, the federal parliament (Bundestag) passed several laws to accelerate the pace of extension. The position of most political parties in Germany regarding power grid expansion is supportive. Especially the two major parties, the conservative party (CDU) and the social democrats (SPD) foster the extension plans. But also, the green party (Die Grünen) and the liberal party (FDP) are basically supportive. Only the socialist party (Die Linke) criticises the plans. Despite this general political agreement on the national level, the political representatives in the affected German federal states, regions and municipalities frequently oppose these plans because they negatively affect their regional or local interests (e.g. tourism or the fight against rural depopulation).

The different power lines are planned and built by different grid operating companies, whose willingness to communicate and consult the local population varies considerably. In fact, some of the network operators have started to implement comprehensive informal consultations even before the institutionalised planning procedures begin (e.g. so-called 'information markets').

The German federal states have no institutionalised power to impede extensions of the power grid. However, their respective administrations are responsible for the concrete planning and collaboration processes concerning the high-voltage power lines passing their territory. Furthermore, all local authorities are consulted formally. According to German planning laws, the local authorities are responsible for distributing information related to the planning process to the public. But precisely how a local authority publishes such information is completely contingent. The mayor of a municipality, for instance, can initiate a town hall meeting or just post a brief message on the notice board in front of the town hall. Such variances in publication strategies demonstrate that the political opportunity structures can vary considerably, even on the local level. Local authorities have a lot of room to manoeuvre. They are free to distribute just the minimal necessary information to the citizens; but they can also go the other way, supporting and cooperating with the citizen action groups.

Perceptions of Political, Societal and Media Opportunity Structures

All interviewed activists have a positive attitude towards democracy and relatively high normative expectations regarding the general openness of the political system and the responsiveness of the political actors concerning their objections. But they perceive a gap between their normative expectations and the political reality. They characterise the political representatives – especially on the state level (Bundesstaat) – as volatile, especially prior to elections, and criticise their behaviour as 'pseudo-openness'.

In our case studies, the interviewees identified two different ways the local political authorities were dealing with extension projects:

1 *The foundation of citizen action groups as result of local political agenda setting*

In some cases, the local political representatives were not only open for the interests and demands of the citizen action group but actually supported them actively. In several villages, local political representatives are core members of the citizen action groups, some of which were even founded by the mayors. As the mayors have easy access to local infrastructures, they organised town hall meetings and comprehensively informed the population about the state of the planning process. Relations between local political institutions and the citizen action groups can be characterised as cooperative. Existing channels of representation are fully exploited.

2 *The foundation of citizen action groups as result of missing local political agenda setting*

In some municipalities, the political opportunity structures were closed. The representatives were either not willing to cooperate or simply added the topic to their political agenda. This situation regarding local political opportunity structures led to local protests e.g. pickets in front of town halls. Such pickets raise public awareness and put the local political decision-making system under pressure.

But also forms of collaboration focused on channels of representation were applied in these cases. As a rule, local council meetings in Germany are public and citizens are allowed to attend the meetings. Furthermore, the citizens are allowed to put questions to the councillors. However, in practice most local council meetings take place behind closed doors. Hence, the 'massive' numbers of activists present when the grid project is on the council's agenda puts the members under scrutiny.

With the help of this mix of protest and collaboration, public oriented versus representational strategies, the pressure on representatives of the political system was built up. In all analysed cases, these protest strategies were successful: The local political representatives were perceived as responsive towards the citizen action groups. This engagement created opportunities for activist groups and the prevailing strategies of political representatives changed from exclusion to inclusion. Whether these openings are permanent, having the potential to change the political culture of a municipality and creating opportunities for further claim makers, remains an open question.

The second relevant dimension of the political opportunity structure is the institutionalised planning procedure. All interviewees evaluated this process quite negatively. The corresponding proceedings are perceived as discouraging. Especially the lack of information, the old-fashioned communication processes (no online-communication) and the fact that the voluminous documents are only physically available in the town hall during office hours is criticized. From the perspective of the activists, these standards demonstrate that *participation is not desired.*

Despite – and sometimes because of – these negative evaluations the members of the citizen action groups initiated a great number of activities using both channels of representation and channels of public awareness: The residents were informed via leaflets, interpersonal communication and road shows. The leaflets often contain sample objections that meet the formal requirements of the planning authority, including a list of acknowledged arguments against the power line project. The aim of these activities is to mobilise a maximum of involved persons to submit formal objections. In these cases, citizen action groups serve as *facilitators* and *catalysers* of *active participation* of the citizenry (bottom up mobilisation of forms of collaboration driven by the political system).

Since the reunification in 1990, East and West Germany have adjusted in many areas. Also, the demanded level of participation is quite similar, as the data from Table 11.1 illustrate, there are only negligible differences between the populations in East and West Germany. Nevertheless, the East German activists argued that their fellow citizens are apathetic because of not being socialised in a democratic system and accordingly unaware of their civil rights. However, it needs to be mentioned that also the members of West German action group described their regional population as apathetic and disinterested. Thus, the criticised level of interest might not necessarily be due to differences in political socialisation.

Another factor influencing the activities of the citizen action groups might be how the population identifies with its home region, the landscape, regional culture and nature. The case studies revealed that in one region the regional identity was a powerful mobilising factor, while in the other regions only a loose identification was observed. Some activists argued that the inhabitants in their region are harder to mobilise than the population in other regions due to a lack of identification with their home region.

Protest strategies require a critical mass of participants in order to attract journalists' attention and provoke news media coverage about their manifestations. In the analysed cases, the activists were not constantly able to mobilise enough people. The general low likelihood of engaging a broader population in protest activities was the reason why the groups perceived their protest activities as predominantly ineffective.

In general, mass media cover only a small number of the protests that take place (McCarthy et al. 1996) and those selected are often portrayed in a specifically biased way, focussing on persons and spectacle (Cammaerts 2012). Especially the NIMBY-frame is frequently applied to the topic (Bräuer and Wolling 2014). On the other hand, regional media sometimes decide to advocate the voices of the region and put the issue on the top of their agenda (Nowacki 2015).

Regarding the perception of *media opportunity structures,* the activists claimed that media quickly lost interest in the topic. Furthermore, many groups mentioned that they had made bad experiences with mass media, especially with television, which often portrayed them as NIMBY protestors. A general bias against their action was perceived in many media outlets. As reasons for this slant, the interview partners named different explanations: among others, they assumed that media are directly steered by corporate and political interests. However, in some cases certain regional newspapers were also praised for their support.

The action groups are faced with a dilemma: They know that they need mass media to create awareness. Hence, all groups try to adapt to the perceived logic of mass media. Some groups are very professional in the way they attend to the needs of journalists. They write elaborate press releases, provide images with credits and organise photogenic nocturnal demonstrations with torches along the planned route of the power line. However, some groups also argue that it should be a normative obligation of local and regional newspapers to advocate their case.

Comparative Analysis of Anti-Infrastructure Mobilisations

Summarising the results, one can see that the perceptions of the opportunity structures may well shape but they don't determine the collective action of citizen action groups. These perceptions are active reflections of individuals' own experiences and the communicated experiences other activists have made with politics, media and local populations. The proposed theoretical approach can thus be regarded as suitable. The results show that activist groups apply both options of protest as well as options of collaboration. Nevertheless, it must be taken into consideration that the results stem from a highly contextualised study on specific infrastructure projects in specific regions in Germany at a specific moment in time and including specific types of population.

In this concluding section, a tentative set of important dimensions will be introduced that should be taken into consideration when conducting future research on action groups, especially in the field of anti-infrastructure mobilisations.

The findings indicate that political and societal opportunity structures varied, even within a small region. Similar to the results from Eisinger (who studied different protests in different communities, i.e. big cities in the United States in the 1960s) it was observed that the way local authorities dealt with the citizen action groups differed considerably. This *local context* comprises an important set of factors that must be considered in order to better understand the collective action selected by the citizen groups. Furthermore, it must be taken into account that the *specific type of planned infrastructure* (power grid extension) makes it probable that the local political representatives cooperate with protestors or even initiate protests as the interests of the local political system and the citizen action groups are almost identical. One would expect a different situation when it comes to infrastructure projects that are in the interest and *responsibility of the local political system*, like industrial or business parks.

Furthermore, it is reasonable to expect that the degree of *consensus among the political representatives* plays an important role. Dissent would probably open opportunities for protestors (Tilly and Tarrow 2007) but also put the protestors under the risk of being co-opted.

Important elements of the *political opportunity structure during the policy implementation* are the participatory options provided by planning regulations. This was obviously a relevant determining factor in this case. As the formal options of citizen consultation for other projects are different, the role of participatory activities might be less on other occasions, and the intensity of protest might be higher. On the other hand, over the past decade some municipalities proactively established non-institutionalised participatory procedures. The intention of these activities is to prevent confrontational protest. Under which conditions this strategy is successful will be an important topic for future research.

Regarding the *societal opportunity structure*, the results from this study show the importance of the overall emotional *identification of the population with the local landscape, nature and traditions*. This aspect should be integrated in theoretical thinking and empirical research in a conscious and systematic way. In this study, some activists from East Germany mentioned a specific East German mentality that would constrain the willingness of the population to take part in collective action. Putting this into a broader context, one would expect *differences between the old member states of the European Union and the transformation countries*. The data presented in Table 11.1 seem to support this idea.

The protests against the building of high-voltage power lines presented here are predominantly a rural protest phenomenon. Often the activists were not able to mobilise a sufficiently critical mass of demonstrators for effective protest. One reason for this lack of resonance and support might be the total number of affected persons. Protests against the extension of airports in urban regions are more visible as more citizens in a defined area are affected. In these cases, also the media organisations are located closer to the projects and to the protest events. Hence, the *urban-rural differentiation* should be taken into consideration in any further analysis of infrastructure protests. But the relevance of the media

Table 11.2 Dimensions for the Further Comparative Analysis of Anti-infrastructure Mobilisations

Political Opportunity Structure	Media Opportunity Structure	Societal Opportunity Structure
• Amount of consensus between the political representatives • Amount and type of formal options for participation (regulation) • Amount and type of informal options for participation • Democratic tradition: Transformation country vs. established democracies • Relevance of planned projects for the local administration (advantages vs. disadvantages)	• Proximity of local and regional media organisations • Position of the media organisations regarding the project	• Location of the project: rural or urban / amount of affected persons • Degree of the population's identification with the region • Political culture • Relevance of planned projects for the local population (advantages vs. disadvantages)

opportunity structure is not limited to this aspect. In the analysed field, some media decided to advocate the action groups whereas especially the national media were regarded to have a negative bias towards the action groups. Further studies should consider the *availability of local and regional media stations* and the *general level of trust in media*.

These aspects highlight the importance of considering systematically the potential variations of the regional/local opportunity structures also *within* one country. A careful elaboration is needed on these dimensions in the phase of the development of comparative research designs and regarding the interpretation and generalisation of the obtained results. Especially comparative studies that seek to make valid claims about different countries should be aware of such inner-state differences. A systematic comparative analysis should also consider the *amount of consensus between political representatives on the different levels of the political system*, the *different regulation processes* regarding different kinds of infrastructures, and the *varying amounts of formal and informal participation options*. Table 11.2 presents the dimensions that need to be reflected for comparisons of anti-infrastructure protests in different countries. This list has so far only a tentative character. Further conceptual and empirical elaborations are needed. Nevertheless, it should have become clear that limiting the role of citizen action groups to sheer protest would lead their counterparts and also social scientific research to misconceive the nature of participation of such groups.

Acknowledgement

The chapter is based on the research project "communication strategies of local environmental groups", funded by the German Science Foundation (WO 842/6-1).

References

Barnes, M., Newman, J., and Sullivan, H. (2006). Discursive arenas: Deliberation and the constitution of identity in public participation at local level. *Social Movement Studies, 5*(3), 193–207.

Beck, U. (1997). Subpolitics. *Organization & Environment, 10*(1), 52–65.

Bräuer, M., and Wolling, J. (2014). Regionaler Protest und Massenmedien: Die Bedeutung von Massenmedien aus der Sicht von Bürgerinitiativen. In F. Oehmer (ed.), *Politische Interessenvermittlung und Medien. Funktionen, Formen und Folgen medialer Kommunikation von Parteien, Verbänden und sozialen Bewegungen* (326–343). Baden-Baden, Germany: Nomos.

Cammaerts, B. (2012). Protest logics and the mediation opportunity structure. *European Journal of Communication, 27*(2), 117–134.

Crossley, N. (2002). *Making sense of social movements. Contemporary Sociology* (Vol. 32). Buckingham, UK: Open University Press.

Della Porta, D., and Diani, M. (2006). *Social movements. An introduction.* Malden, MA: Blackwell Publishing.

Eisinger, P. K. (1973). The conditions of protest behavior in American cities. *The American Political Science Review, 67*(1), 11–28.

Gerhards, J., and Neidhardt, F. (1991). Strukturen und Funktionen moderner Öffentlichkeit. Fragestellungen und Ansätze. In S. Müller-Doohm, and K. Neumann-Braun (eds.), *Öffentlichkeit, Kultur, Massenkommunikation* (31–90). Oldenburg, Germany: BIS-Verlag.

Hilgartner, S., and Bosk, C. L. (1988). The rise and fall of social problems: A public arenas model. *The American Journal of Sociology, 94*(1), 53–86.

Inglehart, R., and Flanagan, S. C. (1987). Value change in industrial societies. *The American Political Science Review, 81,* 1281–1319.

Kaase, M. (1995). Partizipation. In D. Nohlen (ed.), *Wörterbuch Staat und Politik* (521–527). Bonn, Germany: Bundeszentrale für politische Bildung.

Kitschelt, H. P. (1986). Political opportunity structures and political protest: Anti-nuclear movements in four democracies. *British Journal of Political Science, 16*(1), 57–85.

Kriesi, H. (2004). Political context and opportunity. In D. Snow, S. Soule, and H. Kriesi (eds.), *The Blackwell companion to social movements* (67–90). Malden, MA: Blackwell.

Kubicek, H. (2014). "Mitreden" beim Netzausbau: Erwartungen, Wissensstand und Empfehlungen. In Bundesnetzagentur (ed.), *Wissenschaftsdialog 2014. Technologie, Landschaft und Kommunikation, Wirtschaft* (69–92). Germany: Bonn.

Lipsky, M. (1969). Protest as a political resource. *The American Political Science Review*, 62(4), 1144–1158.

Marg, S., Hermann, C., Hambauer, V., and Becké, A. B. (2013). "Wenn man was für die Natur machen will, stellt man da keine Masten hin". Bürgerproteste gegen Bauprojekte im Zuge der Energiewende. In L. Marg, S. Geiges, F. Butzlaff, and F. Walter (eds.), *Die Neue Macht der Bürger. Was motiviert die Protestbewegungen?* (94–138). Reinbek bei Hamburg, Germany: Rowohlt.

McCarthy, J. D., McPhail, C., and Smith, J. (1996). Selektionskriterien in der Berichterstattung von Fernsehen und Zeitungen: Eine vergleichende Fallstudie anhand von Demonstrationen in Washington D.C. in den Jahren 1982 und 1991. *Forschungsjournal NSB*, 9(1), 26–45.

Nowacki, A. (2015). *Bürgerproteste und Journalismus: wie wirken sich Beziehungen zwischen Bürgerinitiativen und Journalistinnen und Journalisten auf deren journalistisches Handeln aus?*. Ilmenau, Germany: Technische Universität Ilmenau.

Snow, D., Soule, S., and Kriesi, H. (2004). *The Blackwell companion to social movements*. Malden, MA: Blackwell.

Tarrow, S. (1996). States and opportunities: The political structuring of social movements. In D. McAdam, J. D. McCarthy, and M. N. Zald (eds.), *Comparative perspectives on social movements* (41–61). Cambridge, UK: Cambridge University Press.

Teorell, J., Torcal, M., and Montero, J. R. (2007). Political participation. Mapping the terrain. In J. W. Van Deth, J. R. Montero, and A. Westholm (eds.), *Citizenship and involvement in European democracies. A Comparative Analysis* (334–357). London, UK and New York, NY: Routledge.

Tilly, C. (1978). *From mobilization to revolution*. New York, NY: McGraw-Hill.

Tilly, C., and Tarrow, S. (2007). *Contentious politics*. Oxford, UK: Oxford University Press.

Van Deth, J. (2009). Politische Partizipation. In V. Kaina, and A. Römmerle (eds.), *Politische Soziologie. Ein Studienbuch* (141–162). Wiesbaden, Germany: VS Verlag.

Wolsink, M. (2000). Wind power and the NIMBY-Myth: Institutional capacity and the limited significance of public support. *Renewable Energy*, 21(1), 49–64.

12 Visibility, Voice and Encounter in Cosmopolitan Online Communication. Rethinking Cultural Citizenship in Post-Migrant Societies

Elke Grittmann and Tanja Thomas

Cosmopolitanism in the Digital Age

Increased mobility and forced migration have boosted the interconnectedness and increased "proximity" (Tomlinson 1999) of formerly distant others. In post-migrant societies[1], the encounter between migrants and non-migrants has become a common experience as well as a challenge in everyday life, which has been highly shaped by digital media cultures. In reference to intensive debates about options and constraints of intercultural and transcultural communication among individuals and groups of different cultural, ethnical and religious background, the concept of 'cosmopolitanism' has experienced some revival across various disciplines (Tomlinson 1999; Beck 2002; Breckenridge et al. 2002; Vertovec and Cohen 2002; Appiah 2006; Held 2010). By now, some scholars prefer the term 'another' (Benhabib 2006), 'new' (Strand 2010) or 'critical cosmopolitanism' (Delanty 2006); or some even replace the term with the concept of 'conviviality' (Gilroy 2004; Nowicka and Vertovec 2014) in order to overcome some of the cosmopolitan heritage, such as its Eurocentric bias. Nevertheless, all such concepts are driven by the idea of togetherness and 'recognition of the otherness of the other'.

Many expectations have been expressed towards digital media as a social space that may push the idea of cosmopolitanism, e.g. by offering access and spaces for encounter and debate for a diversity of people (Schachtner 2015) or by fostering the production of a social-structuring level of engagement in loose, temporal and elastic collectives that operate in social media environments (Varis and Bloemmert 2014). Moreover, as Appadurai (2016) recently argued, online communication may provide communicative access for cultural participation and belonging, hence for citizenship. Thereby, some scholars insist on the demand that belonging has to include 'the right to be different' (Rosaldo 1994, 402; Stevenson 2001, 2003) and that such claims could pave the way to new concepts of citizenship within nation states.

Considerations on cosmopolitanism, conviviality and (cultural) citizenship have been introduced and adopted in media and communication studies within the last decade (cf. cultural citizenship: Klaus and Drüeke 2011; Klaus and Lünenborg 2004, 2013; new cosmopolitanism: e.g. Corpus Ong 2009). While most studies on cultural citizenship and media mainly focused on national television programs, cosmopolitan theory has been adopted to explore representations, aesthetics and discourses of mainstream transnational news media (Silverstone 2006; Chouliaraki 2008a,b; Robertson 2010). In contrast to that, we will focus in this chapter on the preconditions, potentials and communicative practices of different online spaces. Presumed that the internet is characterised by what Fraser (1990) called the 'multiplicity of public spheres', the opportunities to enact cultural citizenship in digital media are a result of the cosmopolitan potential provided by different online projects and their (web)sites. Therefore, by making use of critical cosmopolitanism and (cultural) citizenship, we will first outline a theoretical framework. Our goal is to provide a heuristic tool for a critical and systematic understanding of the potential and the lived out communicative practices of different online platforms, which may help to create public spheres and facilitate mutual recognition, thus providing a precondition for participation. Participation is one of the "buzz words" of online communication. For years, the internet has been discussed as an important means that may foster participation in many different ways. Obviously, from such a perspective on communicative practices of online platforms, participation is not limited to political participation in the sense of institutionalised politics. Instead, the political is conceptualised as a dimension of all social processes, including online communication. In line with Carpentier (2015, 24), we argue that democratic participation should be distinguished from access and interaction as this "allows emphasizing the importance of equal power positions in decision making processes for the definition of participation". Nevertheless, from our view, there is a need to deepen our understandings of such preconditions of participation; research on 'cosmopolitan communication' may allow us to find new opportunities to offer and promote them.

In order to do so, in our second section we will introduce the concept of cultural citizenship and discuss how it has been addressed in media and communication studies so far. Until today, the concept is embedded in the idea of nation-states – although more and more people become relocated within a transnational context. Therefore, we will further develop the concept in the third section by linking it to the concept of critical cosmopolitanism, which we will examine in the context of prior media research. In the following, we will apply both concepts to online communication research. It is thus paramount to first introduce three analytical dimension, which allow us to conceptualise the different communicative modes that enable cultural citizenship in online communication: visibility, voice and encounter. Finally, by taking up the 'circuit of culture' (Du Gay 1997) as a model for the analysis of media communication and by studying different examples of online websites, we will systematically display and employ these dimensions.

Defining Cultural Citizenship in Media Cultures

The social position and civic rights of migrants or ethnic minorities in post-migrant societies have always been precarious and a question of inclusion and exclusion, of participation, negotiation and debate. The concept of 'cultural citizenship' offers a broader understanding of these processes in (digital) media cultures (Hermes and Dahlgren 2006). The term 'media cultures' suggests to analyse 'culture' in terms of cultural practices in and with media; it asks for a contextualisation of 'doing culture' within particular socioeconomic and historical settings, thereby taking into account questions of subjectivity and subjectivation, agency and power relations (Thomas and Krotz 2008). Such a focus on procedures, dynamics and practices corresponds with the understanding of cultural citizenship that we want to introduce here: Rosaldo (1994, 402) emphasises that cultural citizenship 'refers to the right to be different and to belong in a participatory democratic sense'. Thus, it compares in a very different way to former concepts of citizenship (e.g. Marshall 1950).[2] As Couldry (2006, 322) has summed up the discussion since then, such an approach 'has been used to make sense of arguments for including new groups of people as citizens in contemporary polities, or including new types of claim or conflict within civic or political space.' Similarly, Stevenson interpreted 'cultural citizenship', as Allan summed it up in his foreword, as 'a newly emerging interdisciplinary concept that is concerned with issues of recognition and respect, of responsibility and pleasure, and with visibility and marginality' (Allan 2003, XI). Hence, the cultural extension of the former political concept offers a productive integration of cultural practices (Stevenson 2003), in particular in everyday life (Klaus and Lünenborg 2012, 197).

However, some very important critical arguments against such a concept of cultural citizenship have meanwhile been brought forth since it is 'too easy to assume that we know what it looks like' (Couldry 2006, 322) and it underestimates the implications of power relationships (Klaus and Lünenborg 2012, 202). To that effect, Klaus and Lünenborg (2012, 204) argue for a non-essentialist interpretation of the concept. According to them, cultural citizenship 'is not so much something everyone *has or should have* [emphasis by the authors], but a set of strategies and practices to invoke processes of empowerment in order to subversively listen and to speak up in the public sphere' (Klaus and Lünenborg 2012, 204). In media cultures, such practices and strategies in everyday life are highly shaped by media institutions and media technologies. Consequently, these conditions must be taken into account in the conceptualisation of cultural citizenship. Klaus and Lünenborg (2004, 2012) suggest a three-dimensional model of cultural citizenship that comprises media production, media text and reception as constitutive parts. This model allows them to illustrate that reality television programs not only enable visibility and the production of meaning (representation) but also participation. Even though with their research on reality TV programs Klaus and Lünenborg provide important insights in forms of cultural citizenship on the representational level, like similar studies they still argue within a national culture. This is why some scholars (cf. Beck 2012) question such a 'methodological nationalism' that is not able to meet the challenges of global migration and media. The fact that communicative flows and encounters emerge beyond the frame of the national state requires a refined concept, which may contribute to a perspective beyond the nation state without at the same time neglecting it: critical cosmopolitanism.

Cosmopolitanization and Critical Cosmopolitanism

Critical cosmopolitanism has been introduced in the field of cosmopolitan studies as a 'critical attitude' (Delanty and He 2008, 324) and ethical response to fundamental questions of an increased globalisation and its social consequences since the 1990s. The term has been mainly coined by Delanty and He (2008) who speak about a 'cosmopolitan turn in social science' (2008, 324). Drawing on a long tradition of philosophy from antiquity and modernity (see Holton 2009), cosmopolitanism has been discussed since the Second World War as a universalistic principle. In its top-down conception, it has influenced international governance and ethics of institutions or laws on a transnational level. Vis-à-vis this still influential understanding as a universalistic normative order, critical cosmopolitanisms have been developed as a critical sociocultural approach (e.g. Szerszynski and Urry 2006; Beck 2011). Critical cosmopolitanism draws on a multiplicity of roots and approaches (Delanty and He 2008, 324; Holton 2009, 210) and tries to adapt to postcolonial critique (Gilroy 2004). Beyond certain specifies, all concepts of critical cosmopolitanisms share the understanding of cosmopolitanism as recognition of difference, hence the "Otherness of Others".

According to Delanty and He (2008, 328), global justice and equality are key features of critical cosmopolitanism. Although critical cosmopolitanism also refers to normative principles, it is nevertheless deeply engaged in the empirical research of current conditions: 'In normative terms' as Delanty and He stated, the approach 'is significant with respect to the current situation in which globalisation has brought about new challenges; it is also crucial in terms of cosmopolitanism itself, that is in interrogating and testing hypotheses of cosmopolitanism in an empirical world.' (Delanty and He 2008, 327)

In consequence, the term 'cosmopolitanization' has been introduced to put more and more emphasis on the empirical sociocultural processes of increasing global connectivity and encounters forced by globalisation and to coin a term which can be differentiated from cosmopolitanism (Beck 2011). Additionally, Beck and Sznaider (2006) also used the term 'banal cosmopolitanism' that strongly emphasises the interdependencies among others without claiming a simultaneous increase of normative cosmopolitan attitudes among those who are experiencing them. From our perspective, this opens up new perspectives for researching migration in general, and in particular for researching communication and its relevance for claiming and gaining cultural citizenship in digital media cultures. It provides a more precise analysis, e.g. of the quality of encounters; i.e. if the encounter goes hand in hand with the recognition of otherness and thereby fostering cosmopolitan ideas.

This is why the concept of critical cosmopolitanism has already been taken up in media and communication studies. The rise of transnational broadcasting news and worldwide news networks has created new forms of interconnectedness and globalised public spheres, thus raising new questions of responsibility and hospitality towards 'distant others' (Silverstone 2006). Some scholars argue that particular media aesthetics (Chouliaraki 2008a,b) and/or modes of representation (e.g. Lester and Cottle 2009; Robertson 2010) have the potential to evoke cosmopolitan obligations and dispositions in (western) audiences (e.g. Corpus Ong 2009; Kyriakidou 2009; Lindell 2014).

Until today, many scholars have highlighted the potential of new digital infrastructures that are perceived as spaces where people from different backgrounds may encounter each other and enter dialogues, thereby opening up opportunities to listen and to be heard. Nevertheless, cosmopolitan communication on the internet has rarely been discussed (Schachtner 2012) and explored (Mihelj et al. 2011).

Conceptualising Cultural Citizenship and Cosmopolitan Communication in Media Cultures

Given the current status of research, we will link the concepts of cultural citizenship and critical cosmopolitanism to enable a deeper understanding of online media's relevance that may foster communicative strategies and practices of cultural citizenship in post-migrant societies. Media are, as we have argued, both at the core of enabling cultural citizenship and recognition. While cultural citizenship entails mediated engagement in forms of (self-)representation and meaning production that 'signifies cultural belonging and constructs cultural identity' (Klaus and Lünenborg 2012, 205), the concept of critical cosmopolitanism focuses on the mutual recognition of difference. These two different concepts are not exclusive. In contrast, a critical cosmopolitanism which is conceptualised as normative without reproducing universalistic claims can be seen to be precondition of cultural citizenship.

In order to develop a heuristic model for an understanding of digital media's potential to create spaces of cosmopolitanism and thereby practices of cultural citizenship, we have to consider that the modes of online communication are not independent from technological features. Generally speaking, the encouragement of 'others' to engage in public and cultural spheres was quite limited in traditional media. Although online platforms share some common features with other media, they differ significantly in others. If we want to explore practices in online media that may foster access to cultural citizenship, we must take into account how the specific characteristics of these media shape the key dimensions that arrange communication in social spaces, thereby opening a path to mediated cultural citizenship.

But how is cultural citizenship enacted in online communication? Former concepts strengthen the rights of information, experiences, knowledge and participation (cf. Klaus and Lünenborg 2012). Taking up a different understanding of participation as outlined above and the important contribution of (mutual) recognition in both concepts of cultural citizenship and critical cosmopolitanism, we will enrich these considerations.

As a matter of fact, we suggest different dimensions to differentiate more precisely between participation as a political aim and its preconditions and practices. Thereby, we introduce the modes of visibility, voice and encounter as key dimensions of cultural citizenship which are fundamentally shaped by power relations and sociocultural norms. We conceptualise these key dimensions as follows:

Visibility: Here, we refer to Judith Butler's considerations about life and grievability. Butler raises awareness for visual experience and social visibility that is organised by normative frames which 'work to differentiate the lives we can apprehend from those we cannot' (Butler 2010, 3). (Social) Visibility is constituted by recognition and depends on its frames as part of social knowledge that is embedded in its historical, socio-economic and cultural context. In this sense, visibility in online communication means to become visible as an intelligible subject who is enabled to participate in meaning production and to be active in societal debates. However, these opportunities are not only but also configured by technical infrastructures of the online platform.

Voice: One of the key words of participation is 'voice'. Voice is connected to ideas of expression in public spheres, in particular in the context of the rights for equal expression and inequalities in public discourse. People actively raise their voices, something particularly connected to empowerment and democracy (Dahlgren 2005; Cammaerts 2008). While voice refers mainly to the active engagement of citizens in political discourse and political processes, we will broaden this understanding. Following Couldry (2010, 1), voice can be understood as a value, a concept, that 'operates both within and beyond politics'. According to Couldry (2010, 100), voice as a 'second order' value enables voice as process. Thus, in online communication it refers to users and producers who can not only vote, like or comment, but rather create their own content and express their own opinion, experiences and ideas. Furthermore, voice also includes the access to means of media production and representation which yields the possibility to raise one's own voice or become literally visible.

Encounter: Interactivity is defined as a key element of online communication (Van Dijk 2012). In contrast to traditional media, which are defined by their one-dimensional direction of communication, the internet enables interactive forms on blogs, websites or social media. However, while 'interactivity' refers to the technological precondition, we would like to introduce the term 'encounter'. First, encounter is a crucial term in the concepts of cosmopolitanism (Delanty 2011). Second, it refers to the practices of people rather than technological preconditions. Third, it focuses on the reciprocity of those who encounter. Consequently, actors as well as producers of online platforms come into view. While technological features are necessary preconditions to foster visibility, participation and encounter, it is the task of the active producers and produsers to determine how these dimensions are put into practice.

In light of these theoretical considerations, we will explore three online platforms as examples in order to illustrate how cultural citizenship and cosmopolitanism is framed by specific structures and dispositions in online communication websites and how both concepts are put into practice by both network actors, produsers and recipients. To this end, we have chosen three websites whose common aim is to provide and facilitate communication which enables any form of cultural citizenship as defined above (visibility, voice and/or encounter). As questions of cultural citizenship might in particular be recognised and negotiated on websites that are dedicated to migration issues, we searched for websites which focus on these topics. These three websites were chosen because they are explicitly dedicated to inter- and transcultural communication. They are located in three different countries: Forced Migration Online (FMO, Great Britain), Migazin (Germany) and Migrazine (Austria). FMO is an online-collection of resources related to refugees and forced migration hosted by academics.[3] Migazin is an independent online magazine which can be defined as participatory journalism. Finally, we will analyse the independent multilingual online-magazine Migrazine, which is published by Maiz, an autonomous organisation by and for migrant women (Zobl and Reitsamer 2012).

Even though all of these websites are explicitly dedicated to intercultural and transcultural communication, the main question is: how do they enable cosmopolitan communication and provide possibilities to enact cultural citizenship?

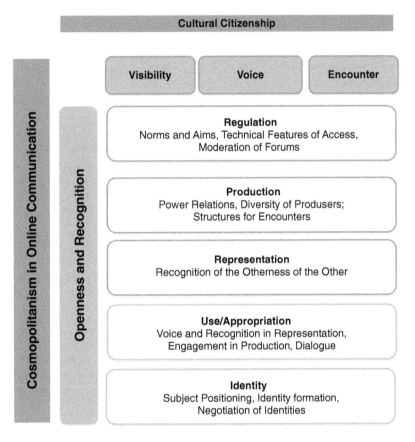

Figure 12.1 Cosmopolitanism in online communication and cultural citizenship: Levels and dimensions of research.

Exploring Cosmopolitanism and Cultural Citizenship

Cultural citizenship and cosmopolitanism in media communication are not only realised in different forms (visibility, voice, encounter) but also on multiple levels. A systematic model of these levels that allows researching practices and the construction of meaning has been provided by Du Gay et al. (1997). Their 'circuit of culture', developed to explore the specific culture of the Sony Walkman, focuses not only on the representation, but also considers the whole 'way of life' and the political, normative and technological context in which a cultural product or act is created and used. The circuit of culture includes five aspects: regulation, production, consumption, representation and identity. The connection of these fields is not linear; they are all related to and shaped by each other.

As illustrated in our figure, openness and recognition are the core characteristics of cosmopolitanism and can be enabled or denied on all five levels: normative regulations define who becomes visible. The diversity among producers may cause a multiplicity of perspectives, while on the level of representation and consumption the recognition of others can enable subject positions or negotiate identities. By addressing these different levels, we will establish a methodological cosmopolitanism that can help not only to define cosmopolitanism as a sole moral aim, but rather to explore it (Figure 12.1).

As openness is the 'crucial defining feature of cosmopolitanism' (Holton 2009, 116), we tried to develop a systematic identification of forms of cross-border openness in online communication on all levels. In the following, we want to provide some answers from our analysis of the aforementioned platforms. Methodologically, we combined qualitative content analysis (e.g. on representation) with document and literature analysis (e.g. to explore the cosmopolitan conditions of production, see below). In the following, we want to provide some answers from our analysis of the aforementioned platforms. By studying our three examples, we will show how cosmopolitanism can be evaluated in those projects and their online communication practices and how cultural citizenship can be enabled and practiced.

Regulation

Forms of regulation can be mainly defined as norms that guide the aims and the practices of the different websites, as well as technological communicative features provided by the producers to facilitate different forms of communications and engagement on the websites.

On the one hand, the normative goals of the three platforms are defined in their self-descriptions; on the other hand, one should examine how these goals can be assessed both by the given infrastructure and the communicative practices of the produsers. All three websites are dedicated to intercultural or transcultural communication; but in order to achieve that they use technical features in very different ways.

While FMO's (2011a) main aim is 'to support and facilitate research and policy making in the field' of forced migration, it refers to visibility via representation. FMO mainly provides information about migration issues. It is more or less a one-way communication (despite a variety of options for produsers to send emails or give some feedback to the provided information). Consequently, FMO does not offer features for dialogue or voice, in particular outside academic communities. Maiz describe their goal as 'to better the lives and work situations of migrant women in Austria and to promote their political and cultural participation, as well as to transform the existing unjust social conditions.' Therefore, we identified *voice* as one of the key issues with which Maiz, or to be more precise, their online magazine Migrazine is concerned. Migazin is a website that is particularly interested in providing possibilities to intensify dialogue of migrants in public discourse (Migazin, n.d.). This way, Migazin tries to promote trans-cultural *encounters*. Thus, there is an explicit cosmopolitan goal or claim of each of the online platforms, although they differ in as far as each of these three websites mainly address either visibility, or voice, or encounter as one of the key qualities that provide a space to enact cultural citizenship.

Production/Produsage

As the boundaries between producers and users are blurring in online communication (Bruns 2008), empirical research has taken the changing processes in decision-making within the production of meaning into account. Although one may argue that webmasters still define the institutional level, produsers are also involved in communicative practices and thus in the production of meaning.[4]

The multiplicity of identities and belongings as well as the plurality of actors in these networks of production and produsage enables the exchange of different experiences. According to Ulrich Beck, one should use the term 'cosmopolitanisation' (2002) to address the fact that the realities and experiences of an increased interconnectedness and encounter of (formerly) distant others can be observed empirically. From his view, cosmopolitanisation can be used to grasp the social consequence of globalisation without claiming that it is accompanied with cosmopolitan attitudes (Beck 2011, 1352).

These processes of cosmopolitanisation can be observed on the production level of the different websites. The editorial team of *Migrazine*, for example, consists of women that have experienced migration; the platform is open to women with different identities and belongings on all levels of production. In contrast, FMO is coordinated by a smaller team of the Refugee Study Centre (RSC) at Oxford University in Great Britain. The RSC has also hosted the website so far. The online magazine *Migazin* invites different producers to contribute with reports and commentaries on the website, however on a limited space compared to other news.

To get deeper insights into the ways these websites may encourage cosmopolitan communication, and cultural citizenship on the production level, further questions should be raised: How do producers and produsers differ regarding categories like social position, experience in different cultural contexts, religion, age, sexual orientation and so on?

Representation/Content

On the level of representation, all three websites are alert to a kind of communication that fosters the recognition of others. Due to the editorial control, the contributions of producers have to meet the given editorial requirements. Instead of mainly offering reports and studies *about others*, as FMO does, *Migazin* enables a wide variety of people to act as subjects by speaking about different experiences, participating and engaging in dialogue, though to a limited degree. More than any other platform, *Migazin* enables cultural citizenship in any dimension. While some research on social media noticed that communication across differences lacks reciprocal communication (Mihelj et al. 2011), websites like Migazin are able to provide different ways of encounter by carefully managing the communication processes and contributions, e.g. concerning one topic. To illustrate the quality of these encounters, we summarise the outcome of our qualitative content analysis of a debate on Muslim women wearing the headscarf at German schools (Migazin 2013). As a result of our analysis, we argue that the commentaries and discussions about an article were not only characterised by a respectful way of talking, but also by reciprocity (although in a limited way). The question of reciprocity is only one criterion of mutual recognition in commentaries. Others, which we cannot discuss broadly in this chapter, are, for example: Which topics are addressed? Can we – for example – notice an increase of discussions on the interrelations in processes of globalisation? Can we notice any debate about the processes and experiences of 'othering' on a meta-level?

Which aspects are made relevant regarding the boundaries of 'us' and 'the others'? Do people address nationality, income, education, job, religion, political affiliation? What kinds of similarities or differences are emphasised that produce distance or closeness toward otherness?

Use, Appropriation and Identities

Despite the fact that the circuit of culture presents use, appropriation and identities as separate units, we want to examine them in combination since they are deeply connected to each other. As we have shown, some websites are more engaged in delivering knowledge about others, as FMO does, or in offering practices of voice for producers, as in the case of *Migrazine*, or, even more, in providing ways to encounter each other, as in the case of *Migazin*. These varieties are bound to different forms of use and appropriation and thus to practices of cultural citizenship. Consequently, regulation, technical infrastructures and norms, production and representation are deeply intertwined with use and appropriation. Use and appropriation can be analysed as processes of meaning production that (dis)encourage norms and dispositions of recognition and openness. For example, mere discourses *about others* only enable negotiations within the dominant code (Hall 1980) while perpetuating certain intelligible subject positions. In contrast to that, online communication provides communication beyond difference. It thereby creates a potential space to develop a cosmopolitan disposition and attitude by negotiating subject positions that refer to the 'self', identity, belonging and to the 'other'. For example, a survey by FMO about the users of their platform has shown that their users are mainly from Western societies, only a few are forced migrants (FMO 2011b). Textual analysis can reveal how open produsers act towards others (we have mentioned the discussion about wearing headscarves in German schools, Migazin 2013). Can we observe negotiations in conflicts? Can we notice the willingness or ability to assume perspectives? How is each position/perspective emphasised and evaluated? In particular in dialogues, individual dispositions and attitudes become visible. To find out whether those users of the websites who are not active in produsage were to develop cosmopolitan attitudes and practices, empathy or cosmopolitan identities of belonging, would obviously require qualitative audience studies. From our perspective, such studies can be seen as huge challenges of online research on cosmopolitan communication and cultural citizenship.

Conclusion: A Concept for Further Research

Taking up the conditions of mobility, we have raised the question as to whether and how transcultural internet platforms provide spaces for enacting cultural citizenship and critical cosmopolitanism. We have argued that cultural citizenship is not a right but a bond of practices which enable visibility, voice and encounter which brings together the 'Self-and-the-Other' (Couldry 2006). Cultural citizenship is constituted by different strategies and practices which, as we have argued and conceptualised theoretically, could be evaluated along the different dimensions of meaning production according to the 'circuit of culture'. In online practices, the technological structures (Dahlgren 2005) and media regulation (du Gay et al. 1997) of the internet as well as the transcultural or cosmopolitan dispositions, norms and aims of the platform providers shape the spaces of communicative practices for all actors, (prod-)users, participants and recipients, and thus shape the modes of cultural citizenship and cosmopolitanism. By studying these different levels, one can assess the openness and the mode of recognition enabled in digital media. As we have demonstrated, it is the interplay of regulation, technological infrastructures, production, practices of representation, as well as use and appropriation that shapes online communication in this particular field. Furthermore, we have offered an enhanced way to explore the potential of online communication to enable cultural citizenship through the lens of new critical cosmopolitan theories. As our research has shown, openness and recognition as key characteristics of cosmopolitanism could be realised on different levels and by different strategies. Even though online communication on websites offers a broad potential for cultural citizenship and cosmopolitanism, each of the platforms practice cultural citizenship and openness differently, enabling visibility, voice and encounter on the levels of regulation, production, representation, use/appropriation and identity. However, the analysis of the three platforms has also demonstrated certain boundaries and limits to cosmopolitan online communication. The possibility to engage is partly restricted and produsage is limited.

Although we have explored exclusively websites, the main insights can also be transferred to the research of other types social media. Furthermore, the concept may offer an intriguing approach for social movements and organisations in respect of how to conceptualise and enhance online communication that is dedicated to values of cosmopolitanism and cultural citizenship.

Notes

1 The prefix 'post' does not signify the end of migration but describes social negotiation processes after migration has occurred:

> Post-migrant societies are societies in which: (a) Social change towards a heterogeneous underlying structure has been acknowledged ('Germany is a country of immigration') regardless of whether this transformation is seen as positive or negative, (b) Immigration and emigration are recognized as phenomena that have a tremendous impact on the country, which can be discussed, regulated and negotiated but not reversed, (c) Structures, institutions and political cultures are adapted ex post to the identified migration reality (i.e. post-migration), resulting in, on the one hand, greater permeability and upward mobility but, on the other hand, also in defensive reactions and distributional conflicts.
>
> (Foroutan 2015)

2 T.H. Marshall has already introduced a differentiated understanding of citizenship in 1950 (Marshall 1950) – he distinguished three forms of citizenship: civil, political and social, proceeding each other chronologically since the eighteenth century.
3 FMO is currently (August 2017) under revision.
4 While producers have the power to decide what kind of knowledge they will create on their platforms, producers collaborate in this process or create their own open-access communities/platforms in order to develop more equality oriented collaborative forms of knowledge production (Bruns 2008).

References

Allan, S. (2003). Series editor's foreword. In N. Stevenson (ed.), *Cultural citizenship. Cosmopolitan questions* (xi–xii). Maidenhead, UK: Open University Press.
Appadurai, A. (2016). Streben nach Hoffnung. Das Narrativ der Flucht und die Ideologie des Nationalstaates. *Blätter für deutsche und internationale Politik, 1/2016*, 95–103.
Appiah, K. A. (2006). *Cosmopolitanism. Ethics in a world of strangers.* New York, NY: Norton.

Beck, U. (2002). The cosmopolitan perspective. Sociology in the second age of modernity. In S. Vertovec, and R. Cohen (eds.), *Conceiving cosmopolitanism: Theory, context and practice* (61–85). Oxford, UK: Oxford University Press.

Beck, U. (2011). Cosmopolitanism as imagined communities of global risk. *American Behavioral Scientist, 55*(10), 1346–1361.

Beck, U. (2012). Global inequality and human rights. A cosmopolitan perspective. In M. Heinlein et al. (eds.), *Futures of modernity. Challenges for cosmopolitical thought and practice* (109–127). Bielefeld: transcript.

Beck, U., and Sznaider, N. (2006). Unpacking cosmopolitanism for the social sciences: A research agenda. *British Journal of Sociology, 57*(1), 1–23.

Benhabib, S. (2006). *Another cosmopolitanism. Hospitality, sovereignity, and democratic iterations*. New York, NY: Oxford University Press.

Breckenridge, C. A., Pollock, S., Bhabha, H. K., and Chakrabarty, D. (eds.) (2002). *Cosmopolitanism*. Durham, NC: Duke University Press.

Bruns, A. (2008). The active audience: Transforming journalism from gatekeeping to gatewatching. In C. Paterson, and D. Domingo (eds.), *Making online news: The ethnography of new media production* (172–184). New York, NY: Peter Lang.

Butler, J. (2010). *Frames of war. When is life grievable?* London, UK and New York, NY: Verso Press.

Cammaerts, B. (2008). Critiques on the participatory potentials of web 2.0. *Communication, Culture & Critique, 1*, 358–377.

Carpentier, N. (2015): Differentiating between access, interaction and participation. *Conjunctions, 2*(2), 7–28.

Chouliaraki, L. (2008a). The mediation of suffering and the vision of a cosmopolitan public. *Television & New Media, 9*(5), 371–391.

Chouliaraki, L. (2008b). The symbolic power of transnational media. Managing the visibility of suffering. *Global Media and Communication, 4*(3), 329–351.

Corpus Ong, J. (2009). The cosmopolitan continuum. Locating cosmopolitanism in media and cultural studies. *Media, Culture, Society, 31*(3), 449–466.

Couldry, N. (2006). Culture and citizenship. The missing link? *European Journal of Cultural Studies, 9*(3), 321–339.

Couldry, N. (2010). *Why voice matters. Culture and politics after neoliberalism*. Los Angeles et al.: Sage.

Dahlgren, P. (2005). The internet, public spheres, and political communication: Dispersion and deliberation. *Political Communication, 22*, 147–162.

Delanty, G. (2006). The cosmopolitan imagination: critical cosmopolitanism and social theory. *The British Journal of Sociology, 57*(1), 25–47.

Delanty, G. (2011). Cultural diversity, democracy and the prospects of cosmopolitanism: A theory of cultural encounters. *The British Journal of Sociology, 62*(4), 633–656.

Delanty, G., and He, B. (2008). Cosmopolitan perspectives on European and Asian transnationalism. *International Sociology, 23*(3), 323–344.

du Gay, P. et al. (1997). *Doing cultural studies. The story of the Sony Walkman*. London, UK: Sage.

Foroutan, N. (2015). Post-migrant society. *Bundeszentrale für Politische Bildung*. Accessed August 1, 2017. www.bpb.de/gesellschaft/migration/kurzdossiers/205295/post-migrant-society.

Fraser, N. (1990). Rethinking the public sphere: A contribution to the critique of actually existing democracy. *Social Text, 25/26*, 56–80.

Gilroy, P. (2004). *After empire: Melancholia or convivial culture?* London, UK: Routledge.

Hall, S. (1980): Encoding/decoding. In S. Hall, D. Hobson, A. Lowe, and P. Willis (eds.), *Culture, media, language* (57–72). London: Hutchinson.

Held, D. (2010). *Cosmopolitanism. Ideal and realities.* Cambridge, UK: Polity Press.

Hermes, J., and Dahlgren, P. (2006) (eds.). Cultural studies and citizenship. Themed issue *European Journal of Cultural Studies*, 9(3), 259–265.

Holton, R. J. (2009): *Cosmopolitanisms. New thinkings and new directions.* New York, NY: Palgrave MacMillan.

Klaus, E., and Drüeke, R. (2011). More or less desirable citizens: Mediated spaces of identity and cultural citizenship. *Global Media Journal*, 1(2), 1–16. Accessed August 1, 2017. http://www.globalmediajournal.de/de/2011/12/09/more-or-less-desirable-citizens-mediated-spaces-of-identity-and-cultural-citizenship/.

Klaus, E., and Lünenborg, M. (2004). Cultural citizenship. Ein kommunika-tionswissenschaftliches Konzept zur Bestimmung kultureller Teilhabe in der Mediengesellschaft. *Medien & Kommunikationswissenschaft*, 52(2), 193–213.

Klaus, E., and Lünenborg, M. (2012). Cultural citizenship. Participation by and through media. In E. Zobl, and R. Drüeke (eds.), *Feminist media. Participatory spaces, networks and cultural citizenship* (197–212). Bielefeld, Germany: transcript.

Kyriakidou, M. (2009). Imagining ourselves beyond the nation? Exploring cosmopolitanism in relation to media coverage of distant suffering. *Studies in Ethnicity and Nationalism*, 9(3), 481–496.

Lindell, J. (2014). *Cosmopolitanism in a mediatized world: The social stratification of global orientations.* Karlstad: Karlstads universitet.

Marshall, T. H. (1950). *Citizenship and social class and other essays.* Cambridge, UK: Cambridge University Press.

Mihelj, S., Van Zoonen, L., and Vis, F. (2011). Cosmopolitan communication online: YouTube responses to the anti-Islam film Fitna. *The British Journal of Sociology*, 62(4), 613–632.

Nowicka, M., and Vertovec, S. (eds.) (2014). Special Issue. Convivialities. *European Journal of Cultural Studies*, 17(4), 341–486.

Robertson, A. (2010). *Mediated cosmopolitanism.* Cambridge, UK: Polity Press.

Rosaldo, R. (1994). Cultural citizenship and educational democracy. *Cultural Anthropology*, 9(3), 402–411.

Schachtner, C. (2012). Cultural Flows and virtuelle Öffentlichkeiten. Die Rolle digitaler Medien in transkulturalen/transnationalen Diskursen. *Medien & Kommunikationswissenschaft*, 60(4), 536–560.

Schachtner, C. (2015). Transculturality in the internet: Culture flows and virtual publics. *Current Sociology Monograph*, 63(2), 228–243.

Silverstone, R. (2006). *Media and morality.* Cambridge, UK: Polity Press.

Stevenson, N. (ed.) (2001). *Culture and citizenship.* London, UK: Sage.

Stevenson, N. (2003). *Cultural citizenship. Cosmopolitan questions.* Maidenhead, UK: Open University Press.

Strand, T. (2010). The Making of a new Cosmopolitanism. *Studies in Philosophy and Education*, 29(2), 229–242.

Szerszynski, B., and Urry, J. (2006). Visuality, mobility and the cosmopolitan: Inhabiting the world from afar. *The British Journal of Sociology*, 57(1), 113–131.

Thomas, T., and Krotz, F. (2008). Medienkultur und soziales Handeln. Begriffsarbeiten zur Theorieentwicklung. In Thomas, T. (ed.), *Medienkultur und soziales Handeln* (17–42), Wiesbaden, Germany: VS.

Tomlinson, J. (1999). *Globalization and culture*. Cambridge, UK: Polity Press.

Van Dijk, J. (2012). *The network society*. London, UK: Sage.

Varis, P., and Bloemmert, J. (2014). Conviviality and collectives on social media: Virality, memes, and new social structures. Tilburg: *Tilburg Papers in Culture Studies no. 108*, 21. Accessed August 1, 2017. www.tilburguniversity.edu/upload/83490ca9–659d-49a0–97db-ff1f8978062b_TPCS_108_Varis-Blommaert.pdf.

Vertovec, S., and Cohen, R. (2002). *Conceiving cosmopolitans. Theory, context, and practice*. Oxford, UK et al.: Oxford University Press.

Zobl, E., and Reitsamer, R. (2012). Feminist media production in Europe. A research report. In E. Zobl, and R. Drüeke (eds.), *Feminist media. Participatory spaces, networks and cultural citizenship* (21–54). Bielefeld, Germany: transcript.

Sources

FMO (2011a). Forced migration online. Accessed August 1, 2017. www.forcedmigration.org/about/about-us.

FMO (2011b). Survey 2010. Accessed August 1, 2017. www.forcedmigration.org/about/about-us/survey.

Maiz.at (2013). Maiz is … Accessed August 1, 2017. www.maiz.at/de/node/5.

Migazin (n.d.). About us (German: Über uns). Accessed August 1, 2017. www.migazin.de/uber-uns/.

Migazin (2013). Das Kopftuch. Verschleierte Probleme. Accessed August 1, 2017. www.migazin.de/2013/05/23/das-kopftuch-verschleierte-probleme/comment-page-9/#comments.

www.Migrazine.at (n.d.). Online magazine by women migrants for all (German: online magazin von migrantinnen für alle). Accessed August 1, 2017. www.migrazine.at/.

13 Mapping the 'Search Agenda'

A Citizen-Centric Approach to Electoral Information Flows

Filippo Trevisan, Andrew Hoskins, Sarah Oates and Dounia Mahlouly

New Media Ecologies for Informed Voters

In the digital age, the idea that voters can use technology to set their own informational agenda and learn about the issues that truly interest them, reaching beyond the slogans offered by political campaigns, sounds rather compelling. However, scholars of political communication continue to be divided on this point. On the one hand, authors, such as Chadwick (2013), have argued that interactive platforms can open up opportunities for 'non-elite' political agents to influence the 'political information cycle'. On the other hand, several scholars have expressed doubts about the pluralising effects of new media in the context of election campaigns. Since Howard Dean's pioneering 'crowd-sourced' campaign in the 2004 US Democratic primaries, sceptical scholars have argued that, by 'redlining some constituents and communities and then narrowcasting political content, hypermedia campaigns diminish the amount of shared text in the public sphere' (Howard 2006, 183). This arguably creates an informational environment where "the decidedly undemocratic view of *controlled interactivity* is how most campaigns operate" (Stromer-Galley 2014, 2), giving voters only very limited opportunities to engage with a range of different views.

Evidence has been gathered that supports both these arguments. Yet, given that many studies have focused primarily on the 'supply-side' of online electoral information (Lilleker and Vedel 2013) – i.e. the online activities of candidates and the content of official campaign messages – it is essential to look more in detail at the demand-side: How do issues gather prominence on contemporary election agendas? And, crucially, are voters granted a greater role than that of target audiences in this process? This chapter makes an initial contribution towards answering these broad questions by reviewing how voters use search engines in today's constantly evolving media landscape. As Hoskins (2013, 4) noted, 'the influences and impact of any medium cannot be understood in isolation from other media.' Instead, voters interact simultaneously with multiple forms of media that enable them to personalise the information

230 *Filippo Trevisan et al.*

they receive and interact with it in a variety of ways. To describe this changing environment, the idea of 'media ecology' – i.e. the idea that different forms of media can be understood and studied like organic life forms as though existing in a complex set of interrelationships within a specific balanced environment – has been reviewed in recent years. For Postman (1970, 161), media ecology is

> the matter of how media of communication affect human perception, understanding, feeling, and value; and how our interaction with media facilitates or impedes our chances of survival. The word ecology implies the study of environments, their structure, content, and impact on people.

The balance of the media ecology is important as what has been seen as the 'dominant' medium of a given "entelechy" (i.e. the structuring of (the) common experiences of each generation, see Mannheim 1952; Volkmer 2006) shapes the mediated engagement with election campaigns. Technological developments, it is argued, change all these interrelationships, transforming the existing balance and thus potentially impacting upon the entire ecology.

In light of this, it is essential to investigate empirically how new and emergent forms of media upset and re-define the traditional media balance, possibly affording voters' opportunities to set a specific information agenda for themselves that is less tied to the issues that dominate traditional news coverage. In recent years, several studies focused on the relationship between Twitter and television, particularly regarding the use of Twitter during televised debates between candidates (e.g. Anstead and O'Loughlin 2011; Chadwick 2011; Elmer 2013). Although this work yielded some interesting results, its main limitation lies in the fact that Twitter users are a relatively small and unrepresentative minority of internet users. In order for this type of research to embrace a broader demographic and dig deeper into the 'demand' side of the political information 'market,' this chapter presents a new method that combines the analysis of open access Google Trends data (www.google.com/trends) with the exploration of relevant content drawn from established news media outlets.

This book sheds light on the changing nature of political participation in democratic nations at a time of increased interaction between institutions, novel forms of media and citizens. Early analyses of internet politics were dominated by theoretically driven paradigms that presented the internet as either an agent of deep democratisation (Stromer-Galley 2000) or yet another venue for 'politics as usual,' which would reinforce existing elites (Margolis and Resnick 2000). While literature in this area has become increasingly more sophisticated in recent years, particularly regarding the relevance of social media for citizen participation, we continue to know little about the role that search engines play in today's political processes. In particular, we know very little about how voters search for information about elections online, and whether this provides them with resources that enable them to participate in elections more effectively or feel more empowered. This is despite the observation that search remains the most popular (Purcell et al. 2012; Dutton and Blank 2013) and trusted (Sanz and Stancik 2014) way for people to find information online. By looking at the electoral information environment from the point of view of voters immersed in an ever-expanding array of media, this chapter seeks to conceptualise how search engine use could boost their ability to participate in elections by extending their informational agendas beyond the issues set by official campaigns and traditional news media outlets. In particular, this chapter asks whether voters have used search engines to fulfil informational needs that were not immediately addressed by established news outlets in recent democratic elections. Three different case studies are analysed to test the idea of a 'search agenda.' These include the 2010 UK general election, the 2012 US presidential election and the 2013 Italian parliamentary election.

The Search Agenda

Internet search, one could argue, expands the purposive nature of information gathering (Molotch and Lester 1974) as it enables citizens to sort through virtually limitless amounts of content and find the information that best suits their interests. Arguably, this could boost the ability of voters to learn about issues other than those promoted by elite players, such as journalists, campaign strategists and PR firms. Nevertheless, any study investigating this hypothesis ought to remember that 'the Internet is growing in popularity but this is not at the cost of television's popularity as a news source [in elections]' (Vergeer 2013, 10). Online information gathering in the new media ecology occurs oncurrently with the continued contribution of print and broadcast media to electoral contests.

In light of this, it is useful to conceptualise information flows in contemporary elections as resulting from the interaction of three different and competing, but also partially overlapping, 'agendas,' each of which is defined in function of the type of actors that influence it. These include: the 'news media agenda,' the 'official campaigns agenda,' and, finally, the 'user agenda.' While the roles of news media, parties and politicians in agenda setting have been addressed for decades by political science and public relations researchers (McCombs and Shaw, 1972), the changing role of citizens in this process is yet to be addressed appropriately. Multiple online platforms, including social media sites such as Facebook and Twitter, present users with opportunities to interact with topics and issues that the news media and official campaigns have ignored or, at best, covered only in part, fostering the growth of a distinct user agenda.

That said, social media platforms push information towards users through their contacts, creating a more directed experience. In contrast, search engines require individual citizen-users to take the initiative and look up information online, affording them a more 'entrepreneurial' role and greater freedom to build their own information agenda. This 'search agenda' is best understood as the sum of multiple individual searches that generate a pattern without being centrally coordinated in the same way as political campaigns and news editorial processes. Citizens who use search engines to find information related to an election make a deliberate choice to find out more about a given topic, event or person. However, search is likely to be all but independent of external influences, including from news media and official campaigns. This generates a highly dynamic informational space in which issues that originate from one specific agenda can translate rapidly into others.

In other words, to what extent, if at all, did the 'search agenda' depart from the issues covered in traditional news outlets and official campaigns? The key to answering this question lies in the ability to establish a clear timeline of when new issues gain prominence on different forms of mass media as this can provide useful hints as to who (or what) drives election information flows in contemporary elections. This task requires a methodology capable of tracking the informational trajectories of key electoral issues across both search engines and established forms of media. Our use of Google Trends plays a key role in this process.

Google Trends as a Method

Google Trends is a free tool that elaborates archived search data to show fluctuations in the popularity of any given keyword or set of keywords on Google, as long as users have carried out a minimum number of relevant searches. Its output consists of normalised data measured against the total number of searches registered during the period under examination. Individual Google Trends scores derive from actual search records normalised on a scale from 0 to 100, where 100 is assigned to the day, week or month – depending on the length of the period under scrutiny – in which the given keyword(s) were searched most frequently. All the other values are calculated in function of their distance from the highest volume value. Thus, Google Trends identifies swings in user-interest in specific topics, people or events by carrying out longitudinal comparisons of the search frequency for inter-related terms within one or multiple countries. Additional geographical filters can be applied to focus on specific regions or even cities in certain countries.

By logging into Google, it is possible to download Google Trends data as CSV files and use them to build additional visualisations. This tool also identifies the terms that were associated most frequently with those inputted by the researcher in Google search queries, which may offer insights into how users move across topics or between different aspects of the same topic. Superimposing this type of information on a timeline of key campaign events and relevant news media coverage could provide important insights for assessing information flows in contemporary elections.

As Google Trends output is normalised, the actual number of relevant searches carried out for a certain keyword remains undisclosed. In addition, we do not know which websites users were likely to visit as a result of their Google queries. The fact that Google Trends does not provide search volume data invites scepticism towards work on public opinion in which Google Trends output has been used in place of survey data (e.g. Scharkow and Vogelgesang 2011). For this reason, it is unsurprising that recent studies also showed it is not possible to use Google Trends scores to predict election results (Lui et al. 2011; Yasseri and Bright 2014), given that this approach ignores some of the tool's main limitations, including doubts over the representativeness of its output, which one of the authors has discussed in detail elsewhere (Trevisan 2014). As with other digital data, it would be misleading to assume that search engine records could simply stand in for significant population indicators.

Instead, Google Trends provides a relative measure of how likely users are to search for information about a certain topic, person or event within a specific period of time. As the keyword(s) and timeframe selected for the analysis fundamentally influence Google Trends outputs, these should never be interpreted in isolation. Rather, they need to be analysed in conjunction with the broader political and media environments that surround them as it is important to account for contextual factors that may have influenced what people searched for and how they did it. Given the ability of established news media outlets to increase the perceived salience and urgency of a given issue, a useful first step is to ascertain whether searches for information on certain topics occurred before or after these gained traction in traditional media coverage. One way to do this is by creating a normalised measure of news popularity that uses the same scale as Google Trends results and can be superimposed directly on the relevant Google Trends chart to generate a visualisation of whether internet search patterns mirrored news coverage trends, or, Google users pursued a different informational agenda. In order to do this, we propose using online news databases to retrieve all the news items that focused on the issue(s) under scrutiny and then normalising the frequency scores obtained for each day on a scale from 0 to 100, where 100 represents the day with the highest number of relevant news items and all the other values are derived from it. For the purposes of the study discussed in this chapter, comparable news popularity indexes were created by searching the main collections of national newspaper articles and TV news transcripts on Lexis Nexis. All the news items that mentioned the main issue(s) associated with the biggest search peaks in their headline or first paragraph during the pre-election period were included in the sample. This step was taken in order to ensure that the analysis concentrates on news items that focused specifically on the issue in question rather than those that mentioned it only in passing.

Comparing Political Information Search in Different 'Media Ecologies'

Given that the use of search engines and online media more generally is likely to be influenced by the broader political, media and cultural context, the empirical portion of this chapter looks at three country case studies, namely: the United Kingdom, the United States and Italy. There are important differences between these three democracies that can affect the use of search engines and their relationship with traditional mass media.

First, the United Kingdom features a parliamentary system. In addition, commercial players dominate the British print media sector while public sector broadcasters (the BBC) are major producers of TV, radio and online news that audiences arguably tend to perceive as 'objective'. Second, the United States is characterised by a presidential system and commercial ownership across both print and broadcast media. Third, the Italian media system, given its high concentration of ownership and direct government influence on state TV, has been described as only 'partly free' by international observers (Freedom House 2015, 222–226).

For these reasons, these countries are approached here as having different media ecologies. In particular, it seems reasonable to expect perceived media bias and the ability to trust established news outlets to influence the ways in which citizens interact with more novel and less directed forms of online media, including search engines. A media system that is less free may act as an incentive for audiences to behave more entrepreneurially on new media platforms, seeking alternative perspectives or information about entirely different issues than those represented in traditional media coverage. In turn, more active audiences may also affect the way in which established news media operate, fundamentally challenging the traditional balance of a given media ecology.

Google Trends was used to investigate the popularity of searches involving the names of the main political leaders in each country over a period of three months surrounding recent elections: the 2010 UK general elections, the 2012 US presidential election and the 2013 Italian parliamentary elections. Google Trends queries were carried out in the local language, and the appropriate geographical filters were applied to focus on searches from each country individually. Findings from this initial part of the study informed a deeper investigation of country-specific trends, such as the potential connection between internet searches for information about politicians' gaffes and related policy 'themes' in the United States and the United Kingdom, as well as the consolidation of a new type of populism in Italy. Undoubtedly, looking at searches for information about political leaders is only one of many possible ways to investigate the 'search agenda.' While this makes for a good starting point in this nascent research area, the considerations presented in this chapter are certainly not meant to be exhaustive. Future work in this area could also focus on a broader set of election-related internet searches, including those for political parties and flagship policies.

Search Peaks on Google and Candidates' Gaffes

In order to better understand the role of internet search in equally solid but politically different democracies, it is useful to discuss key search trends for the United Kingdom and the United States in parallel. In broad terms, search patterns of information about presidential candidates in the United States (Barack Obama and Mitt Romney) and the leaders of the three main British political parties, and therefore candidates to the role of prime minister (David Cameron, Gordon Brown and Nick Clegg), identified some interesting similarities. However, a more detailed exploration of seemingly equivalent search spikes and a contextual analysis of related news coverage revealed some fundamental differences between these two countries.

Except for polling day (6 May 2010 in the United Kingdom and 6 November 2012 in the United States), the most substantial search peaks in the three-month period examined for this study were associated with TV appearances by presidential candidates and party leaders in the two countries (Figures 13.1 and 13.2).[1] In particular, the televised election debates – a longstanding tradition in the United States, but a complete novelty in the United Kingdom in 2010 – seemed to be major drivers of citizen interest in politics in both countries. The continued influence of TV in electoral contests is noteworthy at a time of unprecedented connectivity and hypermedia campaigns. However, it is worth noting that these search peaks occurred at slightly different moments in each country. In Britain, users tended to Google for information on party leaders on the very same days as the televised debates (15, 22 and 29 April). Conversely, Americans were more likely to search for information on Barack Obama and Mitt Romney on the days immediately after each of the TV debates (4, 17 and 23 October).

While we provided a more extensive discussion of the significance of this and other differences between US and UK contexts in a separate paper (Trevisan et al., 2016), it is useful to note here that time differences in otherwise similar search patterns may indicate different approaches to search engines on the part of local users. One possible explanation could be that British voters used search engines to learn about party leaders before each debate and check their statements, background and policy positions in 'real time' during the debates. Instead, US voters might have turned to Google following the TV debates in order to review and reflect on what the candidates had said, possibly looking for clips, transcripts or commentary.

In addition to candidates' TV appearances, other notable 'search catalysts' included both official campaign events, such as party conventions in the United States (Figure 13.1)[2] and the announcement of the election date in the United Kingdom (Figure 13.2), as well as less predictable non-political events that granted candidates intense media exposure. Most notably, searches for Barack Obama peaked when he visited the areas worst affected by Hurricane Sandy, particularly on 31 October 2012. That said, some search peaks did not appear to be connected to any immediately identifiable campaign or media event. In particular, two peaks stood out, namely: the one registered for Mitt Romney on 18 September 2012 in the United States, and the one registered for Gordon Brown on 28 April 2010 in the United Kingdom.

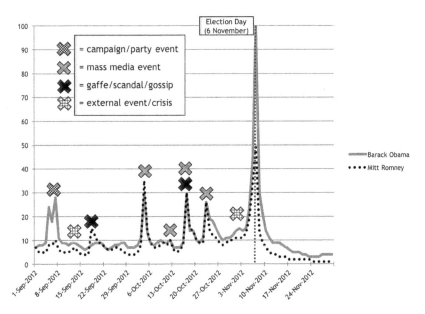

Figure 13.1 Google Trends scores for Barack Obama and Mitt Romney in the US, Sept.–Nov. 2012.

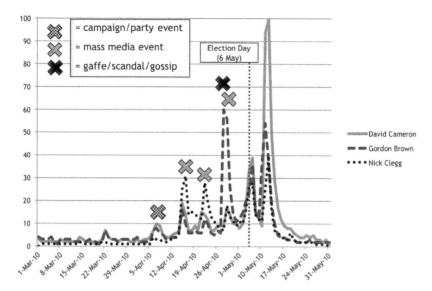

Figure 13.2 Google Trends score for UK party leaders, March–May 2010.

No key campaign events or planned candidate media appearances occurred on those days. Instead, on each of those dates, Romney and Brown respectively found themselves at the centre of two widely publicised gaffes. On 28 April 2010, Gordon Brown was overheard describing a Labour party supporter whom he had spoken to during a campaign visit as a "bigoted woman". This conversation, which was meant to be a private exchange between Brown and his aides, was caught by a Sky News microphone that had inadvertently been left on the then British Prime Minister's jacket and immediately became breaking news branded as 'bigot gate.' With little more than one week to go before the election, British media dedicated a great amount of coverage to this episode to the point that *Time* magazine included 'bigot-gate' among its 'Top 10 Over-reported Stories of 2010' (Fastenberg 2010). In another embarrassing incident, Mitt Romney was secretly recorded while he was talking with contempt about the '47 per cent of the people who will vote for the president [Obama] no matter what'[3] during a private fundraising event. This video was posted on the website of the progressive magazine Mother Jones on 17 September 2012 and generated a huge amount of interest online, including through a series of popular memes. In fact, looking through the search peaks identified for this study revealed that at least one more was connected to a further gaffe by Romney. That is, his remark during the second presidential debate about 'binders full of women', which generated a considerable number of comments about Romney's supposed sexist attitudes.

While it may be tempting to characterise the amount of interest that these gaffes and other mundane episodes, including Donald Trump's bombastic campaign in the 2016 US presidential election, generated among users as further evidence of a general trivialisation of politics, it is important to also ask whether there is more than that to them. In particular, is it possible that seemingly frivolous gaffes acted as springboards for Google users to search for information about policy issues associated with these episodes? In other words, could moments such as the '47 per cent' video, 'binders full of women' and 'bigot-gate' have inspired voters to use search engines to make a 'thematic leap'? If so, did they do that independently, looking at issues that thus far had been off the election agenda or were their searches influenced by the content of established news media? We addressed these questions by querying Google Trends for searches about policy issues that voters might have associated with these episodes and comparing their popularity on Google and in the news media in each country. Policy issues that may have been at the centre of a thematic leap were identified as those that were most closely connected to the nature of each episode and for which candidates were criticised most harshly in their immediate aftermath. These included gender equity and women's rights ('binders full of women' gaffe) and immigration ('bigot-gate').

The 'Thematic Leap' in US Searches

For comparative purposes, it is useful to analyse in depth the 'binders full of women' gaffe as it, like 'bigot-gate' in the United Kingdom, occurred on mainstream TV. Indeed, the '47 per cent' video could be a relevant case study, too. However, the fact that that gaffe appeared first on the website of a liberal niche magazine made it less suitable for comparison with the British case. In addition, at its peak 'binders full of women' was nearly five times more popular than the '47 per cent' incident among Google users in the United States, suggesting perhaps a stronger catalysing ability of television compared to online content. Therefore, we used a broad set of keywords closely connected to women's rights and gender equity issues in order to verify search trends for information on these topics before and after Romney's gaffe during the second televised debate.[4] This generated some surprising results. Most notably, searches for information on women's rights and gender equity rapidly climbed to their maximum level on the day that followed the 'binders full of women' gaffe (17 October, Figure 13.3). Although levels of interest for these issues fluctuated during the period analysed in this study, on average American Google users were substantially more likely to search for information on women's rights and gender equity following the gaffe (mean = 40.5; median = 41) than during the previous weeks of the campaign (mean = 34.48; median = 34.5).

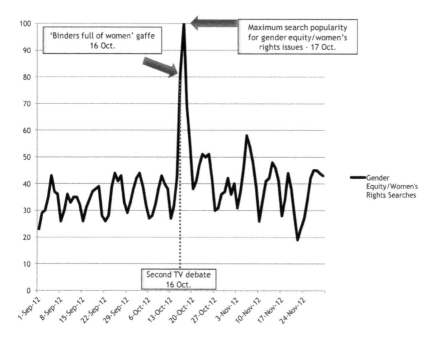

Figure 13.3 Search popularity for gender equity and women's rights issues in the US, Sept.–Nov. 2012.

Intuitively, these results seem to suggest that US Google users interpreted Romney's gaffe not only as an entertaining moment, but also as an opportunity to look more deeply into a set of policy issues that thus far had received little attention on the campaign trail, at least from the Republican camp and conservative media outlets. That said, it would be premature to simply assume that Google users made this 'thematic leap' independently. Rather, one needs to ask whether they were influenced by other factors, particularly the way in which the news media reported on Romney's gaffe, how they framed it and which policy connotations, if any, they attached to it. In order to verify this, the news items that focused specifically on these issues – i.e. those that mentioned gender equity, sex equity, women's rights, women's pay, pay equity, the pay gap, the gender gap and the glass ceiling in their headline or lead paragraph – between the beginning of October and Election Day (6 November) were identified with Lexis Nexis. Daily frequencies were then normalised to create a news popularity index for women's rights and gender equity to be compared with Google Trends data, as was discussed earlier in this chapter.

Perhaps unsurprisingly, the amount of coverage dedicated to women's rights and gender equity issues grew very rapidly after the second presidential debate. Specifically, 205 US news items mentioned women's

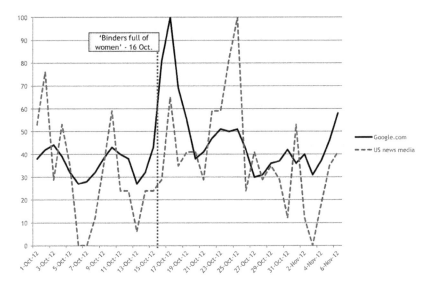

Figure 13.4 Popularity of women's rights and gender equity issues in google. com and news media.

rights issues in their headline or lead paragraph between the 'binders full of women' gaffe and Election Day compared to only 99 in the first half of October. However, the popularity of women's rights and gender equity issues in news media reports peaked only several days after Romney's gaffe (22–26 October). This was in direct contrast with the timeline for Google searches on the same issues, which peaked immediately after the 'binders full of women' episode, as was outlined above. In other words, it was the voters who were the first ones to show increased levels of interest in women's rights and gender equity, turning to Google before established media outlets grasped the newly augmented salience of these issues. In contrast, when the news media eventually expanded the space dedicated to the 'thematic' issues associated with Romney's gaffe, this shift did not lead to more searches for these topics, which instead decreased as traditional media interest peaked.

In this case, citizens behaved as trendsetters in the electoral information space while, on the other hand, the news media were comparatively slow at picking up on the renewed salience of women's rights and gender equity issues in the wake of Romney's gaffe on live TV. Many factors can explain this delay, which could be connected to editorial guidelines, but also more simply due to the time that news organisations need to 'make sense' of an event and shape their coverage accordingly. Nevertheless, this does not change the fact that traditional media outlets were not able to react to the growing public interest in these issues immediately, and, in the meantime, citizens were able to use search engines to locate the relevant information rather than wait for news organisations to catch up.

The Lack of a Policy Connection in UK Searches

In order to test for a 'thematic leap' in the United Kingdom, Google Trends was queried for a set of keywords associated with immigration issues and immigration policy plans.[5] Immigration was selected as a potential policy issue associated with this episode because Gordon Brown had called the Labour supporter at the centre of this episode 'bigoted' after discussing with her Eastern European migrants working in the United Kingdom, which prompted both commentators and scholars to speculate that this incident had strengthened the centrality of immigration to voter concerns in the 2010 general election (Bates 2010; Flynn et al. 2010; Hancock 2010; Denver et al. 2012). However, in contrast to these assumptions, Google Trends results showed that there had not been a noticeable change in the likelihood that British users would search the internet for information on immigration-related issues following Gordon Brown's gaffe (Figure 13.5). In fact, results indicated a slight drop in Google searches for specific information on immigration policies during the week in which 'bigot-gate' occurred (mean weekly Google Trends score = 44) compared to the previous week (mean weekly Google Trends score = 61), when users were actually more likely to search for information on immigration policies.

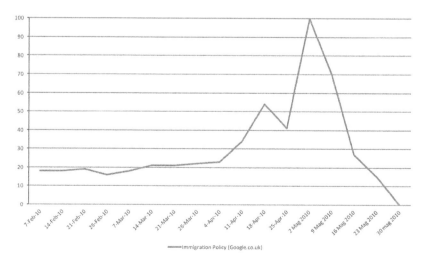

Figure 13.5 Search popularity for immigration policy issues on Google.co.uk, Feb.–May 2010.

These results contradict the analyses that interpreted 'bigot-gate' as a trigger of renewed voter interest in candidates' plans on immigration, suggesting instead that this episode fell short of fuelling a demand for 'thematic' information among Google users. Ultimately, while Google Trends data evidenced a 'thematic leap' in US searches, results for the United Kingdom showed the opposite. Indeed, Gordon Brown found himself at the centre of a 'media storm' in the wake of his 'bigoted' comment. This led several scholars to describe 'bigot-gate' as a turning point in the 2010 UK general election, claiming it delivered a blow to political spin and 'staged' campaigns (Wilkinson 2010, 45; Lilleker and Jackson 2011, 122; Stevens et al. 2011, 129). Although investigating the content of these reports in detail would go beyond the scope of this chapter, it seems reasonable to assume that some of the news coverage linked this episode to Brown's alleged reputation as a 'bully', which had been at the centre of another widely reported incident that involved some of the then Prime Minister's aides just weeks earlier (Chadwick 2011). Thus, Google Trends data seems to corroborate the hypothesis advanced by some researchers that the news media narrative around 'bigot-gate' encouraged citizens to associate Gordon Brown's words with his 'dysfunctional' personality and perceived inability to connect with ordinary people (Wring and Ward 2010; Cantijoch et al. 2013; Higgins and Smith 2013), promoting an 'episodic' interpretation of this incident and helping to veer public attention away from policy themes.

While it would be premature to suggest that internet search necessarily plays different roles in UK and US elections, these results nonetheless raise a number of useful points to drive future research in this area. First, they raise the question of whether the lack of a 'thematic leap' following 'bigot-gate' signals an underlying tendency for British voters to trust, and therefore rely on, established news media reports more than Americans do. In addition, this could also indicate a more general difficulty in engaging with broader policy 'themes' in an era of highly personalised politics. Second, results from this study point at the possibility that citizens in different democratic settings might perceive and approach online media – in this case search engines – in different ways, with Americans displaying a more entrepreneurial attitude. While testing these hypotheses will require more research, including in-depth ethnographic studies with Google users, it is useful to consider the role of internet search in elections in a democratic context with an even more different media system. The next section, therefore, reviews the key search trends associated with the 2013 Italian parliamentary elections.

Internet Search and Populist Celebrity Politics in Italy

The 2013 Italian parliamentary elections took place at a time of deep economic crisis and high political uncertainty. Alongside Silvio Berlusconi's

People of Freedom party and the centre-left Democratic Party, several new parties participated in this contest including the hastily founded Civic Choice centrist party led by then prime minister Mario Monti and the new Five Star Movement (M5S) led by popular comedian-cum-activist Beppe Grillo. M5S stood out both for its self-styled 'digital grassroots' structure based on local groups organised via MeetUp.com and its choice to disengage entirely from traditional mass media. Journalists were often prevented from accessing M5S rallies. Instead, M5S relied exclusively on its own online channels (i.e. a blog, online streaming channel, Facebook and Twitter) and Grillo's 'Tsunami Tour' in 100 Italian cities to promote its campaign. The M5S code of conduct stated that candidates would be struck off party lists if they had taken part in TV or newspaper interviews during the campaign. This generated frustration among members of the press, who regularly described Grillo's movement as political amateurism and a 'joke'. Nevertheless, M5S went on to win more than 25% of the votes, which was more than any poll had predicted. This combination of factors invited a particularly close examination of search trends for information about Grillo, his party and its policies.

Overall, search trends for information about Italian political leaders in the period analysed for this study were divided in two distinct phases. The first phase, which spanned the first six weeks of the campaign from early December 2012 to mid-January 2013, featured markedly irregular search patterns (Figure 13.6). This reflected the general climate of uncertainty that characterised these weeks, when parliament was dissolved

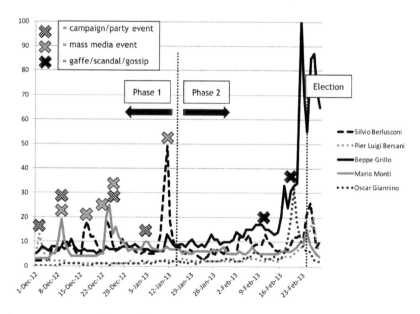

Figure 13.6 Google Trends scores for searches about Italian party leaders, Dec. 2012–Feb. 2013.

unexpectedly following a vote of no confidence against Monti's government, and for some time it was not even clear which leaders and parties would contest the election.

The most prominent search peaks registered during this first phase were linked with TV appearances by party leaders,[6] 'institutional' mediated events, such as Monti's customary end-of-the-year press conference as prime minister and his eventual resignation that led to new elections (21–23 December). In smaller measure, campaign events, such as the Democratic Party's primaries (2 December) and the launch of Monti's 'Civic Choice' party (4 January), also catalysed the attention of Google users. This fairly chaotic dynamic appeared to favour Berlusconi more than other leaders as he took part in several extended one-on-one interviews in prime-time TV programmes following a self-imposed media 'exile' since his resignation as prime minister in November 2011. Berlusconi's interviews were especially powerful drivers of Google search (in particular on 16, 17 and 23 December, 10 and 14 January), confirming more generally the centrality of TV appearances to his political strength and the continued role of TV as a catalyst for search engine use.

Conversely, in the second phase of the campaign, when the political landscape had stabilised, search patterns became more regular. A mini-scandal erupted very near the election weekend. On 18–19 February, it was revealed that the leader of the tiny fringe party 'Fare' and veteran TV commentator Oscar Giannino had lied repeatedly on the record about having university degrees he in fact does not have. As for the gaffes of UK and US candidates, this incident coincided with a sharp increase in Google searches for information about Giannino (Figure 13.6). However, the strictly personal nature of this revelation meant it was unlikely to trigger a 'thematic leap' in Google searches. Moreover, this was an isolated incident, as the rest of this period was not characterised by other sudden search peaks/drops for any of the other leaders.

In contrast, Grillo's popularity on Google.it grew steadily, outperforming other leaders by a very large margin in the last week of the campaign. This trend revealed a remarkably fast-growing demand for information about Grillo, who did not engage directly with traditional news outlets. At the same time, Google data also showed that Italian users were particularly likely to look for information about Grillo and M5S directly at source. Grillo's blog (www.beppegrillo.it), the online streaming portal that covered his campaign ('La Cosa') and the 'Tsunami Tour' were among the top 10 terms most frequently searched together with Grillo's name, indicating that users with an interest in the comedian-turned-activist were often likely to look for information directly on the online channels maintained by the M5S instead of established news portals. Furthermore, M5S's flagship policies (e.g. cuts to elected officials' pay, guaranteed minimum income, withdrawal from EU austerity deals, etc.) had spurred enough interest among Google users to be captured by Trends. This was remarkable, as none of the flagship policies put forward by the other parties generated a sufficient volume of search to be captured by this application. This was particularly noticeable for Berlusconi's supposedly popular proposal to scrap the much-disliked property tax on main homes ('IMU' in Italian). While this proposal was the focus of a targeted and expensive campaign by Berlusconi's People of Freedom party, it nevertheless failed to capture the attention of Italian Google users, who tend to be younger than the average voter and thus less likely to own the properties they live in.

Intuitively, these results appeared to corroborate the widely held assumption that the M5S's messages and rhetoric resonated particularly well with young 'wired' citizens dubbed by Italian journalists 'il popolo del Web' ('the WWW's people' in English), with whom other politicians – especially Berlusconi – struggle to connect as they tend to address an older and less educated type of electorate. The tendency for voters to search for the M5S's online platforms challenged the dominance of established Italian media outlets, which are often criticised due to their proximity to traditional political parties (Hallin and Mancini 2004, 108–109). In this framework, it could seem reasonable to conclude that 'the internet has become a political battleground for Italian progressives who have acknowledged that it constitutes a more hospitable communication environment than Berlusconi-dominated television' (Vaccari 2012, 156). This appears to have weakened the ability of traditional print and broadcast media to influence the election agenda and frame campaign narratives.

However, these results need to be considered against broader trends in Italian politics too. As such, the success of Grillo's movement could arguably be characterised as a step towards the consolidation of 'celebrity populism' – initiated by Berlusconi in 1994 – as the new norm in Italian politics. The ascent of the M5S occurred at the same time as a decline in the popularity of other anti-establishment and anti-EU groups, such as the Northern League, which became embroiled in a series of financial scandals in the year before the elections (Carbone and Newell 2013; Dehousse 2013), although it has since re-bounced in more recent polls. More importantly, Grillo's centrality to this process and his leadership style appear to be particularly well-suited to the Italian electoral system, which encourages the concentration of power in the hands of a charismatic leader, echoing the 'personal party' model introduced by Berlusconi (Mancini 2011; Diamanti 2014), whose own brand of populism seems to have run out of steam in recent years (Fella and Ruzza 2013). From this perspective, neither the M5S nor its leader could be seen as completely new or alien to Italian politics.

Overall, this suggested that Italian internet users were sufficiently confident or frustrated with the limited range of information available through traditional media channels, to look beyond print and broadcast outlets for electoral information. This marked a loss of influence for traditional news media and supported the simultaneous rise of online channels controlled by a political movement that to this day continues to denounce journalists as integral to Italy's political patronage system. Having said that, it would be imprudent to equate this with the emergence of increasingly 'emancipated' voters on the basis of this evidence alone. Rather, one has to ask whether M5S could have achieved such prominence among internet users without Grillo's huge popularity and personal fan-base, which he built during more than 30 years in show business, many of which he has spent touring Italian theatres and piazzas with a range of popular "politically charged" monologues. In this context, Italian voters used Google to access a different election narrative from the one provided by traditional news media. Yet, they did so in a way that fitted pre-existing political and campaign models adapted for the digital era rather than using the internet to pursue a truly independent 'search agenda.'

Conclusion: The Rise of Local 'Search Agendas'

The evidence discussed in this chapter showed that American and Italian Google users were able to take advantage of search engines in ways that challenged the traditional dominance of established media organisations in the electoral information space. This trend took on specific connotations in each of these countries. On the one hand, American Google users completed a 'thematic leap' in which they seemed inspired by an arguably trivial episode – Mitt Romney's 'binders full of women' gaffe – to look for information about policy issues – specifically gender equity and women's rights – that the traditional news media failed to cover in a timely fashion. On the other hand, Italian voters went even further, using Google to retrieve electoral information directly from a new political leader, Beppe Grillo, and his radical movement, the M5S.

As the M5S clashed openly with the Italian mass media establishment both during the elections and in the years since, search trends in Italy corroborated the impression that a significant portion of the electorate sought ways to bypass the narrative promoted by the Italian press and looked for a more direct relationship with this nascent political force. Although in some ways this strengthened a pre-existing model of populist leadership, at the same time it also curtailed the ability of both established media and traditional political leaders to control the electoral information space. While this does not necessarily show that Italian Google users set their 'search agenda' independently, it certainly demonstrates that Grillo and his movement's adversarial attitude towards TV and the newspapers resonated with a broader sense of frustration towards the press and determination to find alternative sources of information among many Italian voters. This also echoes the trend observed during the 2016 US presidential election for voters to turn to new sources of information online.

In contrast with both the US and Italian cases, British Google users seemed less likely to stray from the campaign narrative put forward in traditional news outlets. In particular, they did not complete a comparable 'thematic leap' following Gordon Brown's 'bigot-gate' gaffe. Indeed, more research is needed to clarify whether this episode signalled a broader tendency for UK voters to be satisfied with the interpretations offered by the British press and renounce opportunities to engage with alternative sources of electoral information. Yet, a particularly relevant hypothesis to explore is that the British general public tends to trust its local print and broadcast media more than people in other democratic countries, including Italy and the US. In turn, this might make people less likely to use tools, such as search engines, to look for alternative sources of information at key political moments, including elections.

Although case study research cannot support broad generalisations, we believe that the use of search engines in democratic elections is particularly influenced by perceptions of democratic institutions and processes, as well as media systems in individual countries. Indeed, search engines, such as Google, have the potential to disrupt established media ecologies by providing internet users with the tools they need to pursue different informational priorities. At the same time, however, this process is strongly influenced by the pre-existing structure of the media ecology in each country, with users more likely to set their own 'search agenda' when they believe that traditional forms of media are failing them as citizens, and less likely to do so when public trust in established news outlets is high. This makes search engines a powerful channel for challenging dominant election narratives in countries where traditional media are – or at least are perceived as being – dysfunctional because they appear to be too close to, or actively controlled by, political elites and other powerful interest groups. By building an alternative 'search agenda,' whether independently or due to the influence of nascent political forces as in the Italian case explored in this chapter, citizens have an opportunity to challenge and shake the informational status quo. To interpret these phenomena correctly, it is essential for scholars of political communication to approach search engines – and other internet service providers – as 'domestic media' platforms that are likely to influence and at the same time be constrained by the national media ecology (Oates 2011). As shown in this chapter, Google Trends can be a powerful tool in this emerging area of research.

Acknowledgement

This work was supported by the Economic and Social Research Council: *Google: The role of Internet search in established and challenged democracies* [grant number ES/K007890/1].

248   *Filippo Trevisan et al.*

Notes

1 Figures 13.1, 13.2, 13.3, 13.4 and 13.5 were first published in Trevisan, F., Hoskins, A., Oates, S. and Mahlouly, D. (2016). The Google Voter: Search engines and elections in the new media ecology. Information, Communication and Society, 1–18, published online before print. These figures and the data they contain are reproduced here under the terms of the Creative Commons Attribution License.
2 On the chart, a search peak is shown in conjunction with the 2012 Democratic Convention held on 4–6 September. Although the 2012 Republican Convention took place just before the period analysed in this chapter (27–30 August), a separate query in Google Search returned a similar search peak for Mitt Romney on those days.
3 www.motherjones.com/mojo/2012/12/47-percent-remark-quote-year.
4 Gender equity, sex equity, women's rights, women's pay, pay equity, pay gap, gender gap, glass ceiling.
5 Immigration/migration policy, immigration/migration plans, immigration/migration proposals, immigration Brown.
6 There were no leaders' debates during this campaign; instead, each party leader, except for Grillo, participated in talk shows and one-to-one interviews.

References

Anstead, N., and O'Loughlin B. (2011). The emerging viewtariat and *BBC Question Time*: Television debate and real-time commenting online. *The International Journal of Press/Politics, 16*(4), 440–462.

Bates, D. (2010). Making the white folk angry: The media, 'race' and electoral politics in the United Kingdom in 2010. *Platform: Journal of Media and Communication, 3*(1), 8–25.

Cantijoch, M., Cutts, D., and Gibson, R. (2013). *Internet use and political engagement: The role of e-campaigning as a pathway to online political participation.* Center for the Study of Democracy, UC Irvine Working Papers.

Carbone, M., and Newell, J. (2012). Italy on the eve of the 2013 general elections. *Bulletin of Italian Politics, 4*(2), 205–208.

Chadwick, A. (2011). The political information cycle in a hybrid news system: The British prime minister and the 'bullygate' affair. *The International Journal of Press/Politics, 16*(1), 3–29.

Chadwick, A. (2013). *The hybrid media system: Politics and power.* New York, NY: Oxford University Press.

Dehousse, R. (2013). Negative Europeanisation: European issues in the Italian elections. *Contemporary Italian Politics, 5*(2), 166–178.

Denver, D., Carman, C., and Johns, R. (2012). *Elections and voters in Britain.* Basingstoke: Palgrave Macmillan.

Diamanti, I. (2014). The five star movement: A political laboratory. *Contemporary Italian Politics, 6*(1), 4–15.

Dutton, W. H., and Blank, G. (2013). *Cultures of the internet: The internet in Britain,* Oxford, UK: Oxford Internet Institute.

Elmer, G. (2013) Live research: Twittering an election debate. *New Media and Society, 15*(1), 18–30.

Fastenberg, D. (2010). Top 10 over-reported stories of 2010. *Time*, 9 December.

Fella, S., and Ruzza, C. (2013). Populism and the fall of the centre-right in Italy: The end of the Berlusconi model or a new beginning? *Journal of Contemporary European Studies*, 21(1), 38–52.

Flynn, D., Ford, R., and Somerville, W. (2010). Immigration and the election. *Renewal*, 18(3–4), 102–114.

Freedom House (2015). *Freedom of the press 2015: Harsh laws and violence drive global decline*. Washington, DC: Freedom House.

Hallin, D. and Mancini, P. (2004). *Comparing media systems: Three models of media and politics*. Cambridge, UK: Cambridge University Press.

Hancock, A. (2010). Asylum and refugee policy: Still a political football? London, UK: LSE Politics and Policy Blog. Accessed August 1, 2017. http://blogs.lse. ac.uk/politicsandpolicy/asylum-and-refugee-policy--still-a-political-football/.

Higgins, M. and Smith, A. (2010). 'My husband, my hero': Selling the political spouses in the 2010 general election. *Journal of Political Marketing*, 12(2–3), 197–210.

Hoskins, A. (2013). Death of a single medium. *Media, War and Conflict*, 6(1), 3–6.

Howard, P. (2006). *New media campaigns and the managed citizen*. Cambridge, UK: Cambridge University Press.

Lilleker, D., and Jackson, N. (2011). *Political campaigning, elections, and the internet: Comparing the UK, US, France and Germany*. London, UK: Routledge.

Lilleker, D., and Vedel, T. (2013). The internet in campaigns and elections. In W. Dutton (ed.), *The Oxford handbook of internet studies* (401–420). Oxford, UK: Oxford University Press.

Lui, C., Metaxas, P. T., and Mustafaraj, E. (2011). On the pre-dictability of the US elections through search volume activity. Unpublished research paper. Wellesley, MA: Wellesley College.

McCombs, M. E., and Shaw, D. L. (1972). The agenda setting function of the mass media. *Public Opinion Quarterly*, 36(2), 176–187.

Mancini, P. (2011). *Between commodification and lifestyle politics: Does Silvio Berlusconi provide a new model of politics for the Twenty-First century?* Oxford, UK: Reuters Institute for the Study of Journalism.

Mannheim, K. (1952). *Essays in the sociology of knowledge*. London, UK: Routledge and Kegan Paul.

Margolis, M., and Resnick, D. (2000). *Politics as usual: The cyberspace "revolution."* London, UK: Sage.

Molotch, H., and Lester, M. (1974). News as purposive behavior: On the strategic use of routine events, accidents, and scandals. *American Sociological Review*, 39(1), 101–112.

Oates, S. (2011). Going native: The value in reconceptualizing international internet service providers as domestic media outlets. *Philosophy and Technology*, 24(4), 391–409.

Postman, N. (1970). The reformed English curriculum. In A. C. Eurich (ed.), *The shape of the future in American secondary education* (160–168). New York, NY: Pitman Publishing Corporation.

Purcell, K., Brenner, J., and Rainie, L. (2012). *Search engine use 2012*. Washington, DC: Pew Internet and American Life Project.

Sanz, E., and Stancik, J. (2014). Your search – 'ontological security' – matched 111,000 documents: An empirical substantiation of the cultural dimension of online search. *New Media and Society, 16*(2), 252–270.

Scharkow, M. and Vogelgesang, J. (2011). Measuring the public agenda using search engine queries. *International Journal of Public Opinion Research, 23*(1), 104–113.

Stromer-Galley, J. (2000). Democratizing democracy: Strong democracy, US political campaigns and the internet. In P. Ferdinand (ed.), *The internet, democracy and democratization* (36–58). London, UK: Frank Cass.

Stromer-Galley, J. (2014). *Presidential campaigning in the internet age.* New York, NY: Oxford University Press.

Trevisan, F. (2014). Search engines: From social science objects to academic inquiry tools. *First Monday, 19*(11). Accessed August 1, 2017. http://firstmonday.org/ojs/index.php/fm/article/view/5237/4157.

Trevisan, F., Hoskins, A., Oates, S. and Mahlouly, D. (2016). The Google Voter: Search engines and elections in the new media ecology. Information, Communication and Society, 1–18, published online before print.

Vaccari, C. (2012). Online participation in Italy: Contextual influences and political opportunities. In E. Anduiza, M. Jensen, and L. Jorba (eds.), *Digital media and political engagement worldwide* (138–159). Cambridge, UK: Cambridge University Press.

Vergeer, M. (2013). Politics, elections and online campaigning: Past, present... and a peek into the future. *New Media and Society, 15*(1), 9–17.

Volkmer, I. (2006). *News in public memory: An international study of media memories across generations.* New York, NY: Peter Lang.

Wring, D., and Ward, S. (2010). The media and the 2010 campaign: The television election? *Parliamentary Affairs, 63*(4), 802–817.

Yasseri, T., and Bright, J. (2014). Can electoral popularity be predicted using socially generated big data? *Information Technology, 56*(5), 246–253.

List of Contributors

Mai Beilmann is a Junior Research Fellow in Social Policy at the Institute of Social Studies, University of Tartu, Estonia. Her research interests include social capital, (social) trust, cultural values, social and political participation and youth studies.

Marco Bräuer, PhD, is currently consultant at the Federal Office for the Family and Civil Society Tasks. From 2009 to 2016 he was Research Assistant at University of Technoloy Ilmenau, Germany. The title of his doctoral thesis is: *Energy system transition and protests: a study of the communication strategies of protestors against the extension of the German high voltage power grid.*

Sander De Ridder is a Postdoctoral Fellow of the Research Foundation Flanders (FWO). He is currently based in Ghent University Belgium at the Department of Communication Studies, where he is a member of the Centre for Cinema and Media Studies (CIMS). His work is situated within the field of digital media culture and sexuality.

Udo Göttlich, Phd M.A., Professor for Media and Communication Studies, Zeppelin University, Friedrichshafen (Germany). Main research interests: Sociology of Culture and Media, Media and Communication Studies, Cultural Studies. Publications: *Ko-Orientierung in der Medienrezeption. Praktiken der Second-Screen-Nutzung*, Edited together with Martin R. Herbers and Luise Heinz (2017, Springer), E-Mail: udo.goettlich@zu.de.

Elke Grittmann, PhD, Professor in Media and Society at University of Applied Sciences Magdeburg-Stendal, Germany. Her research interests include media and migration, visual communication, photojournalism, transcultural media communication, gender media studies and journalism and memory and visual methodology. She is Editor of "Anerkennung und Sichbarkeit" ("Recognition and Visibility") with Tanja Thomas, Lina Brink and Kaya de Wolff, forthcoming, December 2017.

Max Hänska is an Assistant Professor at De Montfort University. His research explores the role of digital technologies in political communication and citizen journalism. Furthermore, some of his work centres on normative questions that arise at the intersection between communication and collective choice. He is the founding editor of the Euro Crisis in the Press blog: http://blogs.lse.ac.uk/eurocrisispress/. For more information see: www.haenska.net.

Martin R. Herbers, Dr, is a Postdoctoral at the Chair of Media and Communication Management at Zeppelin Universität, Germany. His research interests include the theory of the public sphere, media production and political entertainment. Contact: martin.herbers@zu.de.

Andrew Hoskins is Interdisciplinary Research Professor in the College of Social Sciences at the University of Glasgow, UK. His latest books are: *Digital Memory Studies: Media Pasts in Transition* (ed., 2017, Routledge), and (with John Tulloch): *Risk and Hyperconnectivity: Media and Memories of Neoliberalism* (OUP, 2016). His *Broken Media* (with Catherine Happer) is forthcoming with Palgrave Springer. http://brokenmedia.net.

Sven Jöckel, PhD, is Professor for Communication with a focus on children, adolescents and the media at University of Erfurt. His research interests are use and effects of digital media, particularly by adolescents, media and morality as well as privacy research.

Veronika Kalmus is Professor of Sociology at the Institute of Social Studies, University of Tartu, Estonia. Her research focuses on socialization, inter-generational relationships, social and personal time, patterns of media use, and cultural values and mental structures.

Klaus Kamps, PhD, is Professor for Communication at the Media University Stuttgart. His research focuses on Political Communication, Political Participation, Digital Media and Media Policy.

Sigrid Kannengießer, Dr, is Research Associate at the Centre for Media, Communication and Information Research at the University of Bremen, Germany. Her research focus is in media sociology, political, environmental and transcultural communication and gender media studies. In her current research project, she analyses media practices which are aiming for sustainability.

Anne Kaun is an Associate Professor at the Department for Media and Communication Studies at Södertörn University, Stockholm. Her research combines archival research with interviews and participant observation to better understand changes in how activists have used media technologies and how technologies shape activism in terms of temporality and space.

Maria Kyriakidou is a Lecturer at the School of Journalism, Media and Cultural Studies at Cardiff University. Her research focuses on the relationship between media and globalisation, with a particular focus on the mediation of distant suffering, cosmopolitanism and media coverage of crises. She holds a PhD in Media and Communications from the London School of Economics and is co-editor of the blog Euro Crisis in the Press.

Ragne Kõuts-Klemm is a Lecturer in Sociology of Journalism at the University of Tartu, Estonia. She teaches courses in media theories and in media systems. Her main research areas are changing media usage patterns among audiences and transformations in the field of journalism.

Dounia Mahlouly is a Postdoctoral Researcher at King's College London War Studies Department. Before contributing to the European Research VOX-Pol Network of Excellence, she completed her PhD in sociology at the University of Glasgow, College of Social and Political Sciences. Dounia also works as an external consultant for the Open University on a research project commissioned by the British Council and Goethe Institute.

Maria Francesca Murru, PhD, is lecturer in Sociology of Media and Communication at Università Cattolica di Milano, Department of Media and Performing Arts. Her research interests are focused on online public spheres and mediated civic participation and she is currently engaged in research projects dealing with mediated civic literacy and emergent publics.

Sarah Oates is Professor and Senior Scholar at the Philip Merrill College of Journalism at the University of Maryland, College Park (USA). She has published widely on Russian media, political communication and the digital sphere. Her most recent book is *Revolution Stalled: The Political Limits of the Internet in the Post-Soviet Sphere* (2013, Oxford University Press).

Karoline Oelsner, since January 2010 is a Research Assistant at the department of Public Relations & Communication of Technology at the Ilmenau University of Technology. Her research interests are the fields of public relations, European public sphere, online communication, political communication, and comparative research. Currently she is writing on her doctoral thesis dealing with the relevance of social media for the building of a European public sphere.

Perrin Öğün Emre, Assistant Professor, she has received her PhD degree in Journalism from Marmara University (Turkey) in 2012, her thesis was about peace movements and internet activism. She had a master's degree in Free University of Brussels where she presented her thesis entitled "The Integration Process of Turkey in European Union Through The Lens of French Press (Le Monde, Le Figaro, La Liberation)". Her research interests include internet and political participation, activism, alternative media and gender studies.

José Javier Olivas Osuna lectures and teaches at The London School of Economics and Political Science. He is a co-editor of the academic blog Euro Crisis in the Press, as well as founder of the civic engagement and e-learning platform Netivist.org. He holds a PhD in Government and an MSc in Public Policy and Administration from the LSE and also advises several organizations on Spanish politics, public policy and higher education. He is the author of *Iberian Military Politics: Controlling the Armed Forces during Dictatorship and Democratisation* (2014, London: Palgrave MacMillan).

Signe Opermann is a Post-Doctoral Research Fellow in Media Sociology at the University of Tartu, Estonia. She conducts research on social generations and their perceptions of "high- or double-speed society" and accelerating pace of life. She also has research interests in the areas of media consumption and (news) media repertoires.

Elena Pilipets is University Assistant at the Department of Media and Communications at the Alpen-Adria-University Klagenfurt, Austria. She studied cultural studies and media theory at the University of Klagenfurt where she currently works on her PhD project about serializations in digital culture. Her research and teaching focus is on media/cultural studies, affective turn and actor-network theory.

Andu Rämmer is a Researcher and Lecturer of Sociology at the University of Tartu, Estonia. His interests are the formation of values, political culture and public acceptance of new technologies. He has published on social, political and work values, and technological optimism.

Annika Schreiter, MA, is a PhD student at University of Erfurt and head of department of civic education at the Protestant Academy of Thuringia. Her research interest is the political communication of adolescents and the exchange between scientific research and practice in media and civic education.

Gülüm Şener, Assistant Professor, teaches media and communication studies for 13 years. She has received her PhD at Marmara University in 2006 with a thesis on the use of the internet by new social movements. Since then, she continued to study the role of the internet and social media in labour unions, social movements, political parties. Also, she investigates new forms of digital activism, citizen journalism, alternative media and political participation in social media. For her publications, see: https://hku-tr.academia.edu/GulumSener.

Tanja Thomas holds a Professorship in Media Studies with a focus on Transformations in Media Cultures at Eberhard Karls University Tübingen. Tanja Thomas' main research interests are (Critical) Media Theory, Communication Theory and Cultural Theory, Feminist Theory and Gender (Media) Studies, Cultural (Media) Studies, Transcultural Media Communication and Media Research. In her current projects, Tanja Thomas works on Media, Doing Memory and Participation in Post-Migrant Societies.

Filippo Trevisan is Assistant Professor in the School of Communication and Deputy Director of the Institute on Disability and Public Policy at American University in Washington, DC. His work focuses on digital grassroots advocacy, online political communication and disability. His most recent book is *Disability Rights Advocacy Online: Voice Empowerment and Global Connectivity* (Routledge, 2017).

Julie Uldam is Associate Professor at Roskilde University, Denmark. She researches the power of communication and media at the business-society nexus.

Sofie Van Bauwel is an Associate Professor at the Department of Communication Studies at Ghent University Belgium where she teaches cultural media studies, gender and media and television studies. She is part of the Centre for Cinema and Media Studies (CIMS) and her main fields of interest are gender, media and film and television.

Cornelia Wallner, Dr, is Postdoctoral scholar at the Department of Communication Science and Media Research, LMU Munich, Germany. Her research focuses on media systems and media culture, public sphere and social change and comparative research. https://www.researchgate.net/profile/Cornelia_Wallner.

Jeffrey Wimmer, Dr, is Professor for Communication Science with emphasis on Media Reality at the University of Augsburg, Germany. His main research interests are sociology of media communication, digital games and virtual worlds, public and counterpublic spheres, mediatisation and participation. From 2009 to 2015 he was chairing the ECREA-section 'communication and democracy' and the DGPuK-section 'sociology of media communication'.

Rainer Winter is Full Professor of media and cultural theory and Head of the Department of Media and Communications at the Alpen-Adria-University Klagenfurt, Austria. Since 2012 he has been honorary adjunct professor at Charles Sturt University in Sydney and visiting professor at Capital Normal University in Beijing, Southwest University in Chongqing and Shanghai International Studies University. He is the (co-)author and (co-)editor of more than 30 books and the (co-)editor of four book series.

Jens Wolling is Professor for Communication Research and Political Communication at the University of Technology Ilmenau, Germany. His main research areas are political communication research, research on media effects and media use, online communication research, research on media quality, and environmental communication research and research on methods.

Index